UNIVERSITY OF WESTMINSTER

Failure to return or renew overdue books on time will result in the suspension of borrowing rights at all University of Westminster libraries. To renew by telephone, see number below.

Due for return on:

# ONE WEEK LOAN

- 3 MAR 2004

2 6 MAR 2004

- 4 OCT 2005

Information Systems and Library Services **Harrow LRC**
Watford Road  Northwick Park  Harrow  Middlesex HA1 3TP
Telephone 020 7911 5885 (direct line)

26 0114249 8

# Broadcast Voice Handbook

## How to Polish Your On-Air Delivery

### Third Edition

**Ann S. Utterback, Ph.D.**

Bonus Books, Inc., Chicago

04  03  02  01  00                                                5  4  3  2  1

Library of Congress Control Number: 00-107292

ISBN: 1-56625-153-2

**Bonus Books, Inc.**
160 East Illinois Street
Chicago, Illinois 60611

Phonetic typeface courtesy SIL International Publishing Services

Printed in the United States of America

*Voice is probably the #1 criterion used in hiring. When news directors punch the eject button 15 seconds into an applicant's tape, they do it because that applicant sounds like an amateur, not a professional. If you're going to make your living with your voice, you should learn to use your voice effectively. It is as basic as learning how to type, and for a broadcaster it is just as important.*

**David Cupp**
**News Director, WVIR-TV**
**Charlottesville, Virginia**

*The effect of a broadcaster's voice is immediate and overpowering. No amount of excellent writing or good on-air presence can compensate for a poor voice.*

**Susan L. Stolov**
**President, Washington Independent Productions**
**Washington, D.C.**

Courtesy of Bruce Whiteaker, News Director, KXAN-TV, Austin, Texas

Courtesy of Desirée Berenguer.

*Even the most brilliantly written and produced
news story can be ruined by a poor delivery or
an untrained voice.  Likewise, a skillful,
expressive delivery can liven up a mediocre
package and make it seem special.*

**Patrick F. Dolan
News Director, News 12 Long Island
Woodbury, New York**

*Bad delivery is the biggest reason I find not to
hire an applicant.  The voice communicates so
much, yet there's an overemphasis on
appearance.  I find a lot more voice problems
than appearance problems.*

**Dave Busiek
News Director, KCCI-TV
Des Moines, Iowa**

# Contents

# Contents

# Quick Reference to Common Broadcast Voice Problems

# Acknowledgments

A project like this book is always based on the support of many people. My thanks date back thirty years to my colleagues at Memphis State University. I thank Mike Osborn for shoving a voice and diction book in my hand and telling me I was going to begin teaching voice and diction, and Jack Sloan for providing continuing opportunity to teach at Memphis State. David Yellin taught me to respect the television medium and the people who work in it. Working with Yellin's friends, such as Fred Freed and Paul Bogart, was invaluable to my development, and I treasure the time I had with his wife, Carol Lynn Yellin, who showed me what might be possible in my life. I am grateful to Betty May Collins Parker and Lea Queener for sharing their extensive knowledge and inspiring me with their continuing interest in the field of voice improvement.

I was fortunate to have the opportunity to attend Isaac Brackett's classes during my doctoral work at Southern Illinois University. As an outstanding speech pathologist, Dr. Brackett's help was immeasurable.

News directors across the country have contributed to this project. You will see many of their names throughout the book and in Appendix B. I would especially like to thank Jim Rutledge, former Assistant Bureau Chief of the CNN Washington Bureau, who, in 1985, first suggested I concentrate my professional interests in broadcast voice. Mike Freedman has been supportive of my work for many years, and I am honored to include his foreword in this book. Other news directors including Dave Cupp, Jeff Alan, Dan

Shelley, John Macdonald, George Clark, Bruce Whiteaker, and Bob Priddy have been supportive since the beginning as well, and I thank them.

I am grateful to Michelle McCoy and Gary Hanson of Kent State University for administering the news director survey and compiling the statistics presented in Appendices A and B.

I wish to thank my clients, who are often my most important teachers. They have all taught me about the realities of working in broadcast news, and I honor them for sharing their thoughts and feelings with me. For this edition, three of my clients were especially helpful, and I want to thank Pierre Thomas, Chris Black, and Desirée Berenguer. They shared their experiences and knowledge about live shots with me and broadened my knowledge immensely. I am also especially grateful to the broadcasters at the Voice of America who come to me from fifty-three different language services. They have taught me not just about voice but about the world as well.

I am grateful to the people at Bonus Books, and I am indebted to the Radio-Television News Directors Association for their continuing support of my work.

My deepest gratitude goes to the people whose love and support have changed my life:

To J who helps me discover all that my life can be,
To Elizabeth who guides me to a deeper understanding of life,
To Anne and Allen Quay who provide a loving community,
And finally, as always, I dedicate this book to my husband and closest friend, Jim, whose constant love and encouragement have shown me, "It can be."

Ann S. Utterback, Ph.D.

# Foreword to the Third Edition

The voice is to the broadcaster as the hands are to the pianist. Just as a musical score is enhanced by the expertise and enthusiasm of the artist, the written word is transformed into compelling, meaningful information for the ear by the eloquence and style of the broadcaster.

In today's broadcast world, "relatability" rules. The days of the rich, baritone "voice of authority" as the professional standard are gone. Conversational style has finally been accepted in the mainstream. As a result, broadcasters today represent the diversity of the audience better than ever before.

Still, just as many of the best ad-libs are carefully crafted, an effective broadcast voice requires training, practice, and care. The finest in the profession understand their roles as communicators and the importance of the voice in the process.

We may not sound alike anymore, but all good broadcasters share common traits. We understand the difference between simply reading copy and conveying information in a way that draws in the listener or viewer. These are the constants, the fundamental elements that haven't changed over the course of time. It is an art. As such, the voice becomes the brush that paints pictures for the mind's eye. And what pictures can be painted!

Listen to the classic broadcasts of Edward R. Murrow from London or Walter Cronkite following the death of President John F. Kennedy. These riveting reports are packed with emotion, yet maintain a sense of calm through calamity.

At CBS Radio News today, we pride ourselves on sharp writing, excellent use of sound and our ability to provide compelling, contemporary broadcasts that continue to set the standard for the industry. The voices of Christopher Glenn, Bill Whitney, Cami McCormick, and Sam Litzinger, for example, are very different. But all four, and all the other CBS radio voices, are extraordinary story tellers who use their voices to make their broadcasts special.

Aspiring broadcasters are trained to articulate, enunciate, breathe from the diaphragm, stay calm under fire and, all the while, sound conversational! This must seem an impossible combination at first. Yet, through training, practice, and care, the voice becomes polished and the procedures routine. Notice it is usually the novice who sounds quite different on the air than off. Professionals sound the same in normal conversation as they do when the microphone is on.

When the best in the business seek voice guidance, the person they turn to is Ann Utterback. A consummate professional, Ann not only understands the voice, she understands the industry, the demands placed on broadcasters and the sensitivities involved.

I have seen the results of Ann's work firsthand. As managing editor for the broadcast division of United Press International, I invited Ann to visit with staff members of our radio network. The improvement was remarkable. Those who worked with Ann not only sounded better on the air, they felt better about themselves. They learned that all voices are special and distinctive and often, minor modification and practice can transform an adequate voice into an excellent one.

It is an honor to contribute to this important handbook, now in its third edition. With it, Ann Utterback plays a significant role in helping radio and television journalists improve the delivery of the message through "The Broadcast Voice."

Michael Freedman
General Manager
CBS News / CBS Radio Network

# Meet
# Dr. Utterback . . .

Photograph by Brian Ashdown, Ashdown of London

As a long-time friend and admirer, it is my pleasure to introduce Ann Utterback to readers of this new edition of her *Broadcast Voice Handbook*.

I met Ann the first time she did a seminar at an international Radio-Television News Directors Association convention in Las Vegas in 1988. The RTNDA organizers cautioned Ann, realistically, to expect no more than 30 people. After all, she was an unknown quantity—"Broadcast Voice" didn't sound like a particularly sexy topic—this was Las Vegas, where nightlife ruled—and Ann's seminar was scheduled for an ungodly early morning hour— around 8 a.m., as I recall. So, she was told, don't be disappointed if you only get about 30 people.

Three hundred people came to Ann's seminar. I was one of them. Like me, most of the others ran broadcast newsrooms. What would convince hundreds of bleary-eyed, hung-over news directors to crawl out of bed in Las Vegas to go to an early morning voice seminar? Desperation, maybe.

Vocal problems are rampant in this business. In all likelihood every newsroom has some. Why? Lack of education is partly to blame. Nationwide, most broadcast journalism programs don't even teach basic voice and diction. Colleges crank out broadcast journalism graduates by the thousands, expecting them to earn livings with their voices, without teaching them the fundamentals. Many graduates don't know how to speak effectively, or even how to breathe to support their voices correctly.

When those graduates get jobs and carry their vocal problems onto the airwaves, the people expected to fix their problems are news directors. And these are problems we don't know how to fix. That's why, bleary-eyed, by the hundreds, we crawled out of bed on an early Las Vegas morning. We needed help ourselves in this critical area.

If you are looking for such help, you've come to the right place. Ann Utterback literally wrote the book. In fact, she's written two. The first, this one, will give you the best self-help guidance in vocal improvement you are likely to find anywhere. The second, *Broadcaster's Survival Guide*, carries voice work to the next level. It is filled with tips to help keep you healthy and sane in the notoriously unhealthy and insane business of broadcast journalism.

Ann Utterback has been giving good advice for over 25 years. She's worked from Alaska to Europe. Her list of clients reads like a broadcasting Who's Who. It includes all the networks, CNN, FOX, NPR, the Voice of America, The Associated Press, Reuters, Bloomberg News, and individual TV and radio stations around the United States and Canada.

Ann has done some remarkable work for my station. She coached one young woman whose voice was so problematic she was not even hirable. That young woman joined us as an intern because, given her vocal shortcomings, we couldn't even consider hiring her as a reporter. When Ann finished with her, she had grown to become our primary substitute anchor, and she eventually moved on to a top ten market.

And in addition to her talents and skill, Ann is a delightful person. I hope you will get the chance to meet her someday. But whether or not you do, you will find this book a big help. Whenever a voice question arises, I reach for my dog-eared copy. So will you. The answers are here.

Dave Cupp
News Director
WVIR-TV, Charlottesville, Virginia

*"Always be a first-rate
version of yourself instead
of a second-rate version of
somebody else."*

**Judy Garland**

# Introduction to the Third Edition

As we move into a new century, experts are debating exactly what broadcast journalism will consist of in the coming years. But two things are certain: vocal delivery will remain important and "live" work will be on the increase. And as technology changes at a rapid rate, it is comforting to know that the vocal mechanism we use has been around for millions of years. Learning how your voice works and how you can improve and care for it is information that will last a lifetime.

This third edition of *Broadcast Voice Handbook* gives me an opportunity to share my professional growth in the last ten years. My work with broadcasters has expanded, and it is rewarding to be able to expand my book as well. You will find two new chapters in this edition. Chapter 6, "Going Live," deals with live shots, which are always one of the biggest challenges in broadcast delivery. Chapter 7, "Other Live Experiences," discusses live experiences besides actual live shots, such as interviews and anchor cross-talk and tosses.

Chapter 9, "Coping With Stress," represents a major focus of my professional growth since I wrote the first edition of *Broadcast Voice Handbook*. I once felt that to improve voice you could concentrate on the vocal mechanism. Fix the problems there, and you fix the voice. I now take a much more complete approach to voice. I have found that I can teach clients everything I know about the mechanics of voice, and they will not improve if their body or mind is physically or emotionally stressed. We speak with our whole bodies, and effective broadcast voice work must be holistic in its approach. Chapter 9 gives ways to deal with the stress of working in the news business and methods for keeping your workplace healthy. You can find more about this topic in my book, *Broadcaster's Survival Guide: Staying Alive in the Business.*

When the first edition of *Broadcast Voice Handbook* came out in 1990, I had been working almost exclusively with broadcasters since 1985. Before that I had spent sixteen years teaching college students, corporate executives, and government officials how to use their voices well. Before I began working with broadcasters, I assumed that because they make their livings with their voices, they would have been trained to use their voices more effectively than most professionals.

After working almost fifteen years with hundreds of radio and television broadcasters in this country and around the world, I am sad to report this is not the case. I continue to see increasing numbers of clients who do not know how to breathe correctly or use their voices to enhance the meaning of their copy. These clients range from recent college graduates to broadcast veterans with thirty years of experience who have risen to the network level. Most have a basic lack of knowledge of how to care for their voices and use them effectively. What broadcasters do have is a real desire to learn more about voice.

In addition to the need for voice work for professionals who are on the air, I have learned that there is much frustration among news directors about the lack of voice training that broadcast journalism students get while in college. As one Baltimore, Maryland, news director puts it: "The proper use of the voice is paramount and is probably one of the most overlooked areas in college training." Many of my clients have voiced this same frustration. I remember one young woman telling me her father was not pleased that he had to pay a consultant to work with her during her last semester of college when he was already paying tuition. Unfortunately, her university did not offer any assistance with voice improvement.

This book provides the information that is needed in the newsroom and the classroom to help broadcasters develop and maintain healthy voices that enhance meaning. You will not find a quick technique in this book that will give you an instant broadcast voice. Breaking old habits and developing new ones takes time. In order to have a better broadcast voice, you must learn how your vocal mechanism works and practice the exercises that will allow new habits to be formed.

I tell clients I give them the tools like someone might give a carpenter a hammer and nails. What each client does with the tools is up to him or her. Just as a carpenter can build something beautiful, my clients can use the tools to improve their voices. Occasionally, it seems the client leaves the tools in my office. You have the same challenge. You can take what you learn in this book and improve your delivery or you can leave the tools here. The choice is really yours.

Luckily, in this country we no longer have a set broadcast model. The days of training everyone to sound the same are gone. I call that old announcer's voice the "Ted Baxter" delivery from the character on *The Mary Tyler Moore Show*. That voice was revived by the "Jim Dial" character on the sitcom *Murphy Brown*. Both of these characters mimic the staid, low-pitched delivery that was once a standard in broadcasting.

There is much more acceptance of different types of voices in broadcasting now than there was twenty years ago, but this acceptance does not mean that voice is unimportant. I hear this warning from more and more news directors. They feel that just because we are not teaching all newscasters to sound like Edward R. Murrow, this does not negate the need for training.

In order to get the most out of any voice, you must know the basic anatomy of speech and the fundamentals of how you can use your voice effectively. Basic knowledge about breathing, producing sound, resonating sound, and shaping sound into words is essential for good vocal production. Broadcasters can not begin to develop a method of stressing words, for example, without knowing how breathing relates to stressing.

In addition to the challenge of knowing the anatomy of speech in order to maintain a healthy voice, broadcasters need to develop a relaxed, conversational delivery. Establishing this natural, conversational delivery is not something that most people can accomplish without a systematic approach. Such a delivery involves breath control, pacing, and stress and intonation. Broadcasters must learn how to sound as if they are talking with someone when they are actually reading. And, as a California news director points out, this situation is as important in television as in radio: "Ninety-five percent of TV news reporting is voice-over. . . . Competent and compelling story tellers are the people we look for, people who can not only write to video but can hold the audience with the power of their voice."

The old notion that broadcasters are "announcers" is gone. Comfortable "communicators" are what the public wants in both taped and live broadcasting. The challenge to broadcasters is to be able to relax enough in a tense situation to maintain a healthy voice and sound relaxed. In addition, listeners want them to pull out the meaning of the story with their voices. This is a difficult challenge. It demands what I call *enlarged conversation.*

This book provides the information needed to meet this challenge. The book is as simple and straightforward as possible. The contents are organized in a sequential manner. Beginning with the production of the breath, which is the energy for speech, and moving through the production and resonating of sound waves to the articulation of the sound and, finally, the methods of stressing for meaning and sounding conversational. You will find specific information on how to sound conversational in live situations. You will also learn how stress affects delivery and how to combat the chronic stress of being in the news business.

The International Phonetic Alphabet is used as a method of presenting the sounds of our language. All phonetic symbols in the book appear in slash marks (e.g., "/k/").

It is recommended that you read the chapters in the order presented so that you will understand how the processes are interrelated. Even if you read the material quickly without completely retaining it, you will get an important basic understanding of vocal production.

In addition to gaining a basic understanding of vocal production, it is also necessary to develop a respect for your voice. After all, if you are a broadcaster, you are making your living on two tiny pieces of muscle in your throat. Broadcasters need to recognize the importance of a healthy voice. Think of your voice as an instrument. Not many concert pianists would abuse their fingers or ballet dancers their legs, but many broadcasters abuse their voices daily.

If you ask even a young ballerina about the hamstring or the Achilles tendon, she can usually tell you where it is and its function. I do not find this basic knowledge of vocal anatomy with many of my clients. Most are amazed when they see photographs of the vocal folds and realize how delicate the tissue is. These same newscasters would want to fire a cameraperson who did not know the basic mechanics of how television equipment works. They expect a cameraperson to have respect and knowledge of television equipment while they lack the same respect and knowledge of their own vocal equipment.

Knowing the fundamentals of vocal production is only the beginning of the process of voice improvement. Just as a pianist or a dancer must practice daily to maintain their skill, broadcasters must learn that voice improvement is a lifetime pursuit. Maintaining a good broadcast voice takes hours of practice and a lifetime of respect.

The Warm-Ups at the end of each chapter can become part of your daily routine. These sections have been marked by black arrows in the margins in this book for your easy reference. Each Warm-Up section is preceded by some exercises that help you become familiar with the chapter concepts. These are called "Focus on Breathing," "Focus on Phonation," etc.

Once you are familiar with the concept, you might want to put your favorite Warm-Ups on index cards or a sheet of paper to post over your desk or in the sound booth to help you remember to practice them. Many of my clients find they like to do Warm-Ups while driving. It is especially helpful to do articulation Warm-Ups in the morning while driving to work. This is usually one time for practice that works in even the busiest schedule. You should find other times as well because continued practice is of utmost importance in changing or maintaining vocal habits.

This book can serve as a lifetime reference companion as you continue to respect your voice by monitoring your vocal production throughout your career. It gives you the basic knowledge you need to maintain a healthy, effective voice.

One of the ironies of a good broadcast voice is that the better it is the less it is noticed. As one news director pointed out, "Voice in a news story should not be noticed. If it is, something is wrong!" Your goal should be to develop your voice and delivery to the point that your audience is aware not of your voice, but only of the information you are delivering.

News directors think of voice as a primary factor in hiring. Dave Cupp, News Director of WVIR-TV in Charlottesville, Virginia, explains his approach:

> Vocal concerns are so important to me that when I'm hiring, the first thing I do is literally turn my back on each applicant's tape. I don't want the distraction of pictures. I don't even want to know what an applicant looks like until I have had a chance to listen carefully.

A broadcaster's voice should be a medium that delivers information to the listener. It should never get in the way of this information. Only a healthy voice that is controlled by a broadcaster can be effective in this task. Through continued monitoring of your broadcast voice and practice to keep it healthy and effective, you can make your vocal instrument work for you.

By permission of Dave Coverly and Creators Syndicate.

*Building a good voice is like building a house. They both must have a good foundation to be strong. Learning correct diaphragmatic breathing is the foundation. Breath control techniques are as essential for an announcer as they are for an opera singer. The singer must control a note for effect—an announcer must control to complete a message. Without proper breathing techniques as a base for delivery, there is no way an announcer can get his or her message across.*

**Robert Runda**
**Former Chief, Broadcast Announcing Division**
**Trainer, Military Broadcasters**


*Don't overlook the importance of pauses in an audio passage—conversation is filled with pauses—breathing space.*

**Mick Jensen**
**News Director, KVOA-TV**
**Tucson, Arizona**


*More than anything else, reporters must learn to breathe. If necessary, even to mark places to breathe in their scripts.*

**John Matthews**
**News Director, WMAL Radio**
**Washington, D.C.**

# Breathing— The Key to Good Vocal Production

"Try to relax." That is the advice I give to clients everyday. But the truth is, if you are a journalist working in broadcasting, it is difficult advice to follow. Radio and television news professionals work in a world of live reports, crises, and deadlines. The pressures and tension in television and radio broadcasting are enormous, and, for the most part, they are unavoidable. Many of you may feel the phrase "relaxed broadcaster" is an oxymoron.

A television reporter, for example, works on a schedule that demands tension and pressure. To meet a 5:00 p.m. news show deadline, a typical reporter has from 9:00 a.m. to around 4:30 p.m. to produce one or more packages. Most of the day, the reporter must run all over the city interviewing people to develop a story. As the deadline approaches, the reporter must shoot a stand-up looking and sounding composed and in control. The voice track must be recorded as the deadline gets ever closer. This same reporter may be called on to do a live shot to lead into the package. The tension that has helped this reporter succeed in the fact-gathering part of the day now becomes a handicap (see Chapter 9).

This hectic schedule is accepted practice for broadcasters.

**Few other businesses demand the daily output that news broadcasting faces.**

Courtesy of Jeff Alan, News Director, KDNL-TV, St. Louis, Missouri.

Few other occupations demand this level of output. Most business executives have weeks between deadlines. Writers, actors, and other artists have months before they have to present their creative product. But broadcasters work with daily deadlines week after week.

For a broadcaster's voice to work effectively, however, relaxation is the key. Because your voice depends on various muscles in your body, it reflects the degree of tension you are feeling. Stress affects all your muscle tone, which affects posture, respiration, and voice control. A tense body usually means a tense voice.

Proper breathing can be very effective in relieving tension and improving the voice. Stress control workshops teach diaphragmatic breathing for relaxation. Natural childbirth depends on breathing to help alleviate pain. Concentrating on a long, slow inhalation/exhalation is often recommended by doctors to control the tension that exacerbates any type of pain. A long inhalation/exhalation is also helpful in tense social situations such as a job interview, an especially rough airline flight, or before giving a speech.

Yoga and other Eastern philosophies have used breathing

as part of meditation for centuries. The philosophy of yoga holds as a belief that if you can control the breath, or *prana*, you can control the mind. This idea can be adapted for broadcasters: If you can control the breath, you can control the voice.

Once you have learned proper abdominal-diaphragmatic breathing as described in the Focus on Breathing section, you can rely on this process to relax you. Your breath is your best ally as a broadcaster. It revitalizes the body while calming the emotions and bringing clarity to the mind. Proper breathing can help break the tension that builds for many broadcasters as their work days progress.

Proper breathing not only relaxes you; it provides the basic energy for speech. Breathing for life and breathing for speech, however, are not identical processes. Therefore, before you can begin to think of how to improve your broadcast voice by working on stress and intonation, rate, or pitch, you must first focus on the basic function of breathing.

Anchoring a network radio news program involves the pressure of coordinating live reports, late-breaking stories, and deadlines by the minute.

Courtesy of Michael Freedman, General Manager, CBS News, Radio.

# Breathing Anatomy

In order to learn to use your breath properly as a broadcaster, you need to have a basic understanding of how we breathe. It is not necessary to learn all the muscles and nerves related to the respiratory system, but some basic anatomy will help you improve your breathing.

## The Lungs

Most of us assume that we breathe with our lungs. Taking a deep breath is referred to as "filling up the lungs with air." What we may not know is that the lungs are not doing the work of inhalation or exhalation. We depend on various muscles in the chest and abdominal area to keep air circulating into our bodies.

The lungs are important for the transfer of oxygen and carbon dioxide to keep us alive, but without the muscles that control them they could not function. The lungs are like two large sponges in our chest. They are light and porous and float in water much like a natural bath sponge. The lungs fill the area of the chest or thoracic cavity with the heart nestled between them.

Leading into each lung is a tube called a bronchus which, like a tree trunk, spreads roots called bronchial tubes into each lung (see Figure 1). These bronchial tubes branch into smaller and smaller tubes (bronchioles) and end as tiny air sacs (alveoli). These air sacs have capillaries very close to the surface, and this is where the exchange of oxygen and carbon dioxide takes place. This exchange of gases is so fundamental in keeping us alive that it begins as a reflex action as soon as we take our first breath after birth.

The first breath we take is usually accompanied by a loud cry, which indicates the close connection between breathing and speech. To produce that cry, the air exhaled from the lungs goes up from the bronchial tubes into the trachea and passes through the larynx which contains the vocal folds (vocal cords) which create sound waves (see Figure 1). That air must be pushed from the lungs, however, since the lungs have no muscles themselves. This is where your understanding of the anatomy of breathing can help you as a broadcaster.

Figure 1
## Anatomy Drawing of the Organs Involved in Speech

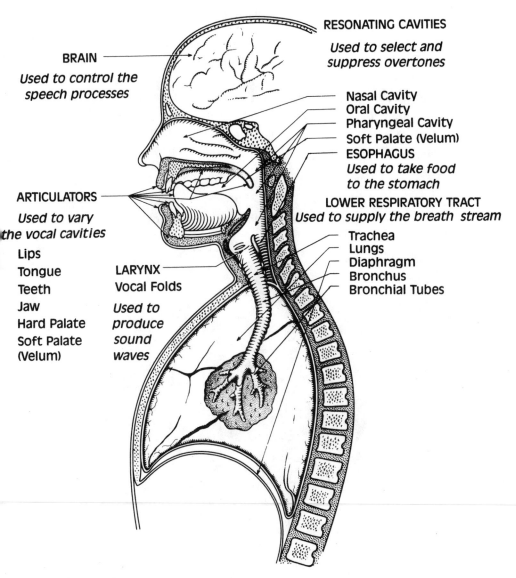

**BRAIN**
*Used to control the speech processes*

**ARTICULATORS**
*Used to vary the vocal cavities*

Lips
Tongue
Teeth
Jaw
Hard Palate
Soft Palate
(Velum)

**LARYNX**
Vocal Folds

*Used to produce sound waves*

**RESONATING CAVITIES**
*Used to select and suppress overtones*

Nasal Cavity
Oral Cavity
Pharyngeal Cavity
Soft Palate (Velum)
**ESOPHAGUS**
*Used to take food to the stomach*

**LOWER RESPIRATORY TRACT**
*Used to supply the breath stream*

Trachea
Lungs
Diaphragm
Bronchus
Bronchial Tubes

Courtesy of AT & T Archives

## The Diaphragm

The most important muscle for speech is the diaphragm. The diaphragm is a large sheet-like muscle that separates the thoracic cavity from the abdominal cavity (see Figure 2). The diaphragm bisects the body horizontally starting at the breastbone. It continues along the bottom of the rib cage around to the spine. The diaphragm forms a complete floor for the thoracic cavity. The broad bases of our cone-shaped lungs rest on the diaphragm. This solid muscle is pierced by three important tubes: the esophagus, which takes food to the stomach (directly under the diaphragm on the left side of the body), the aorta, which takes blood down from the heart, and the vena cava which brings blood up from the lower part of the body to the heart (see Figure 2).

Figure 2
**The Thorax and Diaphragm (cut-away front view).**

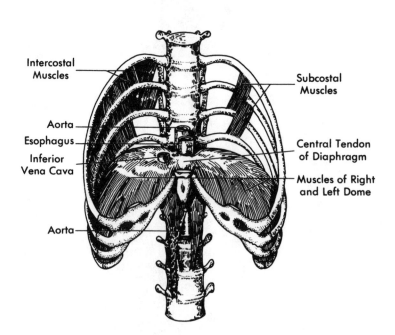

(From *Training the Speaking Voice*, Third Edition, by Virgil A. Anderson. Copyright © 1977 by Oxford University Press, Inc. Reprinted by permission.)

The action of the diaphragm is what allows us to breathe naturally. In its resting state, the diaphragm muscle is dome-shaped, rising up into the thoracic cavity. When we inhale with the diaphragm, this large, sheet-like muscle contracts and flattens out. As it flattens, it moves downward. The ribs flex upward at the same time. The effect of this is to increase the size of the thoracic cavity (see Figure 3). When this happens, a negative air space is created which results in a partial vacuum. Because the air pressure of our atmosphere is greater at this point outside the body, air rushes into the lungs to equalize the pressure.

As the diaphragm muscle flattens out, it also forces the abdominal area to protrude because of the pressure on the stomach, liver, spleen, and other organs beneath it. This movement of the abdominal area makes diaphragmatic breathing easy to monitor (see Focus on Breathing). With a good abdominal-diaphragmatic inhalation, you feel expansion in the stomach area as well as all around the back. The lower chest area may expand as much as 2 ½ inches.

Once the thoracic cavity is enlarged and air has rushed into the lungs, the diaphragm and abdominal muscles work to push the air out with a controlled exhalation. Imagine a bellows filling with

Figure 3
**Increase of Volume of Thorax with Inhalation**

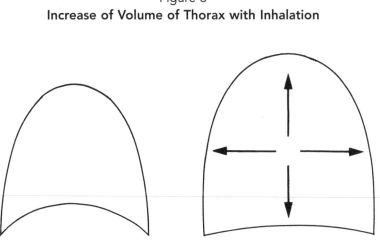

**Rib cage before inhalation**          **Rib cage after inhalation**

air. The first step is to enlarge the cavity of the bellows by separating the handles. When the bellows is filled with air, our arm muscles physically control the force of the air as it is blown out. Our abdominal muscles work much the same way by allowing the diaphragm slowly to rise back into its dome-shaped position and the rib cage to return to its original position. This movement forces the air out of the lungs with control. For relaxed breathing without the demand of speech, exhalation is simply a relaxation without the control of the abdominal and diaphragm muscles. The elasticity of the rib cage and lungs contributes to the deflation of the lungs in relaxed breathing.

The system of respiration is a continuous process that keeps us alive. Our body cannot store oxygen. There is a constant demand for it. When our brain feels the oxygen level has dropped, a signal comes from the brain stem to replenish it. This process is so important for life that we cannot voluntarily stop it. Many children's temper tantrums have ended with the threat, "I'll hold my breath until I turn blue." The child may think this is possible, but the involuntary breathing mechanism will take over to keep the child alive.

We breathe around 15,000 to 20,000 times per day. Our lungs normally contain around three quarts of air. We generally inhale and exhale ½ quart of air in quiet respiration when we are breathing around twelve to sixteen times per minute. The lungs do not ever completely empty of air. They maintain a residual air supply.

# The Importance of Abdominal-Diaphragmatic Breathing

Now that you know the anatomy of breathing, you may be wondering why it is important to you as a broadcaster. If the system described above operated naturally, it would not be important. You would go through life, breathing with the diaphragm aided by the abdominal muscles, and your voice would enjoy all the benefits of this type of breathing. Unfortunately, this is not the case.

At some point in our lives we abandon this comfortable

breathing for what could be called **socialized breathing**. Someone gives us the message that we should hold in our stomachs and stick out our chests. We could blame physical education teachers or army sergeants for this change, but whether we are male or female, a flat stomach and a large chest become our goals.

Knowing the basics of breathing, you can imagine the results of holding in your stomach and expanding your chest. This forces a type of breathing called **upper chest or clavicular breathing**. The muscles of the chest or even the higher muscles in the clavicle or collarbone area and the neck muscles do the work of lifting the rib cage to expand it for breathing. Instead of using one of the largest muscles in the body, the diaphragm, which is constructed for the purpose of expanding the rib cage for breathing, we use smaller, less efficient muscles. These muscles are not there to do heavy lifting, and when we heave up our shoulders to breathe, we ask them to do just that.

When I lecture to convention groups, I often ask the audience to take a deep breath. It is interesting to watch hundreds of people's shoulders heave up and down as they take what they perceive to be a deep breath. Usually only the singers or people who have played a wind instrument know that when taking a deep breath, the shoulders do not move. All of the movement is in the abdominal area below the breastbone.

The fear of developing a big stomach area should not keep you from breathing properly. Ironically, abdominal-diaphragmatic breathing may result in a flatter stomach because it calls for control of the abdominal muscles. They get a better workout when they are used for breathing than when they serve only as a girdle, constantly holding in the stomach area.

## The Benefit to Broadcasters

As a broadcaster, abdominal-diaphragmatic breathing is one of the best ways to maintain a healthy voice. If the diaphragm and abdominal muscles are doing the work during inhalation and exhalation, the tension involved in breathing is positioned far from the delicate structures in the throat, which produce sound waves (laryngeal area). The movement involves the abdominal area moving out and in (see Focus on Breathing). Clavicular breathing, on the other hand, causes the shoulders to rise during inhalation, and increases muscular tension in the neck, which may move into the laryngeal area. Chapter Two explains the importance of keeping tension away from the larynx and vocal folds. In addition to the tension involved in upper chest breathing, it also produces shallow breathing that can be exhausting.

The diaphragm and abdominal muscles give us both the ability to take in a large volume of air and to control exhalation. This ability is called **breath support**. The amount of time involved in a typical inhalation/exhalation at rest is quite different from the requirements for speech. Our ratio of inhalation to exhalation at rest is close to 1:1. We breathe in for about the same duration as we breathe out. For speech, this ratio must change to 1:5, 1:10, or even greater. In other words, exhalation time is greatly prolonged. We can control the air as it is exhaled if we let the diaphragm and the abdominal muscles do the work. Without control of exhalation, after a deep inhalation air would rush from our lungs as it does when we sigh. This would not be conducive to good speech because we could not say many words during the time it takes to sigh. The air rushes out too rapidly.

Think of a sculptor working on a new creation. Given a small amount of clay, the sculptor's choices are limited. Any sculpture created has to conform to the size of the clay. If the sculptor has a large chunk of clay, the choices are greater. All or part of the clay can be used, and the creation can be large or small depending on the sculptor's choice.

Your breath works in much the same way. When reading broadcast copy you need to have a good supply of air, and you need to be able to control that air. A good air supply gives you the raw material to produce good speech. Proper control of that air will help you mold speech into words that are interesting to hear, easily understood, and full of vocal energy.

## Returning to the Natural

You may think at this point that learning to breathe with the diaphragm aided by the abdominal muscles will take months or years of training because it seems so unnatural. Actually, you breathe this way every night when you are sleeping. Have you ever watched a little baby on its back in a crib? The baby's stomach goes up and down, up and down, with each inhalation and exhalation. There is no socialized breathing here. You breathe the same way when you are sleeping, sick, or in a relaxed state unaware of your breathing. Since none of these states applies when you are broadcasting, there is some relearning that must take place, but it need not take long.

A few simple exercises will help you get back in touch with this normal, natural way to breathe. Begin first with the section in this chapter called Focus on Breathing to position your breathing properly. Once you have the correct feeling, proceed to the Breathing Warm-Ups. These should become part of your daily routine to help fight the desire to return to the socialized breathing process.

You should continue practicing abdominal-diaphragmatic breathing in order to increase your breath support. Like any muscle, the diaphragm contracts and relaxes. And like any muscle, it can be strengthened through proper exercising. In the same way that pumping iron builds your arm muscles, breathing exercises build your diaphragm and abdominal muscles.

Part of an opera singer's lifetime training is breathing exercises. A singer will spend time lying on the floor with weight on the abdominal area trying to push the weight up. Voice coaches might even put their foot on top of the weights to increase the pressure. All of this is intended to increase the control of the diaphragm and abdominal muscles. When you hear an opera singer hold a note for longer than seems humanly possible, you can bet that singer has worked many hours building breath support. You are listening to the results.

## Vocal Benefits of Proper Breathing

What advantages does good breath support have for you as a broadcaster? You certainly do not need to sustain one sound for as long as Luciano Pavarotti or Placido Domingo. What you do need is enough air to be in control of what you are saying. You want to be in control of how long your sentences are and what you can do with your voice. Control of exhalation allows you to vary your rate and duration of sounds. You will also be able to use pitch changes to enhance the meaning of your copy (see Chapter 5).

Poor breathing may result in choppy, disjointed speech. We have all heard broadcasters who have to take a breath pause at the wrong time. The meaning is often changed by an inappropriate pause. The effect is like the old example of "What's that in the road—a head?" In addition, you do not want your limited breath supply to determine how you write. I have had more than one client say to me that they write in short sentences because they run out of air. They do not want to run the risk of an inappropriate pause.

Broadcasters with poor breath support suffer from a number of vocal problems as well. One of the most common is a **glottal fry**. This strange name refers to a popping sound that can be heard toward the ends of sentences when breath supply and pitch drop. The glottis is the opening between the vocal folds, which is where this sound originates. This condition may have gotten its name because it sounds like bacon frying with its popping sound. A glottal fry at the ends of sentences usually indicates that breath supply is low, and the pitch is near the bottom of the pitch range. Some speakers have glottal fry elements throughout their speech. Normally, however, the glottal fry will begin a few words before the end of a sentence. Increased air supply and a slight rise in pitch will eliminate a glottal fry as long as it is a functional problem and not organic (see Chapter 2).

Another problem that is very common with improper breathing is a very high-pitched voice. When we get nervous or anxious, our pitch generally rises because of increased tension in the throat area. Think of a broadcaster at a noisy political convention or covering a rally. In order to be heard over the crowd, the reporter may talk louder and increase the tension in the throat. What we hear is a higher-pitched voice.

One of my clients who was reporting from the Preakness horse race found she had this problem. When she got in the sound booth to track the narration for her package, she realized she had been shouting over exuberant spectators at the race. Her pitch in her stand-up had been so high she could not match it in the booth. When the package aired, it sounded like two different reporters because of the differing degrees of vocal tension. The goal is always to have a seamless voicing quality so that the tracking and stand-up sound much the same. With proper breathing, this reporter has now learned how to increase her volume without tensing the laryngeal area (see Chapter 3, Projection).

Tension in the laryngeal area also results from upper chest breathing. The tension it takes to increase the size of the chest cavity using the upper chest muscles can move into the laryngeal area. Chapter Two describes the way the vocal folds work to vary pitch. Basically, tension causes the folds to become thinner, which produces a higher pitch. If you are breathing in your upper chest, you are increasing the likelihood that your pitch is higher than it should be.

Upper chest breathing may also produce an audible intake of air. This occurs when the tension in the upper chest causes the throat to constrict on inhalation. (It may also be caused by the tongue being elevated or the mouth being slightly closed during inhalation.) Normally, we breathe through our nose because this filters, warms, and moistens the air. When speaking, however, it is appropriate to inhale through the mouth. Breathing through the nose is too slow for speech, and causes an audible inhalation.

The mouth and throat should be like an open tube for inhalation to prevent any audible intake of air. Listeners often complain that they are distracted by the gulps of air they hear reporters taking. That whoosh of air can become so predictable it gets in the way of the meaning of the copy. Proper breathing will help eliminate this problem.

Taking a good abdominal-diaphragmatic breath before your countdown and another just before you begin your copy will build your air supply (see Breathing Warm-Up #6). This will allow you to take smaller breaths within the copy. It is not possible to take an abdominal-diaphragmatic breath at every pause in your copy. That would be too time-consuming. You have to take short breaths through your mouth when you need air within your copy. When you go to tape for a sound bite or actuality, you may be able to take in another abdominal-diaphragmatic breath. Use every opportunity you have to let the abdominal muscles and the diaphragm do the work.

## The Value of Standing for Speech

You will find when doing the Breathing Warm-Ups that a standing posture offers the best way to fully expand the chest and back area when inhaling. In a seated position, the abdominal area is pushing up into the dome of the diaphragm. When you stand, the abdominal

This radio studio can easily be adjusted for standing or sitting.

Courtesy of Michael Freedman, General Manager, CBS News, Radio.

area is free to expand all around your body. Good singers know this. You rarely see opera singers sing seated. They know that the diaphragm needs the freedom to move, and standing allows this.

Most radio studios can accommodate a broadcaster who wants to stand, but many television sound booths are not set up for it. An adjustable mic stand is a small expense, however, when you consider the advantages of standing. A few stations have designed standing desks, and several anchors stand even though their desks make them appear to be seated. They have discovered the advantages of standing.

Some broadcasters have found ingenious ways to free up the diaphragm. One television network sports announcer who is a former basketball player reportedly kneels in front of the desk in the sound booth. He is well over six feet tall, and kneeling puts him right at mic level. More importantly, it frees his diaphragm by allowing his abdominal area to expand unrestricted. I do not recommend kneeling because of the stress it puts on your knees, but the sports announcer had the right intent.

Another consideration is to avoid the restriction of tight clothing that might keep the abdominal area from expanding. Many broadcasters loosen belts or unbutton waistbands to facilitate easy breathing. Ed Bliss, a former CBS writer, reports that Allan Jackson, who reported for CBS Radio for over twenty years, always unbuckled his belt and loosened his pants after he sat down for a broadcast. You may find you need to do this, especially if you have just eaten a large meal. Because the stomach is right below the diaphragm, it is difficult to take a deep breath with a full stomach.

## Increasing Vocal Energy

A common problem that I see with clients is a lack of vocal energy. Some clients sound like they are bored with what they are reporting. They tell me that they do not feel that way, but their voices betray them. This is another problem that can be traced to poor air supply. If you feel bad for some reason, it will most likely be heard in your voice. Our voices often reveal our psychological and physiological states. We have all said to someone, "You don't sound like yourself," or "You sound down." Our voices can signal how we feel, and as a broadcaster you must be aware of this.

As a listener or viewer, audience members expect broadcasters to be one step above them in energy level. They want to be convinced that the story they are listening to is important enough to take them away from their everyday lives and into the story. If they are driving, your delivery must be more interesting than the passing scenery. If they are at home or at work, you are competing with an infinite number of distractions. You need to pull your listeners up to your energy level to get them to listen.

I often notice that within a news story the people being interviewed sound like they have more energy and involvement than the reporter does. This indicates low vocal energy and affects the impact of the story. As a reporter, you need to be the tour guide who takes the viewer through your story. Not many of us would want to go on a tour of a city if the guide had low energy. We would most likely wander off and look at the sights ourselves. This is what the viewer will do if the reporter does not have good vocal energy.

Oxygen energizes the mind and body. A good inhalation will not only give you the air you need to speak well, it will also give you the vocal energy you need. You will benefit more from three or four deep abdominal-diaphragmatic breaths than you will from three or four cups of coffee. Yogis have used *pranayama*, the science of breath control, for centuries to achieve a natural high. Proper breathing can help you achieve the vocal energy needed to pull your listener into your story.

# Focus on Breathing

Here is a summary of proper inhalation/exhalation for speech:

**INHALATION**
1. Diaphragm muscle contracts and flattens downward.
2. Ribs flex upward enlarging the chest cavity.
3. Abdominal area protrudes as diaphragm presses on stomach, liver, and other internal organs.

**EXHALATION**
1. Diaphragm begins to relax.
2. Abdominal muscles control relaxation of diaphragm to create breath support.
3. Ribs slowly move down to relaxed position, and abdominal area returns to normal position.

Before you can begin doing Breathing Warm-Ups, you must become familiar with the feeling of abdominal-diaphragmatic breathing. The processes described below will help you focus on the muscles involved.

A) Watch a videotape of yourself taking a deep breath. If you are a television broadcaster, watch one of your air tapes. Otherwise, use a home video recorder to tape yourself reading copy. If a recorder is not available, you may observe yourself in a mirror. Focus on the neck area beneath the chin. Are the muscles of the neck visible when you inhale? Can you see your shoulders move? If either of these is true, you are using your upper chest muscles to inhale.

B) Proper speech production does not begin with the voice being pushed out from the throat or lungs. It begins in the abdominal area. Take a deep breath and sigh. Feel the expansion of the abdomen. Add an audible "ah" sound to the sigh and try to feel the push coming from the abdomen.

C) Various postures and movements force abdominal-diaphragmatic breathing. Try these activities and focus on the movement around the abdominal area, the sides, and the back. Some postures may work better for you than others. In all of them, concentrate on your breathing.

- Bend from the waist at a ninety-degree angle, letting your arms and head hang relaxed. Keep your knees slightly flexed. Remain in this position until you can feel your abdominal-diaphragmatic breathing.
- Squat so that your buttocks are resting a

few inches above your heels. Remain in this position until you can feel the abdominal involvement in your breathing.

- Sit forward in a chair and put your elbows on your knees. Breathe normally and focus attention on the location of the movement.
- Pant like a dog a dozen times. Slow the panting down and notice the abdomen going out as you inhale and in as you exhale.
- Pretend you are Santa Claus and say a strong, "Ho Ho Ho," several times. Notice that the air is pushed from the abdomen.
- Sit up straight on the front edge of a chair. Drop your arms and grab the legs of the chair to lock your shoulders in place so they cannot rise. Push your abdominal area out as you breathe.
- Take a deep inhalation and pretend you are blowing out 100 candles on a birthday cake. Feel the pressure in the abdominal area as the muscles squeeze to blow out all the candles.
- Tilt your head back and yawn deeply. Feel the movement in your abdominal area. Yawning is an excellent way to relax the throat.

D) One of the best postures for feeling abdominal-diaphragmatic breathing is lying down. Find a comfortable carpet or bed and    stretch out on your back. Spread your legs slightly and move your   arms away from your body so that there is open space in your   armpits. Perform the following activities:

- Close your eyes and concentrate on your breathing.

- Place your right hand on your chest and your left hand on your abdomen. Notice that you can keep your right hand still while your left hand rises and falls with the breath.
- Keeping your hands on your chest and abdomen, take in a deep inhalation and purse your lips and blow the air out. Feel your left hand slowly descending as the air is expelled.
- Place a book on your abdomen and watch it rise as you inhale and fall as you exhale.
- Turn over and lie down on your stomach with your hands at your sides. Turn your head sideways and rest your cheek on the bed or floor. Feel your stomach pushing against the surface you are lying on each time you inhale.

E) Working with a partner, put your hand on your partner's abdominal area just above the waist. Ask your partner to inhale and push your hand away. Focus on the movement of the abdominal area. Switch tasks. If either of you has difficulty, forget about breathing and simply push the hand away. Concentrate on moving those muscles, and then put an inhalation with the movement.

# Breathing Warm-Ups

**WARNING: Do not overdo any of the Warm-Ups in this book. If you feel dizzy or uncomfortable at any time, stop and breathe normally. Do not force or strain.**

## General Instructions:

While doing these Warm-Ups, use a vocal volume that is appropriate for your broadcast voice or conversation. If the exercise calls for vocalization, begin the sound immediately. Do not waste any air. When breathing for speech, inhale through your mouth.

These exercises should be done in a standing position. Your posture should be straight, with your knees slightly bent. Try to keep your body as relaxed as possible. As you build your control of exhalation, you will feel the diaphragm rising until it seems to be pushing up into the chest cavity as you reach the end of your vocalization. Do not force vocalization as you deplete your air supply. Always stop if your pitch changes or your tone breaks as in a glottal fry or a hoarse sound.

You may feel slightly dizzy doing some of the Warm-Ups. This is especially true if you are a smoker. Deep abdominal-diaphragmatic inhalations bring large supplies of oxygen to your brain. If your body is not accustomed to this, dizziness may occur. If you become dizzy, sit down and breathe normally for a few seconds. As you continue doing these Warm-Ups, the dizziness should subside. If it does not, see your physician.

Do not worry about hyperventilating during these Warm-Ups. Hyperventilation is fast, shallow breathing that gives a feeling of breathlessness. It is usually associated with anxiety. Hyperventilation causes the carbon dioxide level to drop and lightheadedness, dizziness, or a giddy feeling results. For these exercises, you will be doing the opposite of hyperventilating. You will be breathing slowly, deeply, and with control. Training in controlled breathing is the common treatment for hyperventilation.

You should make these Warm-Ups part of your daily routine. Practice at least ten minutes a day for several weeks to build breath support. Select the ones that you enjoy as your regular routine and add others for variety. You should also begin to use proper breathing whenever you read copy. Using proper breathing will become a habit if you stay aware of your breathing.

1) To feel *improper* breathing, take a deep inhalation in the upper chest area. Exaggerate the lifting of the shoulders and tension in the throat. Say an extended "ah" sound. Time the number of seconds you can sustain an "ah." Listen to the quality of the sound.

Now, take a comfortable abdominal-diaphragmatic breath in a standing position. If you have difficulty with this, go back to Focus on Breathing. Once you have inhaled comfortably with the diaphragm, exhale vocalizing "ah." Again, time your "ah" and listen to the quality. With the abdominal-diaphragmatic breath, your "ah" should sound lower in pitch and vocalization should be longer.

2) Using a child's pinwheel, purse your lips and blow air out making the pinwheel spin. Use your abdominal muscles to sustain a slow, steady spin. Time how long you can make it spin. Try to increase your time as you repeat this exercise.

3) Tear off the corner of a facial tissue. Hold it against a wall with the force of your exhalation. Feel your abdominal area squeezing in as you exhale for as long as possible.

4) With one hand on your abdominal area, take a deep inhalation, pushing your hand out. Sustain any of the following vowel sounds on exhalation:

"ah" as in spa
"aw" as in caw
"u" as in two

Time each vowel production. Stop vocalization when the sound begins to waver or sound weak. At first, your times may be in the ten to fifteen second range. Try to build your control of exhalation by adding a few seconds each time until you can sustain a vowel for twenty to thirty seconds. Keep a record of your progress.

5) Grasp your body so that your fingers touch in the front of your abdominal area and your thumbs reach around toward your back. Take a deep inhalation that pushes your fingers apart. With that breath, vocalize any of the lists below. Make certain that you do not take in any additional small gulps of air. You should be measuring your breath support by exhaling only one inhalation. Keep a record of how far you go each time.

- Repeat the days of the week.
- Count by ones or tens.
- Repeat the months of the year.
- Say the alphabet.

### 6) *Countdown to Calm Down.*
If you practice this enough, it will relieve some of the tension that precedes each taping. Establish a habit of using it in the sound booth and for stand-ups. It will break the tension of the day and get you ready to record.

Take a deep abdominal-diaphragmatic inhalation and say,

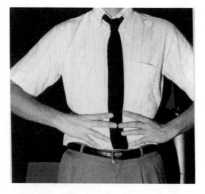 

| Correct beginning hand position after exhalation. | Correct hand position after abdominal-diaphragmatic inhalation. |

Courtesy of Dave Cupp, News Director, WVIR-TV, Charlottesville, Virginia.

"Broadcast Voice Handbook story, Take One." (You can replace this title with your story slug as you make this part of your recording routine.) Now inhale deeply again, and say, "Three, two, one." Inhale a third time and begin your story. For a practice story opener you can say, "Broadcasters are finding that a few simple breathing exercises can make a difference."

This method of beginning your taping may seem too slow or time-consuming at first. I have found with clients, however, that the four or five seconds needed for the additional breathing are well worth it. Many clients report that they do fewer takes of each piece with this method. They often are pleased with their voice in the first reading after using their countdown time to calm down.

7) Take a deep abdominal-diaphragmatic inhalation and say, "Good evening, I'm (*your name*) and this is Eyewitness News." Exhale any remaining air. Inhale again and say the phrase twice. Continue building the number of times you can repeat the phrase on one inhalation maintaining an appropriate pitch and volume. Keep a record of your progress.

8) Take a good inhalation and read as far as you comfortably can in the copy below. Meaning is not important. Do not try to "sound like a broadcaster." Mark your progress and try to add one more word each time as long as you are not dropping into a glottal fry or forcing. If you find it is easy to read the entire selection on one breath, start over and read until you run out of air.

```
A medical researcher says anyone
who drinks five cups of coffee a
day, or more, may be increasing the
chances of developing lung cancer.
The University of Minnesota
scientist says his study is the
first to implicate coffee by itself.
He also says that if someone drinks
too much coffee and smokes, the
combined effects may be far worse.
```

But he says investigators must do
more research.

Reprinted with permission from *Writing Broadcast News—Shorter,
Sharper, Stronger*, Mervin Block, Bonus Books, Inc., 1997.

9) Marking your copy for breath pauses will make it easier to avoid inappropriate pauses. In Chapter Five, breath pauses are explained as an integral part of the process of marking copy to add stress and intonation to your reading. For practice purposes, the following selections have been marked for pauses. There are many different ways copy can be marked, and this marking may seem awkward to you. Tape-record these anyway to practice, beginning each with the countdown from Warm-Up #6. The double slash marks indicate a pause with a fairly deep inhalation. The single slash marks mean a quick intake of air (called a catch-breath) or a pause with no breath intake.

A construction crane in San
Francisco / fell off a 12-story
building into morning rush-hour
traffic / and killed nine people.//
    At least a dozen people were
hurt.// And five construction
workers are missing,/ perhaps
buried in debris.// Part of the
crane hit a school bus/ and killed
the driver and a student.//
    Among the dead was the crane
operator himself.//

A boy fell into a wild-animal
concrete pit in a suburban Chicago
zoo today/—and was saved.// By a
gorilla.//
    The three-year-old boy had
climbed over a fence at the
Brookfield Zoo,/ then fell about 15
feet.//

The zoo says the female gorilla
cradled the injured boy in her
arms/ and carried him to a door,/
where zookeepers took him.// No
word on his condition.//

Reprinted with permission from *Writing Broadcast News—Shorter, Sharper, Stronger*, Mervin Block, Bonus Books, Inc., 1997.

10) Try marking the selections below for breath pauses. As you found in Warm-Up #9, most double slash marks are found at periods, and single slashes are at commas, ellipses, dashes, or to distinguish meaning. Once these are marked, continue the reading process you established in Warm-Up #9.

Oregon police are searching for a
prison escapee who was on board the
United Airlines DC-8 that crash-
landed in Portland last night. The
escapee was being returned by two
guards to the Oregon state prison.
185 persons were on board the
plane. In the crash, at least 10
were killed and 45 hurt, five
critically. And the escapee
apparently escaped again.

Tornadoes and thunderstorms
struck the southeast today and
caused at least two deaths.
Tornadoes in Laurel county,
Kentucky, in the London area,
overturned mobile homes, toppled
trees, battered buildings, peeled
off roofs, killed cattle and
destroyed or damaged a lot of other
property. At least six people there
were hurt.

A fire swept through one of the nation's biggest libraries today. The Central Los Angeles Library was damaged severely, and thousands of books were destroyed. 250 firemen fought the fire, and 22 of them were hurt. Firemen were hampered because they tried to hold down the use of water--to minimize water damage to books.

Reprinted with permission from *Writing Broadcast News—Shorter, Sharper, Stronger*, Mervin Block, Bonus Books, Inc., 1997.

*Don't ignore voice-impairing illnesses. I have found that most radio news people don't realize how fragile their voices can be, until they lose their voices. The recovery time is typically much longer than expected.*

**Carolynn Fedor**
**Bloomberg News—Multimedia**
**Princeton, New Jersey**

*Don't smoke. It's important to work in a smoke-free environment. And don't strain your voice at sporting events— just clap instead of yell.*

**Dan Dillon**
**News Director, KFDI AM/FM**
**Wichita, Kansas**

*Women in particular seem to strain their voices and lose them—perhaps voice training should be part of talent training and education.*

**Deborah R. Halpern**
**Assistant News Director, WFLA-TV**
**Tampa, Florida**

# Phonation— Using the Vocal Folds Effectively

Whether you are making $15,000 a year as a general assignment reporter in a small market or $5 million as a network anchor, healthy vocal folds (vocal cords) are a prerequisite to your work. It would be ludicrous to think of a concert pianist laying bricks several hours a week. Obviously, most pianists take very good care of their hands. As a broadcaster, you should be equally as protective of your vocal mechanism. If you are misusing your voice, you are playing Russian roulette with the part of your anatomy that you must depend on for a lifelong career.

This chapter explains how talking while you are hoarse, coughing, clearing your throat, and shouting can cause physical damage to your vocal folds. More serious damage is caused by smoking, which remains a career and health hazard for broadcasters.

# Anatomy of Phonation

Breathing is your best ally as a broadcaster. It provides the energy for speech while relaxing the body. But breathing alone cannot produce speech. In order for sound to be produced, the air from the lungs must be altered to create sound waves. This is called **phonation**. When we speak, we alter the air in several ways, but the most important alteration involves the vocal folds.

The vocal folds are folds of muscle that are located within your larynx (Adam's apple). Their position varies from a fully open V-formation that allows air to flow through unimpeded, to a closed position formed when the sides of the V come together to create a valve in our throats (see Figure 4). This valving is the primary purpose of the vocal folds. They are not in our throats so we can speak. The vocal folds protect our lungs from foreign matter by closing off the trachea when food or liquid comes down the pharynx (see Figure 1). Since the pharynx splits into two tubes—the trachea that goes to the lungs and the esophagus that goes to the stomach—this valve is very important. Without the vocal folds, our lungs would be unprotected, and food and liquid could go into our lungs when we swallow, resulting in asphyxiation. Our vocal folds keep us alive by protecting our lungs.

It is easy to feel your vocal folds working. Slide your fingers down the front of your neck until you reach your larynx, which will feel like a protrusion directly beneath your chin. You are feeling the thyroid cartilage, which is a shield-like structure that protects the vocal folds. With your fingers on your larynx make a sustained "eeee" sound, and you will feel vibrations. Swallow and feel the larynx rising up in your throat. Yawn and you will feel the larynx moving downward. All of this movement is controlled by an intricate system of muscles in your throat.

The entire structure of the larynx, or voice box, is an alteration of the top two cartilage rings of the trachea (see Figure 1). These rings have altered to protect the vocal folds and to allow them to open and close. The vocal folds are delicate tissue covered with mucus (see Figure 4). Of all our vocal mechanisms, these structures are the most delicate and the most vulnerable.

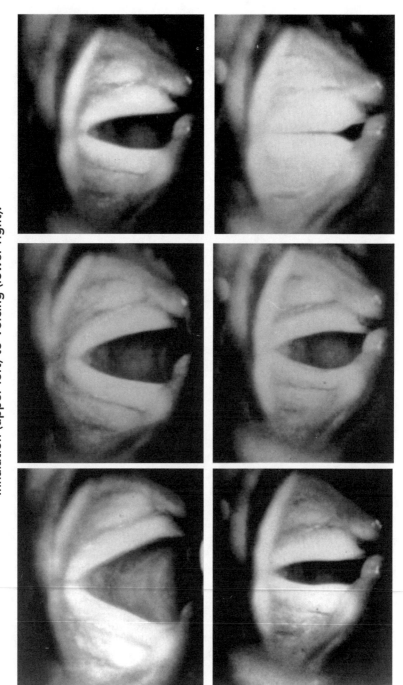

Figure 4
High Speed Photography of Human Vocal Folds Progressing from Inhalation (upper left) to Voicing (lower right).

(Courtesy of AT & T Archives)

Most mammals have similar valve systems in their throats to protect their lungs. Other animals' brains and oral structures are not refined enough, however, to produce speech. Rabbits and deer remain mute even though they have a valve structure. Cats can meow and dogs bark, but our speech is far more intricate than anything even chimpanzees (with whom we share 98.4 percent of the same DNA) can produce.

The larynx is arranged in some animals so that they can swallow and smell at the same time to protect themselves while eating. Humans have lost that ability. We cannot inhale while swallowing because our lungs are completely sealed off as a protective measure by the closure of the vocal folds.

We share an important laryngeal attribute with other mammals, however. This is called the **glottal effort closure reflex**. To feel this reflex, put your palms together and push hard against your hands. To build up pressure to push, you probably closed your vocal folds and trapped air in your lungs. This gives you more upper body strength than you would have with an open airway. Push your hands together and continue breathing as you are pushing, and you will feel much less power.

The primary purposes of the vocal folds are to give us the upper body strength we need and to protect the lungs from foreign matter. When we speak, we are using a life support function that we have adapted.

# How Sound is Produced

To produce sound, we exhale air up from the lungs. The brain signals the vocal folds, which are open for normal breathing, to come together to prepare to produce sound. The air builds pressure under the closed vocal folds. When appropriate pressure has built up, the folds are pushed apart. They are then sucked together to block the air again (see Figure 4). This process continues and produces a fluttering effect that alternately blocks the air and lets it pass through. This causes the air molecules to be condensed and rarefied, which creates a sound wave.

If you think of undisturbed air as soldiers marching in perfect formation, a sound wave is what happens if one trips. The formation is disturbed and some soldiers are closer to others than before. Air molecules respond much like this. Once the sound wave leaves the mouth, it can be heard when the altered movement of air forces our eardrum to move in the same pattern (the same frequency) as the sound wave.

To experience a process similar to phonation, blow up a balloon and stretch the mouth of the balloon. The air pressure from the balloon will cause the latex at the stretched mouth to flutter, producing a high-pitched squeak. The latex being alternately sucked together and pushed apart causes this. Your vocal folds flutter much like the mouth of the balloon as they are pulled together and pushed apart to produce sound waves.

Sound waves produced at the vocal folds are measured in cycles per second (cps). A cycle is a complete opening and closing of the vocal folds. Middle C, for example, is 256 cps. These delicate tissues move very rapidly for speech and are vulnerable to misuse.

# Common Vocal Problems

To produce sound, the vocal folds must be able to come together as a valve. All the problems associated with phonation involve alteration of the folds, which prevents them from closing effectively. The problems range from a fairly innocuous sore throat to laryngeal cancer. Fortunately, the voice lets us know fairly quickly if there is something wrong in the throat. Pain, hoarseness, and a persistent feeling of a lump in the throat are all signs of a problem.

## Hoarseness

The most obvious symptom of a vocal problem is usually hoarseness. It may result from something as simple as a common cold. Hoarseness sounds like a rough, husky, coarse voice. The voice may be lower in pitch than normal and may crack or break as you speak. Any swelling, thickening, or growth on the vocal folds can produce a hoarse voice. Think of the mouth of a balloon being stretched tightly together. If the latex has a bump in it or is thickened, the closure cannot take place. This is what happens when the folds are swollen or a growth exists.

It is impossible to tell from the sound of someone's voice whether hoarseness is caused from a simple swelling or a benign (non-cancerous) or cancerous growth. This is why one of the Seven Warning Symptoms of the American Cancer Society is a nagging cough or hoarseness. In general, if you are hoarse for more than two weeks you should see a doctor. Using a procedure called indirect laryngoscopy, an ear, nose, and throat doctor can look at your vocal folds by inserting something similar to a dentist's mirror in the back of your mouth. Looking down at your folds, the doctor can see what is preventing proper closure.

## Laryngitis

A common cause of hoarseness is laryngitis, which in most cases is an acute infection that may be accompanied by a sore throat and fever. This infection usually does not last long, and once the virus is gone your voice returns to normal. Laryngitis changes the healthy pink-colored vocal folds to swollen, red tissues.

Chronic laryngitis is a more complex condition caused by vocal misuse. Repeated bouts of laryngitis unaccompanied by fever or sore throat may indicate continued misuse of the vocal mechanism. If your hoarseness is usually worse in the morning when you get up, and you cough frequently, you may suffer from chronic laryngitis. This type of laryngitis requires work with a speech professional to change vocal habits.

In either type of laryngitis the worst thing to do is to continue trying to talk as usual. It is very easy to damage the vocal folds when the tissues are reddened and swollen as they are with laryngitis. When you are hoarse, you should talk as little as possible.

Continuing to talk while hoarse creates what has often been called the **vicious circle of vocal abuse**. You are hoarse, so you try even harder to talk, which makes you even hoarser, and on and on. Not many of us would run a marathon with tight shoes and continue running the next day despite the blisters and calluses that had developed. All too many broadcasters, however, insist they can go on the air with a hoarse voice. By doing so, they are damaging their vocal folds in the same way you would damage your feet by running when they are red and swollen. Hoarseness should be taken very seriously. Talking while you are hoarse can have long-lasting effects and may cause permanent damage.

Vocal rest is the best treatment for laryngitis. If you must talk, use a breathy voice, not a whisper (see Focus on Phonation). For whispering, the vocal folds are held tightly together and sound is produced through a limited opening. This forces the swollen tissue to be held tightly, causing more abrasion. As an example of a breathy voice, think about a sexy voice like that of Marilyn Monroe or Zsa Zsa Gabor. The folds are held open and relaxed, and air comes through the folds without closure of the folds.

If you become hoarse, you need to rest your voice. It is much more healthy for your throat to take time off for vocal rest when you first become hoarse, rather than allowing the condition to get worse through the vicious circle of vocal abuse over several days. It is like the old saying, "Pay me now or pay me later." At some point, you are going to have to rest your throat. Since your vocal folds are so important to your future career, I suggest you take time off and rest when you first feel hoarseness developing.

If you must continue to work while you are hoarse, you should limit your talking. If you are a radio news person and must do hourly spot news, try to remain silent between your broadcasts. Get an assistant to make phone calls for you and to go out in the field. Also limit your talking when you are not at work. All of this will help, but if at all possible, take a day off to rest your voice completely.

Take hoarseness seriously. Remember that you are dealing with two delicate pieces of tissue, and abuse of these tissues can cause permanent damage to your body and your career. I have heard incredible stories from clients about bad advice they have been given. One client said that he was not only encouraged to go on the air when hoarse, but was told that shouting with a hoarse voice would lower his pitch. Bad advice like that could easily end his career as a broadcaster. Having healthy vocal folds should be your top priority, and hoarseness is always a sign that your voice is not working correctly.

## Vocal Nodules and Polyps

Continued misuse of your voice when you are hoarse may result in vocal nodules (nodes). If swelling is present in the larynx, as it would be with laryngitis, a thickening of the tissue may occur. If you continue to talk, small wart-like growths the size of a pinhead can develop. These nodules are generally on both sides of the vocal folds (bilateral) and are often directly opposite each other (see Figure 5). The nodules may continue to enlarge, and if vocal abuse continues, speech production may become very difficult.

The vocal symptoms for nodules are similar to laryngitis. The voice is hoarse, low-pitched, and may lack sufficient volume. These symptoms do not go away, however, as they would with acute laryngitis.

Nodules are most common in adult women who speak with a tense, loud voice. The typical candidate for vocal nodules is socially aggressive, talks a lot, and is often in tense situations. All of these characteristics are common traits of broadcasters. The voice may have been high-pitched, but it progresses to low-pitch as the nodules become larger. Nodules, also called nodes, are also common in public speakers, singers, and young children ("screamer's nodes").

Vocal nodules develop from a combination of overtaxing the voice and incorrect use of the vocal mechanism. Many singers reportedly have numerous operations to remove vocal nodules. Harry Belafonte, for instance, whose singing is characterized by a staccato and explosive use of the voice, reportedly had such surgery. This type of vocal production is called **glottal attack** and results from an intense build-up of air under the closed vocal folds that is allowed to explode out, causing trauma to the tissues.

Vocal polyps are similar to nodules (see Figure 5), but they are usually only on one fold (unilateral). The vocal symptoms of hoarseness and low-pitch are the same as for nodules. Unlike nodules, however, vocal polyps may occur from a single traumatic vocal event. This is why it is so important not to scream at a football game or yell across the newsroom. Even an overly vigorous cough or a forceful clearing of your throat can cause a polyp. One loud burst of sound can abuse the vocal folds enough to cause hemorrhaging. Fluid fills the sac caused by the hemorrhage, which produces a polyp.

When broadcasting, remember that an increase in volume may be harmful to your vocal folds. Talk at a conversational level when on-air. The microphone is only a few inches from your mouth, and that should be your point of focus for your volume. There is usually no need to talk louder, even in very noisy conditions, if you project your voice well (see Chapter 3).

## Contact Ulcers

Another benign lesion that can develop on the vocal folds is a contact ulcer. Using a tense voice that has a hard glottal attack causes this condition. The muscular tension used for this type of voice causes the cartilage near the vocal folds to create an ulcer.

Contact ulcers are most often found in hard-driving middle-aged men. Their voices usually began as low-pitched with some glottal fry sounds. Broadcasters who lower their pitch unnaturally are good candidates for contact ulcers.

Unlike vocal nodules or polyps, contact ulcers usually cause pain in the throat, neck, or even in the ears during swallowing. The person may feel a tickle or lump in the throat. The voice may progress from being strong and forceful to breathy. The breathy voice is used after the ulcers are present to avoid the pain from forceful closure of the vocal folds.

Contact ulcers may be aggravated by gastrointestinal problems. A condition called **gastric reflux** may aggravate the ulcers in the larynx. Gastric reflux occurs when liquid comes up from the stomach during sleep. This liquid may enter the pharynx and move into the laryngeal area, causing irritation to the vocal folds. If you suffer from this condition, avoid heavy evening meals, and do not eat at least two hours before going to sleep. Consult your doctor if the problem persists.

Figure 5.

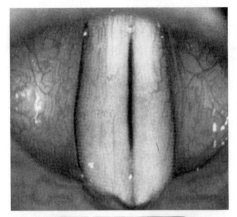

**Normal Vocal Folds** (white structures) seen during sound production. Note that healthy vocal folds have a pearly white color and sharp, well-defined contacting surfaces. They are wet with mucus.

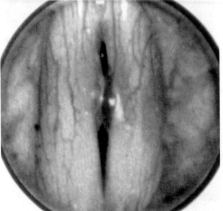

**Vocal Nodules** on both vocal folds. These lesions result from vocal abuse and cause incomplete closure, irregular margins, and added mass to the vocal folds. These contribute to breathiness, hoarseness, lowered pitch, and sometimes roughness in the voice.

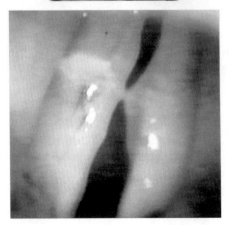

**Vocal Fold Polyp** resulting from vocal abuse in an 18-year-old acting student. Note the irregularities and swelling in the mucosa on the non-lesioned (left) vocal fold.

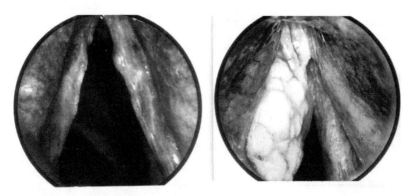

**Smoker's Vocal Folds** Two laryngoscopic views of the vocal folds in long term smokers. Note that this habit can result in inflammation, architectural changes (left photo) and the possible development of cancerous lesions (right photo) on the vocal folds.

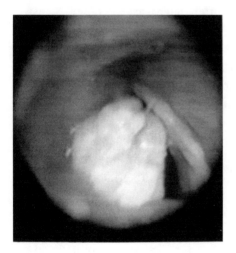

**Laryngoscopic view** of a large benign tumor of the vocal fold (cottonball structure) found in a 28-year-old woman who was first examined after experiencing hoarseness for three months. This case emphasizes the need to receive medical evaluation of hoarseness that persists for longer than 2 weeks.

Figures provided with the compliments of the Memphis Voice Care Center, a comprehensive multidisciplinary medical specialty clinic dedicated solely to the care of voice and voice-related problems. Through medical treatment, long-range vocal management planning, and continued vocal education, the Center helps patients keep their voices in top shape.

## Treatment for Vocal Nodules, Polyps, and Ulcers

The good news about all of the benign conditions described above is that they may not require surgery, and they do not appear to be pre-malignant conditions. They are caused from vocal misuse; when the misuse goes away so does the condition. New diagnostic procedures and equipment, as well as research, have shown that most of these conditions will completely disappear when the voice is used correctly.

Dr. Joshua Oppenheim, an ear, nose, and throat special-ist (otolaryngologist) in the Washington, D.C. area, reports that 90 percent of his patients with nodules, polyps, or ulcers do not require surgery. Often, though, work with a speech pathologist to learn proper vocal production is necessary. This work might last from six months to a year in some cases, and involves reduc-ing tension in the larynx and learning to talk with a relaxed voice. Medical treatment is often necessary to control gastric reflux.

If you become hoarse for more than two weeks, the first step is to get a proper diagnosis. An otolaryngologist might use in-direct laryngoscopy or videostroboscopy. Videostroboscopy in-volves the use of a video camera and a strobe light. By projecting the strobe light down the throat and timing its flash, the video cam-era shows the vibrations of the vocal folds as a wave-like move-ment. This technique allows physicians to view the size and type of the vocal fold problem as well as the resulting interruption in the vibration. Dr. Oppenheim has observed that this equipment allows for a much more precise diagnosis.

If you are having vocal problems, seek a specialist with the latest equipment. Also, always get a second opinion if you are advised to have surgery to remove a benign lesion. In the past, surgery was often recommended, but, as has been pointed out, it may be unnecessary or inappropriate. Surgery is still required in some instances to cure vocal fold lesions that do not respond well to medical or speech therapy, but a second opinion is always appropriate.

## Cancer of the Larynx

All vocal problems are not as easily treated as nodules, polyps, and ulcers. Laryngeal cancer requires surgery or radiation, and is a life-threatening condition. The American Cancer Society reports that laryngeal cancer strikes approximately 10,600 persons in the United States each year and causes 4,200 deaths.

As with the benign conditions described above, hoarseness is usually the first symptom of laryngeal cancer, which most often begins as a growth on the vocal folds (see Figure 5). Other symptoms may be a change in pitch, a sense of discomfort or lump in the throat, coughing, difficulty or pain in breathing or swallowing, and earache. Since these symptoms can also signal benign conditions, it is important to have them diagnosed by a physician if they persist for more than two weeks.

The impact of laryngeal cancer on a broadcaster's voice is profound. Even the non-surgical technique of using radiation therapy can affect the sound of the voice. Surgery to remove a cancerous growth usually affects vocal production significantly. If a laryngectomy is required, the voice is completely lost when the larynx is removed. Following the surgery, the patient breaths through a tracheostoma, a hole made in the lower front of the neck. This is necessary because the important valve provided by the vocal folds has been removed, and the path to the lungs is unprotected. During the surgery it is necessary to block off the trachea permanently from the mouth, and channel the breathing out the tracheostoma. In addition to losing the capability for normal vocal production, laryngectomy patients are also physically weaker because they no longer have the glottal effort closure reflex explained earlier in this chapter.

## Smoking and Cancer

Unlike nodules, polyps, or ulcers, laryngeal cancer is not caused from vocal misuse. The most common cause of laryngeal cancer is cigarette smoking (see Figure 5). In fact, the American Cancer Society reports that almost all those who develop cancer of the larynx use or have used tobacco. Cigarettes contain chemicals that directly irritate the vocal folds when inhaled and exhaled. Alcohol consumption is another important risk factor. People who smoke *and* drink are at highest risk of cancer (see Table 1).

In addition, smoking is the primary factor in oral cancer, which, like laryngeal cancer, can have devastating effects on a broadcaster. According to the American Cancer Society, oral cancer strikes approximately 29,800 persons in the United States each year, causing 8,100 deaths. Male smokers are 27.5 percent more likely to get oral cancer than nonsmokers. The death rate from oral cancer is about six times higher for smokers than for nonsmokers. Pipe and cigar smokers may develop oral cancer even if they do not inhale smoke into their lungs.

### Table 1
### Relative Risks of Developing Throat Cancer (Laryngeal and Hypopharyngeal) for Smokers and Drinkers versus Nonsmokers and Nondrinkers

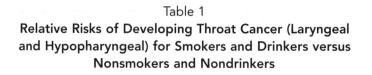

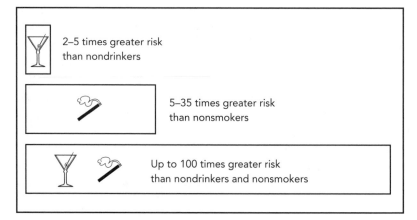

2–5 times greater risk than nondrinkers

5–35 times greater risk than nonsmokers

Up to 100 times greater risk than nondrinkers and nonsmokers

Source: American Cancer Society, Cancer Facts & Figures, 1999

If those cancers are not enough reason to avoid smoking, lung cancer should be. Smoking has been shown to have a direct connection to lung cancer. The American Cancer Society says that smoking is responsible for 87 percent of incidents of lung cancer. They expect 171,600 new cases in 1999 and 158,900 deaths. A person who smokes two packs a day is twenty-five times more likely to die of lung cancer than a nonsmoker.

The dangers of smoking are not limited to broadcasters who smoke. Environmental tobacco smoke, or second-hand smoke is estimated to cause nearly 2 percent of annual lung cancer deaths, according to a National Academy of Sciences report quoted by the American Cancer Society. This amounts to 3,000 persons who die from lung cancer caused from others' cigarettes. The American Cancer Society has found that nonsmokers exposed to twenty or more cigarettes a day at home or work have twice the risk of developing lung cancer. It is also estimated that 35,000 to 40,000 deaths from heart disease are related to exposure to second-hand smoke. In addition, people exposed to second-hand smoke suffer more colds, bouts with bronchitis, chronic coughs and ear infections, and have reduced lung function.

To summarize the devastating effects of smoking, the American Cancer Society reports in their 1999 "Cancer Facts and Figures" that cigarette smoking is the single main cause of cancer mortality in the United States. Smoking is directly related to 1068 deaths *per day* in this country. Compare this to scheduled airline flight fatalities, which totaled *only* 342 *per year* for 1996 (as reported by the National Transportation Safety Board), and you begin to understand the significance.

When I speak to groups of broadcasters, I tell them that smoking is just plain stupid if you value your career and your life. The evidence is overwhelming and irrefutable. It is not even a good gamble. If you smoke, the odds are that you will develop vocal problems. Why spend years training to be the best broadcaster you can be, only to defeat yourself by smoking?

Do not admire the classic "smoker's voice." Smokers generally do have a lower-pitched voice, but that is because of the trauma smoking causes to the vocal folds (see Figure 5). Incredibly, I was told of a news director who advised the women in his shop to smoke because it would lower their pitch. That advice is the equivalent of telling someone to drive while drunk because he or she will be more relaxed. The effects can be deadly.

Remember the danger of environmental smoke as well. We now have smoke-free airline flights, offices, and restaurants. CNN was the first company to make its newsrooms smoke-free worldwide. Now this is common practice, but make certain that your news organization strictly enforces the smoking ban.

The once common image of the smoke-filled newsroom should be history. Far too many broadcasters, including Edward R. Murrow, have died from smoking-related illnesses. Ed Bliss, Murrow's writer at CBS Radio, reports that Murrow smoked three to four packs of unfiltered Camels a day. A former Murrow writer advised Bliss to never use adjectives in his copy and always carry a fresh pack of Camels for Murrow. Murrow died of lung cancer at the age of fifty-seven. All the facts about smoking that are now common knowledge were not available thirty years ago. Broadcasters today should avoid all contact with tobacco smoke.

# Taking Care of Your Voice

In addition to avoiding tobacco smoke, there are other steps you can take to have a healthy voice. Luckily, vocal hygiene and basic good health often go hand in hand.

## Coughing

Straining the voice in any way has a harmful effect on the vocal folds. Perhaps the most common vocal abuse is coughing. When we cough, we build up tremendous air pressure under the vocal folds. The air moves up the trachea very rapidly after being forcefully exhaled by a push from the abdominal muscles. This blast of air is intended to blow any obstruction out of the throat. This might be mucus, if we have a cold, or a piece of food that has started down toward the laryngeal area. When we cough, the air leaving the lungs is moving at nearly 600 m.p.h. The folds vibrate explosively which is what is needed to clear the throat.

The force that makes a cough work may also damage the delicate throat tissue. Excessive coughing can be harmful to the vocal folds because of the forceful closure it causes. The folds may begin to swell and eventually become thickened. Any cold or allergy should be controlled to limit the need for coughing (see Chapter 9 in this book and *Broadcaster's Survival Guide* for information on working when you have a cold).

In certain instances, a blast of air similar to that of a cough can save a person's life. The Heimlich Maneuver (taught by the American Red Cross and the American Heart Association as part of CPR instruction) involves forcing air through the trachea to dislodge food or objects totally blocking the trachea. When foreign matter is caught between the vocal folds, the person cannot make a sound. The universal sign for choking is a gripping of the throat area; a person choking is unable to cough, speak, or breathe. During the Heimlich Maneuver, the choking person's abdominal area is compressed forcefully. The diaphragm rises, and the effect is as if you slammed the handles of a bellows closed. Anything stuck in the tube of the bellows would be blasted out. In a similar manner, food stuck in the person's throat may actually fly across the room if the Heimlich Maneuver is performed correctly.

## Throat Clearing

Throat clearing can also be harmful if done excessively. As when coughing, clearing your throat causes your folds to vibrate explosively. This can cause swelling and may lead to the development of polyps or nodules on the vocal folds. Clearing your throat is like a small cough, and it can become a habit. Some people feel the need to do this repeatedly throughout the day. Try to be aware of how often you clear your throat and keep it to a minimum. You may have to ask a friend to observe how many times you clear your throat, since this action is often unconscious.

Allergies are often a factor in throat clearing. If you find yourself clearing your throat a great deal, it might be helpful to have yourself tested for allergies. An allergy to certain foods or substances may be causing your discomfort.

One food group that commonly makes people clear their throats and cough is milk products. If you like to drink milk in the morning or have cereal for breakfast, you may find yourself clearing your throat all morning. Milk products establish a condition in

**Newsroom noise may contribute to loud speech.**
Courtesy of KSL-TV, Salt Lake City, Utah.

our throats conducive to the development of mucus. If you avoid milk products before going on air, you will find your throat much clearer. Save the consumption of milk products for after your on-air work if you find they contribute to coughing or throat clearing.

## Loud Speech

Vocal nodules and polyps are linked with overly loud speech. For loud speech, the vocal folds come together very forcefully. They open slower but close much more quickly.

Most broadcasters are aware of their volume on the air because of the advice they receive from engineers. What they may not monitor, however, is the volume of their speech at other times. Many people with slight hearing loss, for instance, consistently speak too loudly.

Another condition that may cause loud speech is a noisy newsroom without an intercom. All too often I find myself in a newsroom where police scanners are blaring, several monitors are on, and ten or twenty people are trying to talk on the phone or to others in the newsroom. As calls come in, I hear on-air broadcasters shouting over this chaos to tell someone else to pick up the phone.

For good vocal hygiene, you should limit your talking in noisy places. This includes the newsroom described above, as well as in cars or vans, airplanes, trains, or anywhere that requires an increase in volume. And, of course, avoid shouting at sports or music events. Remember that you are making your living on those two little muscles in your throat, and you must take care of them.

## Vocal Hydration

The vocal folds are covered with mucus. The nose alone produces more than a pint of mucus per day. The entire respiratory tract produces more than a quart a day. This moist condition is important to

Often reporters' assignments require broadcasting from noisy locations such as Dan Rather faced in Tiananmen Square during the Chinese pro-democracy uprising.

Courtesy of CBS News.

aid in proper vocal-fold closure and to protect the tissue. Much like oil in a car, mucus provides a protective coating. If the throat is dry, the folds are more likely to be damaged because they lack the appropriate mucus to protect them. Any condition that dehydrates body tissues also dries out the throat.

Excessive mouth breathing can dry out the throat. It is appropriate to breathe through your mouth when you are talking. At other times, breathing should be through the nose so that the air can be filtered, warmed, and moisturized before it goes into the laryngeal area. If you have any blockage in the nose that causes mouth breathing, it should be corrected. In addition, you should avoid breathing through your mouth when you are asleep. Sleeping on your back will often cause mouth breathing. Since this sleeping posture may cause back pain as well, it should be avoided. Sleeping on your side with your mouth closed is best.

If you have a cold or a stuffy nose, antihistamines will help open a blocked nasal cavity, but they accomplish this by drying out the tissues (see Chapter 9). If the nose is dried out, the throat is also. When you have a cold, it is difficult to avoid drying the throat, since you will most likely be breathing through your mouth if you do not take something. This is one of the reasons why it is so important to drink plenty of liquids and inhale steam when you have cold symptoms.

Forced-air heating and air conditioning are used in most homes and newsrooms as well as on airplanes and trains. This dry air also contributes to a dry throat. If you live and work in this type of condition or in an excessively dry climate, a humidifier should be used to increase humidity to 40 to 60 percent (see *Broadcaster's Survival Guide*). This pumps moisture into the air to lessen the harmful drying effects of the forced air. You can also inhale moisture by using a facial steamer, which gives you the added advantage of moisturizing your facial tissues as well. Simply inhaling steam from a pot of boiling water will also help your throat. (Make certain it does not burn your throat or skin.)

One important chemical that takes water out of the body by acting as a diuretic on the kidneys is caffeine (or technically xanthine, which includes the chemicals in tea and cocoa). You only retain about one-half cup of fluid for every cup of caffeinated fluid you drink. One cup of coffee will not have a tremendous dehydrating effect on your tissues, but if you combine that with other sources of caffeine (see Table 2), you can easily suffer from its usage.

It is easy for caffeine consumption to become excessive. Looking at Table 2, you will see that if you consumed three cups of coffee, a glass of iced tea, an ounce of chocolate, a Diet Coke, and two Excedrin tablets in one day you would be in the range of 610 milligrams of caffeine. Since caffeine also stimulates the central nervous system and your heart, excessive amounts are not good for your throat or your body. Think of coffee as liquid stress. Most recommendations suggest no more than two small (5 oz.) cups of coffee a day or around 200 milligrams. Caffeine does give you a sense of alertness, but as Chapter 1 explained, that can be achieved in healthier ways through proper breathing.

Alcohol also works as a diuretic. It robs your tissues of needed moisture. Dehydration may be the cause of the hangover headache. The classic dry mouth and excessive thirst the morning after signal the degree of dehydration that has occurred. In addition, chronic alcohol abuse is linked with laryngeal and oral cancer. Alcohol is such a significant diuretic that it does not count at all in your daily fluid needs. You have to drink the same amount of water as alcohol just to replace what you lose from the diuretic effect of the alcohol. For a healthy body and voice, alcohol consumption should be limited.

The best way to combat the drying effects of alcohol, caffeine, and environmental factors is by drinking as much water as possible. Calculating how much water to drink is simple if you use the ratio devised by the International SportsMedicine Institute, which works with Olympic athletes. They have done research on the amount of water we need, and their formula has been used for over two decades. They report that our **daily water needs are one-half ounce of water per pound of body weight**. This adjusts water intake for body size.

If you do drink a caffeinated beverage, remember that you retain only half of the fluid. You can see that it is much healthier and more efficient to keep a mug filled with water on your desk rather than coffee. Drink from it all day to keep your body and throat hydrated. Avoid ice water close to air time, as it may constrict the muscles in the throat.

If you feel the need to drink warm liquids, try to avoid

### Table 2
### Caffeine Content Of Beverages, Foods, And Common Drugs

|  | Average milligrams of caffeine |
|---|---|
| Coffee (5-oz. cup) | |
| Brewed, drip method | 115 |
| Brewed, percolator | 80 |
| Instant | 65 |
| Decaffeinated, brewed | 3 |
| Decaffeinated, instant | 2 |
| | |
| Tea (5-oz. cup) | |
| Brewed, major U.S. brands | 40 |
| Brewed, imported brands | 60 |
| Instant | 30 |
| Iced (12-oz. glass) | 70 |
| | |
| Cocoa beverage (5-oz. cup) | 4 |
| | |
| Chocolate milk beverage (8 oz.) | 5 |
| | |
| Milk chocolate (1 oz.) | 6 |

** Source: FDA, Food Additive Chemistry Evaluation Branch, based on evaluations of existing literature on caffeine levels.

| Soft Drinks (12-oz. serving) | |
|---|---|
| Jolt | 71.2 |
| Sugar-Free Mr. Pibb | 58.8 |
| Mountain Dew | 55.0 |
| no caffeine in Canada | |
| Diet Mountain Dew | 55.0 |
| Kick Citrus | 54 |
| (36 mg per 8 oz can, caffeine from guarana) | |

| | Average milligrams of caffeine |
|---|---|
| Mello Yello | 52.8 |
| Surge | 51.0 |
| Tab | 46.8 |
| Battery energy drink | 140mg/1 = 46.7mg/can |
| Coca-Cola | 45.6 |
| Diet Coke | 45.6 |
| Shasta Cola | 44.4 |
| Shasta Cherry Cola | 44.4 |
| Shasta Diet Cola | 44.4 |
| Mr. Pibb | 40.8 |
| OK Soda | 40.5 |
| Dr. Pepper | 39.6 |
| Pepsi-Cola | 37.2 |
| Aspen | 36.0 |
| Diet Pepsi | 35.4 |
| RC Cola | 36.0 |
| Diet RC | 36.0 |
| Diet Rite | 36.0 |
| Canada Dry Cola | 30.0 |
| Canada Dry Diet Cola | 1.2 |
| 7 Up | 0 |

Candy
Chocolate, Bakers—1 oz (28 g)

| | |
|---|---|
| baking choc, unsweetened, | 25 |
| german sweet | 8 |
| semi-sweet | 13 |

Choc chips

| | |
|---|---|
| Bakers—1/4 cup (43 g) | 13 |
| german sweet, | |
| Bakers—1/4 cup (43 g) | 15 |

|  | Average milligrams of caffeine |
|---|---|
| **Candy (continued)** | |
| Chocolate Bar, | |
| Cadbury—1oz (28 g) | 15 |
| Chocolate milk | 8 |
| **Desserts** | |
| Jello Pudding Pops, Choc (47 g) | 2 |
| Choc mousse from Jell-O mix (95 g) | 6 |
| Jell-O choc fudge mousse (86g) | 12 |
| **Beverages** | |
| 3 heaping teaspoons of choc powder mix | 8 |
| 2 tablespoons choc syrup | 5 |
| 1 envelope hot cocoa mix | 5 |
| **Dietary formulas** | |
| ensure, plus, choc, Ross Labs— 8 oz (259) g) | 10 |

** Source: Bowes and Church's Food values by Anna De Planter Bowes. Lippincott, Phila. 1989.

| **Perscription Drugs** | |
|---|---|
| Cafergot (for migraine headaches) | 100 |
| Fiorinal (for tension headaches) | 40 |
| Soma Compound (muscle relaxant) | 32 |
| Darvon Compound (pain relief) | 32.4 |

| | Average milligrams of caffeine |
|---|---|
| **Nonprescription Drugs** | |
| Weight-Control Aids | |
| Dex-A-Diet II | 200 |
| Dexatrim Extra Strength | 200 |
| Dietac capsules | 200 |
| Maximum Strength Appedrine | 100 |
| Prolamine | 140 |
| | |
| Alertness Tablets | |
| Nodoz | 100 |
| Vivarin | 200 |
| | |
| Analgesic/Pain Relief | |
| Anacin, Maximum strength | 32 |
| Excedrin | 65 |
| Midol | 32.4 |
| Vanquish | 33 |
| | |
| Diuretics | |
| Aqua-Ban | 100 |
| Maximum Strength Aqua-Ban Plus | 200 |
| Permathene H2 Off | 200 |
| | |
| Cold/Allergy Remedies | |
| Coryban-D capsules | 30 |
| Triaminicin tablets | 30 |
| Dristan Decongestant tablets & | |
| Dristan A-F Decongestant tablets | 16.2 |
| Duradyne-Forte | 30 |

** Source: The FDA's National Center for Drugs and Biologics. The FDA also notes that caffeine is an ingredient in more than 1,000 nonprescription drug products as well as numerous prescription drugs.

caffeine. You can drink decaffeinated coffee or tea, herbal tea, or warm water with lemon. Singers try spraying their throats with various solutions to increase moisture, but this is not necessary if you drink plenty of liquids. In addition, be aware that gargling may dry and stress the vocal fold area since you are blowing air up forcefully to gargle. The best way to have a healthy, well-hydrated throat is to drink plenty of water.

## The Ideal Newsroom

I often joke with news directors that my ideal newsroom would have sound booths set up for standing, a standing anchor desk, no smoking signs everywhere, spring water dispensers instead of coffee pots, intercoms to prevent yelling, and humidifiers. I am not sure I will see every newsroom making these changes, but as more data becomes available about the harmful behaviors mentioned above, changes will occur.

# Pitch

We not only produce sound with our vocal folds, but we also have the capability to alter the pitch or musical note of that sound. We alter pitch by increasing or decreasing the vibrations per second of the vocal folds. We can go from middle C (256 cps) to high C (512 cps)—one octave—and cover all the pitches in between. Singing this eight-tone scale ("do-re-mi-fa-so-la-ti-do") involves a subtle shortening and lengthening of the vocal folds.

The V-shaped opening of the vocal folds is positioned with the folds connecting in the front of our throat. The apex/bottom of the V is directly behind the thyroid cartilage (Adam's apple). The two ends of the folds that move are toward the back of the throat. They are each connected to a triangular-shaped arytenoid cartilage. These cartilages can pivot, rotate, and tilt backwards or sideways to alter the length of the folds and thus change the pitch.

The length, thickness, and degree of tension of the folds determine the pitch we create. Men's voices are generally around one octave lower than women's because they have longer folds—around three-quarters of an inch, versus one-half inch in women. During childhood, girls and boys have similar pitches. The male larynx, however, goes through an explosion of growth at puberty and nearly doubles in size. During this spurt of growth, boys' voices are very unpredictable and often produce embarrassing voice breaks.

A healthy voice has a range of about one and one-half octaves. Opera singers expand their range significantly, with men reaching two octaves and women often reaching three. A tenor, for example, might sing from middle C (256 cps) down an octave (128 cps) and up an octave (512 cps). This skill comes from practice and training to expand pitch range.

When we lower our pitch, the arytenoid cartilages move so that the folds become shorter and thicker. Short, thick, relaxed folds produce low pitch. For high pitch, the folds are stretched tight, producing thinner, tenser folds. The pitch is determined by the cross-sectional mass. Thick folds move slowly, which produces a low pitch, and thin, tense folds move more rapidly, producing a high pitch.

To achieve this change in pitch, the muscles in the larynx must move. The larynx actually rises in the throat slightly for a high-pitched sound and moves down noticeably for a low pitch. To experience this, put your fingers on your Adam's apple and hum a familiar song such as "Happy Birthday." You will feel the larynx moving as the pitch changes.

It is interesting to watch the head positions of television news reporters and anchors as they change pitch. Many times the head will drop down when the pitch is lowered on a word or phrase. Proponents of the affected "Ted Baxter" voice often lower their chin and compress the neck area before beginning their on-air voice. If you remember Ted on *The Mary Tyler Moore Show*, you know that his conversational voice was much higher pitched than his on-air voice. The Jim Dial character on the *Murphy Brown* show is another good example of this affected voice.

It is important to note that pitch is accomplished by changing the tension in the throat. A higher pitch is produced by greater tension. If you feel your pitch is consistently too high, it may be because of too much tension in the throat. Think of how your voice sounds when you are relaxed and content, such as when you first awaken or after a cozy evening by the fire. You might say you have a "mellow" voice. Compare this to your voice in the sound booth after a frantic day of news coverage. You might characterize both your day and your voice as tense. It is this tension that causes the pitch to rise.

If you feel your voice is too high-pitched, the first step toward improving it is to achieve relaxation in the throat area. Most of us hold our greatest degree of tension in our shoulders and neck area. Relaxing this area is imperative for good vocal production. Using abdominal-diaphragmatic breathing will help a great deal (see Focus on Breathing and Breathing Warm-Ups in Chapter 1). Relaxing your neck by doing simple neck rolls will help as well (see Focus on Phonation and Phonation Warm-Ups at the end of this chapter). Be aware that a tense body usually means a tense voice. For more on relaxation, see Chapter 9 in this book and Broadcaster's Survival Guide.

## Optimum Pitch

Inappropriate habitual pitch can cause vocal abuse. If you are speaking above or below your natural frequency, you are using unnecessary muscular energy, which can result in vocal fatigue and hoarseness. Voice professionals disagree about whether inappropriate pitch can cause vocal nodules, but there is evidence to link excessive low pitch to contact ulcers.

Equally as important to you as a broadcaster is the effect of inappropriate pitch on expressiveness. If you are consistently talking at the low end of your pitch range, you have no room to drop your pitch for emphasis. The same is true of a pitch that is too high.

I rarely see clients who feel their pitch is too low. Most clients complain that their voice is too high-pitched. According to the survey results in Appendix A, news directors agree.

Many times broadcasters adopt an inappropriately low pitch to compensate for a pitch they feel is too high. They drop their pitch when they go on the air. By doing this, they accomplish a low-pitched sound, but the damage they are doing to their vocal folds becomes apparent. They often complain of vocal fatigue, breathiness, or frequent bouts of hoarseness.

The goal for proper voice production is to talk in your optimum pitch range, which is usually around one-fourth of the way up from the bottom of your range. At your optimum pitch, the muscles of the larynx are functioning best, and the voice is the most comfortable to use. Pitch changes are easy to produce and require the least effort when you are using your optimum pitch. The most resonant tones are produced at the optimum pitch because it matches the pitch range of the resonators above the larynx (see Chapter 3).

It is difficult in a book such as this to give instructions on how to find your optimum pitch range. That is more appropriately done by a voice coach, singing teacher, or speech pathologist. Suffice it to say, however, that achieving relaxation in the vocal mechanism is always the first step toward finding your optimum pitch range.

Problems that are perceived as pitch problems are often not related to phonation, but to resonance, which is the enrichment of the sound in our vocal cavities. You are not the best judge of whether your voice is too high-pitched. I often find that clients are using the correct pitch but are limiting vocal resonance in such a way that their voice seems high-pitched and thin. These clients need work on resonance, not pitch. For more on resonance, see Chapter 3.

Beware of anyone who advises you to lower your pitch. As has been noted, finding your best pitch range is a complicated process, and not something with which to experiment. It should only be done with the guidance of a trained professional.

If you came to me as a client and had a fairly high-pitched voice, I could certainly give you a deeper voice by telling you to drop your pitch an octave. Likewise, I could make you seem taller by telling you to walk on your tiptoes all the time. Both of these activities would produce the desired results, but they would do so at the expense of your muscles. Eventually you would not be able to talk or walk without problems.

In lectures to news directors, I often play a tape of a client who came to me because of vocal fatigue. His conversational voice was relaxed and pleasant. As soon as I handed him a microphone, however, he dropped his voice into an unnaturally low pitch. I finally convinced him his natural pitch was appropriate for on-air.

The before and after tape I play usually brings laughter because he sounds so much better in his natural pitch range. Everyone wonders why he suffered so long to produce a tense, unnatural, low-pitched voice on the air.

Your goal should be to talk in a relaxed, well-resonated voice that requires the least amount of energy to maintain. Manipulating the muscles in your throat to achieve a voice you or others think sounds better can result in vocal damage. You might have a great voice for a few years, but your career will be limited by the strain you are putting on your vocal mechanism.

---

### TEN RECOMMENDATIONS FOR A HEALTHY VOICE

1) Practice abdominal-diaphragmatic breathing to decrease tension in the laryngeal area.

2) Do not smoke or expose yourself to second-hand smoke.

3) Avoid excessive alcohol consumption.

4) Avoid eating at least two hours before you go to bed. Avoid milk products before on-air work.

5) Do not talk loudly or in noisy environments such as airplanes, cars, boats, or sports and music events.

6) Keep your vocal tract moist by drinking one-half ounce of water per pound of your body weight a day, using a humidifier or inhaling steam, and avoiding substances and environments that dehydrate. Decaffeinated warm drinks may also be consumed, or hot water with lemon.

7) Avoid mouth breathing except for speech. Limit throat clearing and coughing.

8) If you do become hoarse, limit your talking, and use a breathy voice, not a whisper.

9) Use a pitch that is comfortable and does not cause vocal fatigue.

10) See a physician if hoarseness, pain, or odd sensations in the throat last for more than two weeks.

# Focus on Phonation

Relaxation is the key to good phonation. Many of the activities listed below are designed to achieve maximum relaxation in the laryngeal area.

A) A whisper requires a great deal of tension in the vocal folds. They must come together tightly, and sound is produced in a small opening. To feel the tension this requires, imagine you are leading your crew out of a city council meeting. You must get everyone to follow you to the live truck, but you do not want to disturb the meeting. Whisper loudly, "Come with me, everybody." Whisper this several times and feel the tension in your throat. Now completely relax your throat and attempt to say the same phrase in a breathy voice. Begin with a barely audible sound that feels like the "h" in "hello." For a breathy voice, the vocal folds are left open in their V-shaped position and air rushes over them. The throat remains completely relaxed. The breathy voice will not sound as loud, but the throat will be relaxed. This is the voice you should use when you have any hoarseness or discomfort in your throat.

B) Take a breath using the clavicular muscles, so that the shoulders rise on inhalation. After you have inhaled, hold the breath and feel the tension in the throat. Next, take an abdominal-diaphragmatic breath (see *Focus on Breathing* in Chapter 1). Hold the breath and compare the degree of tension in the throat. You should feel much less tension with the abdominal-diaphragmatic breath.

C) To feel the larynx moving, put your fingers on your Adam's apple and make an "eee" sound as in "bee." Change the pitch of the sound and feel the larynx rise for the higher pitch and move downward for the lower pitch.

D) To compare voiced and voiceless sounds in our language, put your fingers on your Adam's apple. Bring your lips together and make a "p" sound (the initial sound in the word "pot"). Now make a "b" sound (as in "Bob"). You should feel vibrations of the vocal folds for the "b" but not for the "p."

E) If you want to get a feeling of what your optimum pitch might be, sigh deeply with an "ah" sound. This "ah" will usually be in your optimum pitch.

F) To avoid laryngeal tension, you should develop the sense that your voice does not come from your larynx or your mouth, but from your diaphragm in the solar plexus region. Our entire body produces speech. Imagine a bellows with a reed at the end of the neck. All the energy to make that reed vibrate comes from your arms pushing the bellows shut. The reed does not move by itself. In the same way, our voice does not come from the vocal folds, but begins with the breath, which is the energy that produces the movement of the folds. Gaining a sense of body involvement in vocal production can be helpful in eliminating tension and producing the healthiest voice possible. Two authors who have written extensively on body involvement in speech are Kristin Linklater and Arthur Lessac (see Suggested Readings.) In addition, instruction in the Alexander Technique, T'ai Chi, and Yoga can help develop this feeling. Acting classes are also helpful.

## Phonation Warm-Ups

These exercises are aimed at reducing tension in the laryngeal area. They should be performed until relaxation has occurred. Be careful not to exercise the vocal folds too much since vocal fatigue may occur.

1) Yawning has been used for centuries as a technique to relax the throat. A good yawn relaxes the larynx and throat and brings in a good air supply. Practice yawning for relaxation. Drop the jaw and think of what a good yawn feels like. Yawning is sometimes contagious so take the opportunity to yawn when you see others doing so. Add a sigh at the end of your yawn to feel your relaxed, open throat. After yawning, say this phrase with the same open throat, "How many hats does Henry have?" Say this several times trying to preserve the open feeling.

*Most of us tend to hold tension in our shoulders, upper back, and neck. To relieve this tension try the following exercises. Be careful not to stretch your muscles too much.*

2) Clasp your hands behind your back. Squeeze your shoulder blades together and tilt your head back slightly. Hold for five seconds at the point you feel resistance. Release. Repeat this warm-up until your shoulders and upper back feel relaxed.

3) Place your hands on your shoulders. Rotate your shoulders by bringing your elbows together in front, moving them down, back, and up in a circular movement. Rotate five times in one direction and five times in the opposite direction.

4) Very slowly drop your chin to your chest and roll your head up to your right shoulder. Roll your head back down to your chest and roll your head up to your left shoulder. Bring your chin back down to your chest. Repeat slowly three times. (Do not roll your head back. This may cause neck injuries.)

5) Look straight ahead. Rotate your head slowly and look over each shoulder twice as if you were signaling an exaggerated "no." Repeat twice.

6) To relax the throat, take a deep abdominal-diaphragmatic breath and exhale an "ah" sound. Inhale again and exhale an "ou" sound as in "you." Inhale a third time and exhale an "m" sound. Feel the resonance in the nasal cavity for the "m."

7) To gain flexibility in pitch, say "one" at your normal pitch level. Now go up one step in pitch and say "two." Go up another step in pitch and say "three." Go back down to your normal pitch with "three, two, one." Now go down in pitch one step and say "two." Go down another step and say "three." Go back up to your normal pitch. This process would look like this:

```
            three three
      two             two
one                 one one                          one
                           two              two
                         three three
```

You might want to trace the steps in pitch in the air with your hand as your voice produces them. Tape recording this and the following Warm-Up will help you hear if you are really producing the pitch changes you hope for.

8) Continue pitch work by saying the sentences

```
                    up
My voice is going       in pitch.
My voice is going           in pitch.
                  down
```

Repeat these two sentences until you feel comfortable with your pitch changes.

9) Use this phrase to expand your pitch range:

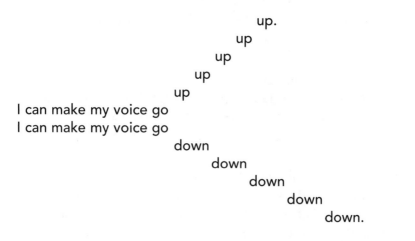

```
                              up.
                        up
                  up
              up
          up
I can make my voice go
I can make my voice go
              down
                  down
                      down
                          down
                              down.
```

Do not push your voice into an artificially high or low pitch during this Warm-Up. Going too high or low can cause vocal fatigue and possible abuse. For a falsetto, for example, the vocal folds are pulled excessively tight, and they lose their wave-like motion. As with any unnatural position of the folds, this can be harmful.

10) Sing up the musical scale until you feel comfortable with these eight tones.

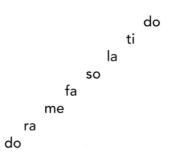

*Voice is critical to a news department . . . because it is the first indicator an audience has to gauge whether a reporter knows what he or she is talking about. . . . If the reporter sounds young and inexperienced the audience is immediately put on notice.*

**David Jensch**
**News Director, KBJR-TV**
**Duluth, Minnesota**

*On-air talent should get in touch with their delivery system—from breathing to diction. But don't "put on," be natural and real.*

**Jonathan Knopf**
**News Director, WLFL-TV**
**Raleigh, North Carolina**

*Reach a "happy medium" that's comfortable for you. Don't overdo it (like a bad 1960's DJ) or underdo it by assuming voice work isn't important.*

**Kim Wright**
**Director of News Coverage, NewsChannel 8**
**Springfield, Virginia**

# Resonance— Enriching the Speech Sound

When people criticize the quality of a broadcaster's voice, they are usually talking about resonance. The vocal folds generate sound waves, but the resonating cavities enrich and augment the sound. Just as no two people look exactly alike, no two vocal mechanisms are exactly alike. The difference in the shape, size, and resiliency of the resonating cavities makes each voice unique.

Resonance not only gives us each a different voice, but it also allows our voices to be heard. To create sound waves, the vocal folds set air in motion in a wave-like fashion, fluttering open and closed (see Chapter 2). If these sound waves were not resonated, they would produce a faint sound barely audible to the human ear. The slight movement of air at the vocal folds must be enriched by the air and resonating structures above it in the throat.

# Characteristics of Resonance

All sound-producing instruments use resonance to enrich their sounds. A guitar string nailed between two pieces of wood would not make a loud musical sound that you could hear easily. Plucking that string would produce a very thin, weak sound. Put that string on a guitar body, however, and the sound is enriched by the body of the guitar and the air trapped in the body. The sound waves become louder and richer.

Resonance is the ability of one body of molecules to set another body into the same wave-like motion. These may be air molecules or a solid structure. Notice how solid objects vibrate when there is a loud crash of thunder or an explosion. If you feel a table or wall when this happens, you can feel the vibration that results from the molecules moving.

Touching a vibrating tuning fork to different surfaces also demonstrates how solid matter resonates sound. A vibrating middle C tuning fork will sound different depending on what you touch it to. The structure of the solid matter determines the quality of the sound you hear. The pitch remains middle C, but the quality changes.

Resonance also results from air molecules being set into motion. Musical wind instruments work on the principle of air chamber resonance. Middle C played on a flute sounds different from the same note played on a tuba because of the resonating qualities of their structures. The fundamental frequency played may be the same, but the quality we hear is very different.

# Anatomy of Vocal Resonance

Our voices work on the same principle as a wind instrument. Sound begins with the vocal folds setting air into motion. These sound waves created at the vocal folds are then resonated in the cavities of the throat, mouth, and nose. The fundamental pitch established at the vocal folds is important, but equally important is the manner in which this pitch is resonated.

## Variables of Vocal Resonance

Sound waves react in specific ways depending on the cavities they encounter. The harmonics or secondary vibrations (overtones) created along with the fundamental pitch are either enriched or damped off (killed) depending on the type of environment they enter. All resonating bodies have a natural frequency at which they resonate best. Consequently, they will damp some harmonics and emphasize the amplitude of those closest to the natural frequency of the resonating body.

A jug band is a good example of this. If you blow over the mouth of a big jug you will hear a deep sound. A small jug produces a high, shrill sound. You may blow over these with the same intensity, but as the air rushes around inside the jug, some sound waves are damped and others are augmented. A larger cavity allows more low-pitched or long sound waves to survive. Smaller cavities damp the long sound waves, and a higher pitch results.

There are four principles of air chamber resonance (tube or cavity resonance) that specifically affect speech:

1) The length of the tube or size of the cavity it passes through—larger cavities resonate lower frequencies.
2) The elasticity of the walls of the tube or cavity—softer, more relaxed surfaces resonate lower frequencies.
3) The size of the lip opening of the tube or cavity—smaller openings resonate lower frequencies.
4) The constriction along the tube or cavity.

These principles apply to the jug band, our speech, and any sound-producing source. Just like the jug band, we can alter the size of our resonating cavities to make our voices sound richer or thinner. We have three basic resonating cavities that affect our vocal sound.

## Pharynx

The pharynx is a soft-sided, muscular tube about five inches long that begins at the larynx and goes up to the nasal cavity (see Figure 6). You see the back wall of this tube in a mirror when you open your mouth and say "ah." If you think of human resonating cavities as being in an "F" shape, the main, upright line would be the pharynx.

```
P    NOSE
H
A    MOUTH
R
Y
N
X
```

The pharynx is important for vocal resonance because it gives tube resonance to our voices. Just like the body of a clarinet or any wind instrument, the tube of the pharynx provides air trapped in a cylinder that will vibrate. Like any resonating body, a tube has a natural frequency it resonates best. A pipe organ or a xylophone is designed with this in mind. The resonating tubes vary in length corresponding to the notes they are to resonate. The longer tubes resonate the lower frequencies.

The length of our pharynx affects vocal resonance. A child's pharynx, for example, is short, which works best for higher frequency resonance. Because a child's vocal folds are also short and produce a high-pitched sound, the pharynx is appropriate to resonate a child's voice.

Adult voices sound more resonant if the pharynx is longer and has a greater diameter. For the most part, this is an anatomical feature and not something that can be controlled during speech.

One adjustment in the pharynx that does take place involves the larynx rising for a higher-pitched sound and lowering for low-pitched sounds (see Focus on Phonation in Chapter 2). This

## FIGURE 6
### Resonating Cavities

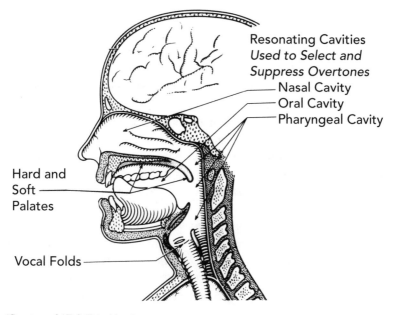

Resonating Cavities
*Used to Select and
Suppress Overtones*
—— Nasal Cavity
—— Oral Cavity
—— Pharyngeal Cavity

Hard and
Soft —
Palates

Vocal Folds ——

(Courtesy of AT & T Archives)

may be an attempt to match the length of the pharynx with the pitch of the sound. This happens automatically just as the larynx rises and the pharynx constricts when you swallow. I have seen broadcasters, however, who purposefully constrict their necks by lowering their chins and pushing their heads back. This action seems to lower the pitch, but it increases tension in the throat area and also shortens the pharynx. These are two things you want to avoid.

The elasticity of the walls of the pharynx also affects the quality of the resonance. A relaxed throat creates the best atmosphere for good resonance. A hard, tense throat may emphasize the higher harmonics of the voice—resulting in a harsh, strident voice. A relaxed throat usually results in a longer, softer pharynx, which produces a mellow, rich voice.

## Oral Cavity

Our mouths are our most flexible resonators. We can vary the shape by moving the tongue, the jaw, the cheeks, and the velum (*soft palate*). The oral cavity is also changed by any addition to the mouth like dental braces, bridge work, or false teeth. Even tooth bonding slightly changes the resonance characteristics of the oral cavity. The tonsils lie directly behind the oral cavity in the pharyngeal area, and their removal greatly changes the shape of the resonating cavities.

The tongue is a major factor in oral resonance. It fills the bottom of the mouth and continues down to form the front of the pharynx. Manipulating the tongue helps us articulate our sounds and resonate them. For the "ee" sound, for example, we raise and tense the tongue to fill part of our oral cavity. Compare the formation of this sound to "ah."

The vowels in our language are produced mainly by adjusting the shape of our oral cavity. We change its size to accentuate certain harmonics and reduce others. The same pitch, therefore, can sound like an "ee" or an "ah" based on our manipulation of the oral cavity that changes the resonance (see Focus on Resonance).

Anyone who can talk like Donald Duck knows that this is accomplished by bunching the tongue in the back of the mouth to limit the size of the resonating cavity. Likewise, a childish voice results from small resonating cavities. Experiment with this feeling by saying your name first with the tongue down and then with it pushed high up in the mouth toward the hard palate. By making the oral cavity smaller you reduce the size of the resonating cavity. Just like the sound coming from the small jug, the voice sounds higher-pitched.

Unfortunately, many speakers have developed a habit of bunching the tongue up in the mouth while speaking. This produces the thin, immature-sounding voice that plagues some female (and occasionally male) broadcasters, and contributes to the nasality or palatal production of certain sounds in the Midwestern and New York dialects. For both of these problems, opening the mouth more and lowering the tongue is the key to improvement (see Resonance Warm-Ups).

The jaw also plays an important role in oral resonance.

Good flexibility of the jaw helps create a better opening. It is not surprising that the jaw often causes difficulties with resonance. The closing muscles of the jaw are some of the strongest in our body because they are designed for chewing. They can produce thousands of pounds of pressure per square inch. We often hold tension in the jaw area and clench our mouths shut. Many people do this while sleeping, and they may even grind their teeth at night. If you tend to hold your mouth tightly closed and clench your teeth at night, it is difficult to relax the jaw for speaking. You should concentrate on exercises to relax the jaw (see Resonance and Articulation Warm-Ups in this chapter and Chapter 4).

For good oral resonance, the jaw should be relaxed and free moving. Eliminating tension from the neck area before speaking is important (see Phonation and Resonance Warm-Ups in this chapter and Chapter 2). Proper abdominal-diaphragmatic breathing assists in maintaining a relaxed throat (see Breathing Warm-Ups in Chapter 1). It is also a good idea to consciously try to keep space between your teeth during the day. Resist clenching your teeth. This will help you sound better and reduce tension in your vocal mechanism.

It is not advisable to smile when speaking. Smiling pulls the cheek muscles back and tenses them, creating a wider mouth opening. The wider the mouth opening, the higher the frequencies resonated. Spreading the lips in a smile can thus contribute to the production of a high-pitched, strident sound. It is not accidental that most beauty pageant contestants sound alike. Their perpetual smiles have a negative affect on their resonating cavities. If you feel you need to smile in an especially upbeat story, do so before and after you speak. Lose the smile while you are talking.

You should make the most of your mouth as a resonating cavity since it is the most flexible resonator. It is amazing what can be accomplished when we improve the way we use our mouths as resonating cavities. When clients come to me saying they want to lower their pitch, what they are usually seeking is more resonance. Remember that the flute and the tuba can play exactly the same pitch, but sounds completely different because each instrument's body creates a different resonance. Changing the resonance of the sound after it leaves the mouthpiece of the musical instrument creates this difference. All of us can change our vocal sound as well by resonating it differently.

## Nasal Cavity

The nasal cavity is another resonating area that can change our sound significantly. We all have heard the whining, honking sound of someone with a nasal voice. This type of voice is unpleasant because the nasal cavity is not as good at resonating as the oral cavity.

Our nasal cavities are the least controllable of the resonating areas. The nasal cavity is about four inches long and is divided by the septum, which is a wall of cartilage and bone running from our nostrils to the soft palate. The septum extends upward from the roof of the hard palate to the bottom of the brain cavity.

The septum and the mucus in the nasal cavity tend to damp (kill) low frequency sound waves. A sound that would be full and resonant coming out of our mouths becomes high and whiny coming from our noses. The frequency of the sound may be the same when it enters the cavities, but the size of the available resonating area in each damps and reinforces different harmonics, thus changing the sound.

The soft palate, or *velum*, works as a trap door at the back of the oral cavity (see Figure 6). It opens and closes to allow access to the nasal cavity. During respiration, the soft palate is relaxed in a downward position, which allows air to enter the pharynx from the nose. When we speak, however, the soft palate tenses and moves up and back to close off the nasal cavity—except for during the production of English's three nasal consonant sounds /m/, /n/, and /ŋ/ (as in sing).

To feel the soft palate working, breathe in through your nose and out through your mouth. To watch this process, hold a mirror in front of your face and open your mouth wide as you breathe. You may see the uvula, the bulb-like extension of the soft palate, pulling up into the velum as it rises. The uvula adds little to our speech or to the action of the velum, but it does help demonstrate the action of the soft palate.

The soft palate is relatively slow moving for a speech

organ. Because it must close the nasal cavity to prevent nasality on inappropriate sounds, its slow action can create difficulties.

# Common Resonance Problems

## Nasality

With the exception of thin voices, nasality is the most common resonance problem I hear from broadcasters. The problem occurs in various ways. Some clients have **generalized nasality**, which means that all their sounds go through the nasal cavity and a true nasal voice results. Others have **assimilated nasality** which occurs only on vowels that precede or follow /m/, /n/, or /ŋ/. This is caused by the slow-moving nature of the soft palate. In a word like "man," for example, the soft palate remains down for the vowel sound instead of rising to close off the nose for the vowel, and then relaxing again for the /n/. Still other clients have nasality or palatal placement of certain vowels, like the Midwestern and New York tendency to become nasal on the vowel sounds /ɑ/ (as in "park") and /æ / (as in "back")

There are some anatomical reasons for nasality. A cleft palate leaves a hole in the hard palate, which allows sounds to enter the nasal cavity. This is generally corrected at birth now, but in the past, cleft palate sufferers had generalized nasality all their lives. Another problem occurs when the soft palate is too short. Also, some neurological diseases like myasthenia gravis affect the use of muscles and, therefore, weaken the muscles of the soft palate, limiting its ability to contract and rise to close off the nasal cavity.

In most cases, however, nasality is either a learned behavior or the result of a lazy soft palate. Learned nasality may come from living in an area where nasality pervades the pronunciation patterns, or from copying a parent or teacher with this resonance. The soft palate may lack the needed tension to close the nasal cavity. It may also result from the mouth not being opened widely enough, which can force the sound into the nasal cavity.

Unfortunately, nasality is one of the hardest resonance problems to correct. Opening the mouth more will usually help. It is also beneficial to work on placement (see Resonance Warm-Ups). I have also had clients who profited from lowering their pitch, but this should only be attempted with the help of a trained speech professional.

## Denasality

Many people mistakenly refer to a denasal voice as nasal. Actually, denasality is the reverse of nasality. A denasal voice sounds less nasal and is often associated with a head cold. A person might say, "I have a cold id by dose," when they are speaking with a denasal voice. For this vocal production, the nasal consonants /m/, /n/, and /ŋ/ are prevented from entering the nasal cavity. This eliminates the degree of nasality that is expected in American speech.

Denasality is usually a structural problem that requires medical attention. It results from nasopharyngeal blockage that prevents sound from entering the nose. This might be a deviated septum or a growth in the nasal cavity. Allergies can also cause blockage in the nose due to swelling and secretions. And, of course, all of us occasionally suffer from head colds that change our voices (see Chapter 9 in this book and *Broadcaster's Survival Guide* for more information on dealing with colds). Colds will go away, but an ear, nose, and throat specialist should check any of the other conditions. Removing the blockage and perhaps follow-up speech therapy will generally eliminate the denasality.

If denasality is not caused from blockage, it may be a learned behavior. Exercises to feel the soft palate movement will aid in correcting the problem (see Focus on Resonance).

## Thin Voice

The most common resonance problem I encounter in broadcasters is a thin voice. This may be referred to as an "immature" or "childish" voice. In women this is often called a "little girl's voice," and in men it can result in an effeminate voice. In broadcasters, a thin voice lacks an authoritative sound. It is difficult to sound credible when you have a child-like voice. In addition, when the volume is raised, this voice usually becomes shrill and strident.

As discussed earlier, bunching the tongue up in the mouth reduces the size of the resonating cavity. When the size of a cavity is reduced, the long sound waves are more likely to be damped. If you fill a vase with water, you can hear this phenomenon. The pitch of the sound will get higher and higher as the water fills more and more of the resonating air chamber. Most of us know when to turn off the water by the sound we hear from the vase.

If you use your tongue to restrict the size of your oral cavity, you will limit the number of long sound waves that can escape from your mouth. Your pitch will sound higher, and your voice will sound thin. You may be speaking in your optimum pitch range, but your small oral resonating cavity is killing the lower-pitched harmonics and emphasizing the ones closest to its natural resonant frequency. Because the cavity is small, its natural resonating frequency is high. What we hear is a thin, high-pitched sound.

Building a rich voice requires opening your mouth more. This does not mean that you will have exaggerated lip movements for speech. Your lips may not have to open any more than they already do. What needs to be accomplished for good oral resonance is a wider opening in the back of the oral cavity. Arthur Lessac, a prominent voice specialist, refers to this as the "inverted megaphone" approach (see Suggested Reading). If you put a small megaphone next to your cheeks, the small end would be at your lips and the wide end by your molars.

Learning to open the mouth wider in the back requires practice. Remember that the muscles that close the mouth are some of the strongest in our bodies. Dropping and relaxing the jaw means letting go of tension in the jaw area (see Warm-Ups and Focus on Resonance). A reduction of tension in this area can be accomplished, however, and the increase in resonance can be dramatic.

If you are told your pitch is too high for broadcasting, the first thing you should work on is your resonance. You may be using your optimum pitch but sending it out through a flute instead of a tuba. Spend time doing the Resonance Warm-Ups before considering artificially lowering your pitch, which can result in problems with your vocal mechanism (and remember, pitch work should always be done with the help of a trained speech professional). You may find, as many of my clients have, that increasing your resonance gives you the sound you desire. Lowering the tongue, eliminating tension in the oral cavity, and opening the mouth and throat more are all necessary steps toward better resonance.

# Placement

Another aspect of resonance is placement. Placement involves where you channel the sound waves as they come up the pharynx. Poor placement contributes to nasality and thin voices. If the sound waves are sent straight up the pharynx, they do not enter the oral cavity and will have very little low-frequency resonance, resulting in a thin voice (see Figure 7, arrow #1). Think of an exaggerated "Valley girl" voice. If the sound waves are aimed at the nasal cavity, they are likely to create a nasal voice (see Figure 7, arrow #2). Since these areas limit good resonance, they should not be your area of placement.

To send your sound waves into the best location for good oral resonance, you should place the sound just behind your lower front teeth. This requires bringing the sound waves up the pharynx and making a 130-degree turn into the oral cavity. It also involves sensing the vibrations extending all the way to the front teeth (see Figure 7, arrow #3). Breath is a key here, since it is the energy for speech. Be certain that you are using proper breathing as described in Chapter 1.

## Projection

Placing the sound correctly in the oral cavity helps create good resonance, but this must be followed by proper forward projection of the sound. Projection is what allows an actor or singer to be heard in the last row of a theatre without a microphone. Many speakers have good resonance, but they hold the sound close to their mouths

Figure 7
**Voice Placement**

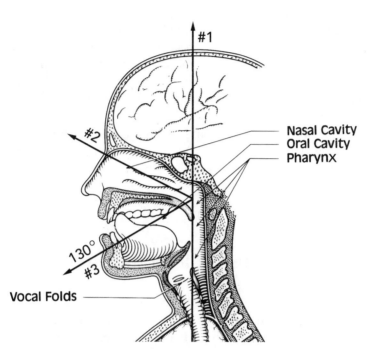

and never project it well. It is as if they are wearing a surgical mask while talking.

Good projection does not involve increasing volume, but moving the sound waves out of the mouth with intensity. Think of volume as a flashlight. In a dark room, the light from a flashlight disperses all over the room. Projection is more like a laser beam. This light is focused and intense, and it can continue for great distances without weakening. This is what good projection sounds like.

I ask clients to visualize their placement in some manner. Some view the sound waves as a garden hose coming up from their lungs and spraying out their mouths. Others see a beam of colored light like a laser beam projecting from their lungs, turning to enter the oral cavity, and extending toward to their lower front teeth and out their mouth. I even had one radio sports announcer who envisioned his placement as a basketball being thrown in an arch-like pattern. Whatever image works for you is fine as long as that beam of light or stream of water you imagine is projecting through the lower front teeth and out into the air (see Resonance Warm-ups).

One final way to imagine good projection is to think of a tour guide at a museum. No one wants to follow a guide who has a weak, ineffectual voice. We expect a tour guide to have a commanding voice that carries to the entire tour group. This voice makes us want to listen and pay attention. As a broadcaster you are much like this tour guide. You need to command our attention, and you do this with projection.

Good resonance should be the goal of all broadcasters. Letting our natural resonators, the pharynx, nose, and mouth, do their optimum work produces the best voice with the least amount of strain.

# Focus on Resonance

To improve the resonance of your voice, you must first learn to feel the involvement of your resonators in your speech production.

A) Use a mirror to watch the movement of the soft palate. Inhale through your nose and exhale through your mouth. Watch the uvula (the bulb-like extension of the soft palate) move up and down. It moves up when the soft palate rises, closing like a trap door to block the nasal cavity as you exhale out of your mouth. When you inhale, the back of the tongue moves up to meet the soft palate as it relaxes in its downward position.

B) Now watch the movement of your soft palate and tongue as you make the following sounds:

- gah, gah, gah, gah
- ng, ng, ng, ng (as in "sing")
- ah, ah, ah, ah (as in "father")
- ah, ng, ah, ng

C) The tightest closure of the soft palate occurs for the consonant "plosive" sounds of /p/ /b/ and /t/ /d/. These sounds are called plosives because the air must be stopped in our mouths and pressure must build up before the air is allowed to explode out. Feel the soft palate's tight closure by making these sounds. Exaggerate the build-up of air before letting it explode out. Now begin the formation of the /p/ sound and build up extra pressure. Instead of letting it explode, release the pressure through your nose. You should feel the soft palate relaxing to let the air out the nose. You may even feel some popping in your ears.

D) To check for denasality, breathe through each nostril alone when your nasal cavity is clear. If one nostril restricts your air intake, you will feel it. Watch in a mirror as you do this. One nostril may seem to collapse when you inhale through it. You may see this at the nostril or higher up behind the bridge of the nose. Closure is a sign that there is some blockage in that nostril. You might want to have this checked by a physician. To hear the effect of denasality, hold your nostrils closed and say this phrase:

```
Now our morning money market
summary.
```

With denasality, it probably sounded like

```
Dow our bordig bodey barket
subary.
```

This illustrates the important role our nasal consonants play in giving our language its distinctive sound.

E) To check for nasality, hold your nose closed and repeat the following sentences:

```
• Authorities agree that the gas
  could have caused the fire.
• The reporter will follow the
  story at six o'clock.
```

These sentences have no nasal sounds in them. When you hold your nose closed and say them, you should not feel any pressure in the nasal area. If you do, you have nasality to some degree.

The pressure comes because you are allowing some sound to enter the nasal cavity. You feel it trying to escape from your closed nose.

F) To feel nasal resonance at work, try making the three nasal sounds. Make a strong /m/ sound by closing your lips and forcing the air into the nasal cavity. Put your index finger and thumb on each side of the bridge of your nose and feel the vibrations as you make the sound. Now make an /n/ sound by putting the tip of your tongue against the alveolar ridge (the ridge behind the upper, front teeth) and blocking the air. Again, feel the vibrations. Now make an /ŋ/ sound as in "sing." Bring your tongue up to your velum, and feel the vibrations. Next alternate between "ah" and /m/, and feel the change in vibrations. You should feel the nose vibrating for the /m/ and no vibrations with "ah."

G) To get a sense of your pharynx moving, induce a comfortable, relaxed yawn. This opens the pharynx for the maximum intake of air. Use this as a natural relaxer for the throat.

H) To illustrate how smiling affects your voice, say the vowel "ah" with the lips pulled back. Now say the vowel without a smile by dropping the jaw straight down. Listen to the difference in the quality of the sound. The first one should sound thinner and tenser than the second. You may think the pitch is different, but you should try to keep it the same. The change in the quality of the sound can be quite apparent, and it can result from the change in resonance only.

I) Changing the shape of our oral cavity, which alters the resonance, forms our vowels. Say these vowels, gliding from one to another and feel the oral cavity adjusting for each vowel:

"ah"—"ee"—"awe"—"oo" as in food.

## Resonance Warm-Ups

When doing the Resonance Warm-Ups, especially the ones that call for opening the back of the mouth more, you should use caution. Do not force the jaw to open too widely. This is of utmost importance if you have TMJ syndrome (temporomandibular joint dysfunction) or have had dislocations of your jaw. Symptoms of these would be pain when chewing or talking, tightness in the jaw, and clicking sounds with jaw movement. If you have any of these symptoms, only open as widely as you can without straining when you do these exercises, and consult a dental specialist to relieve the jaw problem.

1) To improve placement and increase oral resonance, bend forward from the waist at the 90-degree angle. Keep your neck straight so you are looking down at the floor. Flex your knees slightly to prevent strain on your back. (If you have a bad back, do this Warm-Up on all fours with your back straight and your face parallel to the floor.) Repeat this phrase, aiming the sound at the floor as you look down:

- Good evening, this is [*your name*] reporting for Eyewitness News.

Feel the sound resonating in your oral cavity before the sound falls toward the floor. Concentrate on hitting the floor with the sound. Now straighten up and repeat the phrase trying to keep the placement the same.

2) The sound "ah" opens the mouth the widest and lowers the tongue. Doctors use this to look at our throats, and you can use it to increase resonance. Say the following words, preceded by "ah" and try to maintain the wide opening:

| | |
|---|---|
| ah | far |
| ah | father |
| ah | got |
| ah | factor |
| ah | back |
| ah | tackle |

| ah | awesome |
|----|---------|
| ah | awful |
| ah | law |
| ah | go |
| ah | own |
| ah | gold |

3) The word "awe" puts your lips and cheeks in a position to have the best oral resonance. This position is the reverse of a smile, which pulls the lips back and tenses the cheeks. Say the word "awe" before each number as you count from one to ten to feel the relaxed, forward position of the cheeks and lips.

- Awe—1, awe—2, awe—3, etc.

4) To increase the opening in the back of the mouth, make a fist with your hand and extend the index and middle finger slightly. With these fingers still in a bent position, place the knuckles against your cheek with your thumb toward the ground (see photograph). The desired effect is to use the knuckles of your two bent fingers to measure an opening of an inch or more between your molars. Press these fingers against your cheek and open your mouth enough to push your knuckles between your molars. This creates a wide opening in the back of the mouth. With your fingers in this position, say these words (they may sound distorted):

- go, go, go, go
- awe, awe, awe, awe
- ah, ah, ah, ah
- at, at, at, at
- all, all, all, all
- yard, yard, yard, yard

Use the knuckles of your index and middle fingers to measure the opening between your molars.

Courtesy of Dave Cupp, News Director, WVIR-TV, Charlottesville, Virginia.

5) Preserving the feeling of the last Warm-Up, leave your bent fingers against your cheeks. This time let them be a gauge of the amount of opening sustained while speaking. You will feel your teeth come together for some sounds, but try to maintain the wide opening when possible. Repeat these sentences, working to open the back of the mouth:

- Good afternoon. This is News-break, and I'm [*your name*].
- Fighting broke out again today between rival forces.
- Winter promises to bring bitter cold to the Washington area.
- A victory today for abortion rights supporters.

6) **Drop and Talk.**

To increase jaw openness for better resonance, place your chin between your thumb and index finger. Get the feeling that you can "Drop and Talk" with your jaw. You can drop the jaw down like a ventriloquist dummy before you begin to talk. The jaw does not have to open like a pair of scissors that has a tight hinge. You can drop the jaw first. Repeat these words feeling the jaw drop as much as possible before you say the word:

- back, back, back, back
- sack, sack, sack, sack
- bad, bad, bad, bad
- yard, yard, yard, yard
- am, am, am, am
- accent, accent, accent, accent
- sang, sang, sang, sang

7) To avoid assimilated nasality, you must learn to keep vowels that precede or follow nasal sounds from having nasal production. This requires extra work to close the nasal cavity for these vowel sounds. Practice with these comparisons. The first column should be resonated in the oral cavity. Check your production of this by holding your nose closed while you say a word in the first column. You should be able to say all the words in the first column with no air pressure against your closed nose. Next say the corresponding word in the second column, but maintain the oral resonance for the first part of the word. You can hold your nose closed until you get to the nasal sound at the end of the word to monitor your oral placement.

| be | beam |
| tee | team |
| see | seam |
| we | wing |
| law | long |

| | |
|---|---|
| pay | pain |
| owe | own |
| burr | burn |

In the next two columns, say the nasal sound in the first column, but in the second column, switch to oral resonance for the rest of the word after the nasal.

| | |
|---|---|
| m | me |
| m | mud |
| m | mow |
| m | mitt |
| n | no |
| n | near |
| n | new |
| n | need |

8) It is important to continue to work on placement of the sound waves behind the lower front teeth. Decide what imagery you want to use to see the sound beginning at the diaphragm and moving up from the lungs through the vocal folds and into the pharynx. Watch the sound waves making the important 130-degree turn to enter the oral cavity, and see the sound waves hitting the back of the lower front teeth before leaving the mouth (see Figure 7). You might think of a beam of light, a hose, a tube, or anything that helps you visualize this path. Now repeat these vowel sounds with your eyes closed and your concentration on the sound waves making their journey:

- ah, awe, eee
- ah, awe, eee
- ah, awe, eee

Next say this sentence with the same concentration:

- My voice begins at the diaphragm, is pushed from the lungs, passes through the vocal folds into the pharynx, and turns to resonate in my oral cavity.

Keep working with this phrase until you can say it with one exhalation and imagine it moving through the vocal mechanism.

9) An important part of good resonance is projection. Using an extended "ah" sound, begin by imagining the sound coming out of your mouth through your lower front teeth. Next hold your hand about twelve inches in front of your face. Project the "ah" sound and imagine it hitting your hand. Now take your hand away and try to hit a wall several feet away with the sound. Finally, project the sound so that it goes through the wall.

This exercise should not involve an increase in volume. Remember the analogy of the laser beam versus the flashlight. If you allow the sound to originate in your abdominal area, you should get a feeling of the sound projecting forward. Another way to think of this is to imagine how it feels to give a command to an active two-year-old child or a misbehaving puppy. You do not have to scream, which would involve an increase in volume, but you do have to be forceful. Try saying, "Sit down," with forcefulness and intensity. This should give you a feeling of proper projection of the sound.

*The biggest problems I run into among students are sloppy articulation and fast pace. I tell them to relax, slow down, and pre-read so they know what their copy means as well as what it says. If the words have meaning for them, they tend to be more careful how they read.*

**Kevin Allen**
**News Director, WUFT-FM**
**Gainesville, Florida**

*Adopt Standard American diction. Regional identification is good only if a talent wants to remain in a specific area an entire career.*

**Jack Frost**
**Senior Managing Editor, KALB-TV**
**Alexandria, Louisiana**

*Pre-read all scripts out loud before air time. Mark your scripts for inflection. . . . If you don't have a command of the material it will show on the air.*

**Jeffrey S. Raker**
**News Director, WYTV-TV**
**Youngstown, Ohio**

# Articulation— Forming and Shaping the Sound

A healthy, well-resonated sound is worthless to you as a broadcaster and a communicator if you can not articulate the sound into words. Words in our language are made up of phonemes (individual sounds) that combine to give meaning. We use our articulators to shape sound waves into phonemes.

Proper articulation is of utmost importance to you as a broadcaster because your voice must be carried through many different electronic devices (see Figure 8). You speak into a microphone which transfers the sound to an amplifier which is connected to a transmitter. After the sound is transmitted either by wires or satellite, it must go through a receiver and be broadcast through a speaker before it can enter the listener's ears. Every step in this process can diminish the sound. What might be heard perfectly well in face-to-face conversation may be washed out by the time it reaches the listener in electronic media. Careful articulation is imperative.

## Figure 8
### Electronic Communication

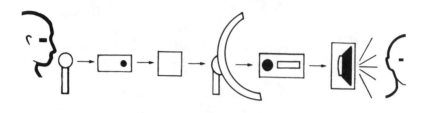

Microphone Amplifier Transmitter Satellite Receiver Speaker

# Articulation Anatomy

To shape sound, we use our lips, teeth, tongue, jaw, hard and soft palate (see Figure 9). These structures are called our articulators. We move our articulators in many ways to speak, and they are most active for consonants.

To feel the articulation of a series of consonants, first make a /p/ sound. The lips come together to stop the air and let it explode out to make the /p/. Now try a "th" sound. Begin to say the word "thin," and feel the friction that results from forcing air through the opening between the front teeth and the tongue. Now make a /t/ sound and feel the tongue tip coming in contact with the alveolar ridge (the ridge behind the upper, front teeth). The soft palate helps with the production of /k/ and /g/ sounds. The tongue comes up to contact the soft palate. Begin to say the word "kick," and feel this movement.

Vowel sounds are made by changing the shape of the oral cavity, thereby changing the resonance. Compare the "ee" sound with "ah." The "ee" sound is produced with a limited mouth opening and a tense, high tongue. For "ah," the jaw and tongue drop to increase the size of the resonating cavity. All vowels depend on the

Figure 9
**Articulators**

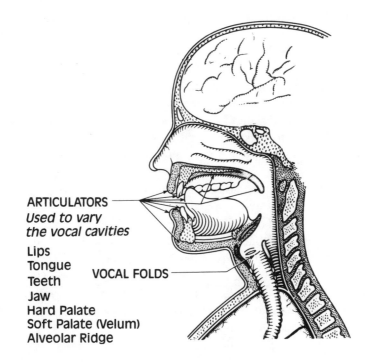

ARTICULATORS
*Used to vary*
*the vocal cavities*

Lips
Tongue
Teeth      VOCAL FOLDS
Jaw
Hard Palate
Soft Palate (Velum)
Alveolar Ridge

(Courtesy of AT & T Archives)

tension of the mouth, the height of the tongue, and the shape of the lips for their production.

## Flexibility

The expressions "lazy tongue" or "lazy mouth" indicate the importance of flexibility for good articulation. If the articulators are sluggish, it is difficult to articulate sounds clearly. Frequently this is also referred to as "sloppy speech." Sometimes this is adequate in relaxed conversation, but poor articulation is never acceptable for broadcast voice.

The agility of our articulators is very important for good

speech. Consider, for example, what your tongue alone has to do to say a simple sentence like, "Let Ted label that truck." Say the sentence slowly and feel the tongue moving from the alveolar ridge to the front teeth and up to the soft palate (see Figure 9). The tongue must make all this movement to produce only five words. At this rate, the tongue will make as many as 400 or more movements per minute to produce speech.

Tongue positions are only one part of the complicated combination of articulation movements required for speech. While the tongue is moving, the jaw must vary the size of the oral cavity and the soft palate must open and close the passage to the nasal cavity. All of this must be done rapidly to create the series of phonemes that make up speech. Watching an x-ray of the speech process is like seeing a fine-tuned machine in motion, making hundreds of adjustments every minute.

The jaw is of utmost importance in the process of articulation. Even the most flexible tongue can not move freely if the jaw is constricting the oral cavity. Clenched teeth not only affect resonance (see Chapter 3), but they limit the movement of the other articulators as well. Developing an open, relaxed mouth is important for both resonance and articulation (see Resonance and Articulation Warm-Ups in Chapter 3 and this chapter).

The articulators depend on lubrication to work properly, just like the vocal folds. Unlike the rest of the vocal tract, however, which produces mucus for lubrication, the oral cavity produces saliva. Glands under the tongue and in the back of the mouth secrete saliva. Dehydration causes a reduction in saliva, which makes articulation more difficult (see Chapter 2). Tension also may reduce the production of saliva. Public speakers are provided with a glass of water for this reason. Taking a few sips of water lubricates the mouth and relaxes the throat. You can also activate the salivary glands by sucking as if you had a mint in your mouth. You will feel the saliva coming out from under the tongue as you pretend you are sucking a mint.

Tension can also cause too much saliva to be produced. A radio client of mine called one day to ask my advice for excessive saliva. She said she had to swallow throughout her newscast because her mouth was flooded with saliva. I imagined her using a towel to wipe her mouth as the saliva poured out, but she assured me it was not quite that severe. She was worried, however, that her new job would be in jeopardy because of the problem. Using breathing exercises to relax, she overcame her tension about her new job. When the tension disappeared so did the excess saliva. See Chapter 9 and *Broadcaster's Survival Guide* for more information on dealing with tension and stress.

# The Sounds of our Language

In order to articulate properly, you must know the sounds we use in our language and how to form them correctly. There are 40 sounds required for General American speech, the dialect most accepted for broadcasters. Because we have an alphabet that uses twenty-six letters to represent 40 sounds, our spelling is confusing. We cannot depend on written words for pronunciation guides. In order to know how to pronounce words, we have to depend on a more accurate system than our alphabet and spelling. We must use a sound-based method as a guide to pronunciation.

The 40 sounds in our language are called **phonemes. A phoneme is the smallest segment of spoken sound that signals meaning**. (They are printed in slash marks to distinguish the symbol for the sound from a letter in our alphabet.) If you omit the /t/ sound from the word "last," for example, you have the word "lass." Therefore, /t/ is a phoneme in the word "last." "Last" contains four phonemes: /l/, the vowel sound /æ/, /s/, and /t/. "Lass" has only three phonemes: /l/, /æ/, and /s/. In another example, if you omit the /r/ from "crash," you have the word "cash." Phonemes signal meaning in our words.

Phonemes and spelling are not always the same, which makes our language difficult to learn to pronounce. Look at the word "thaw." It is spelled with four letters, but there are only two phonemes in the word: the /θ/ ("th" sound) and the vowel sound "aw" /ɔ/. "Bought" has six letters and only three sounds: /b/, the vowel /ɔ/, and /t/. We also have the spelling problem of silent letters like the extra "s" in the word, "lass" /læs/.

Another problem with our spelling that creates pronunciation difficulty is that many of our sounds are spelled with the same letter. The letter, "e," for example, can be pronounced in six different ways: /ɑ/ as in "sergeant," /e/ as in "Jose," /i/ as in "be," /ɪ/ as in "pretty," /ɛ/ as in "pen," and /ə/ as in "item." Consider the different pronunciations of the vowel sounds represented by "ou" in the following words: through, though, thought, rough, could, loud.

There is also the problem of the same sound having different spellings. /i/ ("ee" sound), for example, can be spelled in at least ten different ways including "Caesar," "see," "eve," and "please." A frequently used example of this is often attributed to George Bernard Shaw. He wrote the word "ghoti" and asked for it to be pronounced. When he reported it was the word "fish" he explained that the "gh" was as in "rough," the "o" was as in "women," and the "ti" was as in "nation."

## Finding Proper Pronunciation

Knowing the proper pronunciations of words is a requirement for a good broadcaster. The UPI Stylebook stated that it is as important for a broadcaster to know how to pronounce words correctly as it is for a newspaper writer to know how to spell them. As broadcasters, you have an obligation to the public to set a standard for correct pronunciation.

In the past, networks have often provided help with establishing standard pronunciations. Dr. Cabell Greet, a former professor at Barnard College, was a pronunciation and grammar consultant for CBS for nearly fifteen years. He carefully screened broadcasts and sent memos to reporters when corrections were needed. Today, broadcasters usually are responsible for polishing their own pronunciations.

There are three places you can look when you need to find the proper pronunciation of a word:

1. The dictionary
2. The wire service
3. A phonetic dictionary

## The Dictionary

You are probably familiar with the use of a dictionary for pronunciation. Dictionaries use a system of "diacritical markings" to show pronunciations of each word. These markings can be helpful, but they are sometimes hard to decipher because they vary from publisher to publisher. Also, they depend on unfamiliar markings like macrons (a line above a letter), umlauts (two dots above a letter), and breves (a curved line above a letter). If you are marking your script to help you remember the pronunciation of a particular word, diacritical markings do not always work well. The markings above letters can be difficult to see, and the system may be hard to remember.

## The Wire Service

The wire services offer daily pronunciation guides for difficult words and names (see Figure 10). Phonetic spellings or "pronouncers" are given, using the letters of our alphabet. Here is the key to the AP broadcast pronunciation style, provided by The Associated Press Broadcast Services:

### Vowels:

| | |
|---|---|
| a -- apple, bat | oh -- go, oval |
| ah -- father, hot | oo -- food, two |
| aw -- law, long | ow -- cow |
| ay -- ace, fate | oy -- boy |
| e -- bed | u -- foot, put |
| ehr -- merry | uh -- puff |
| ee -- see, tea | ur -- burden, curl |
| i -- pin, middle | y, eye -- ice, time |

### Consonants:

| | |
|---|---|
| g -- got, beg | sh -- shut |
| j -- gem, job | z -- zoom |
| k -- cap, keep | zh -- mirage |
| ch -- chair | kh -- guttural "k" |
| s -- see | |

Figure 10
**AP-Pronunciation Guide**

News<
Abdurrahman Wahid -- ahb-doo-RAH'-man WAH'-hid
Mumia Abu-Jamal -- moo-MEE'-ah AH'-boo jah-MAHL'
Aceh -- ah-cheh
Fehmi Agani -- FEH'-mee ah-GAH'-nee
Kofi Annan -- KOH'-fee AN'-nan
Ehud Barak -- EH'-hud bah-RAHK'
Stephanie Bellagarrigue -- bel-uh-gah-REE'-gay
Benazir Bhutto -- BEN'-uh-zeer BOO'-toh
Osama Bin Ladin -- oh-SAH'-muh bin-LAH'-din
Capac -- KAY'-pak
Matthew Cecchi -- CHEH'-kee
John Chafee -- CHAY'-fee
Chappaqua -- CHA'-puh-kwah
Charles Chaput -- SHAP'-yoo
Chechnya -- CHECH'-nyah
Viktor Chernomyrdin -- chehr-nuh-MEER'-din
Chetek -- sheh-TEK'
Jacques Chirac -- zhahk shih-RAHK'
Jean Chretien -- zhahn kreh-TYEN'
Loi Chow -- loy chow
Tony Coelho -- KWEHL'-oh
Coos Bay -- KOOZ Bay
John Demjanjuk -- dem-YAHN'-yuk
Lodewijk de Vink -- LOOD'-wihk
E. coli -- ee KOH'-ly
Saeb Erekat -- sah-EEB' EHR'-ih-kaht
Luis Alfredo Garavito -- loo-EES' al-FRAY'-doh
  gah-rah-VEE'-toh
Carlos Ghigliott -- gig-lee-AHT'-ee
Rudolph Giuliani -- joo-lee-AH'-nee
Jose Alexandre "Xanana" Gusmao -- zah-NAH'-nah
  GOOS'-mow (like cow)
Grozny -- GRAHZ'-nee
Hachette Filipacchi -- ha-SHET' fihl-ih-PAH'-kee
Joerg Haider -- yorg HY'-der
Hamas -- hah-MAHS'
Nizar Hamdoon -- nee-ZAHR' ham-DOON'
Hezbollah -- hez-boh-LAH'
James Inhofe -- IN'-hahf
Islamabad -- ihz-LAH'-mah-bahd
Jiang Zemin -- jahng zuh-MEEN'
Bill Kennard -- kuh-NAHRD'
Mohammad Khatami -- HAHT'-ah-mee

Sergei Kiriyenko -- SEHR'-gay keer-ee-YEN'-koh
Dylan Klebold -- KLEE'-bohld
Kosovo -- KOH'-soh-voh
Leonid Kuchma -- KOOCH'-mah
Kosovska Mitrovica -- KOH'-sahv-tskah mee-TROH'-vit-sah
David Levy -- LEE'-vee
New Madrid -- MAD'-rid
Mary Mapes -- MAYPS
Kweisi Mfume -- kwah-EE'-see oom-FOO'-may
Slobodan Milosevic -- sloh-BOH'-dahn mee-LOH'-shuh-vich
Mina -- MY'-nuh
Myanmar -- mee-ahn-MAHR'
Novi Sad -- NOH'-vee SAHD
Pfizer -- FY'-zur
Augusto Pinochet -- pee-noh-CHET'
Pokemon -- POH'-kay-mahn
Primary sclerosing cholangitis -- skluh-ROH'-sing koh-lan-JY'-tihs
Pristina -- PREE'-stee-nah
Yitzhak Rabin -- YIT'-sahk rah-BEEN'
Angel Maturino Resendiz -- ahn-HEHL' mah-tyoo-REE'-noh reh-SEN'-deez
Vazgen Sarkisian -- VAHZ'-gehn sahr-KEE'-see-ehn
Patti Scialfa -- skee-AL'-fuh
Samuel Sheinbein -- SHYN'-byn
Skopje -- SKAH'-pyeh
Barnett Slepian -- SLEHP'-ee-uhn
Sobibor -- saw-BEE'-bur
Javier Solana -- HAH'-vee-ehr soh-LAHN'-ah
Aung San Suu Kyi -- ahng sahn soo chee
Gerardus 't Hooft -- gehr-AHR'-dus hohft
Taliban -- TAL'-ih-bahn
Atal Bihari Vajpayee -- ah-TUL' bee-HAH'-ree VAHJ'-py-ee
Abdurrahman Wahid -- ahb-doo-RAHK'-man wah-HEED'
Wei Jingsheng -- way jeeng-shuhng
Jean-Philippe Wispelaere -- zhahn-fih-LEEP' wihs-pih-LEHR'
Zhu Rongji -- joo rahng-jee
Byran Uyesugi -- oo-eh-SOO'-gee

This system is helpful, but it is limited because it is based on the letters of our alphabet. It is impossible to give a phonetic transcription of every word in our language using only the alphabet. The main advantage of the wire service pronunciation guides is that they deal with proper names and places that are in the current news. It is advisable to save the daily pronunciation guides given by the wire services. You might want to develop your own file or notebook of these guides. This will help you pronounce the many foreign names and places that are in the news every day. It is also a good idea to add local pronunciations to your personal guide. When you first move to a station, ask other reporters about local pronunciations. "Cairo" in Illinois, for example, is pronounced "Kayro." In Maryland, "Grosvenor" is pronounced "Grovner," and in Missouri, "New Madrid" does not sound the same as "Madrid, Spain." The emphasis is on the first syllable in the Missouri pronunciation (see Figure 10). Your credibility with your local audience will be ruined if you mispronounce local names.

## A Phonetic Dictionary

The International Phonetic Alphabet (IPA) contains numerous symbols to transcribe all languages. Some languages have as many as a hundred phonemes while some have as few as a dozen. Forty symbols represent the most frequently used sounds in American speech. These 40 symbols are represented by most of the twenty-six letters of our alphabet, but ten symbols are added to cover all 40 sounds. (The letters C, Q, Y, and X are omitted because they are represented by the sounds /k/ or /s/, /kju/, /j/, and /ɛks/.) The IPA was developed because a group of scholars attending an international convention of language teachers in 1886 were aware of the difficulty of transcribing English without a phonetic alphabet. It has been used since that time as the most accurate guide to pronunciation.

Each phonetic symbol represents only one sound and does not change its pronunciation. The symbol /i/, for example, always represents the sound "ee" as in bee. When you see a word written in phonetics that includes an /i/, you can be confident that sound is "ee." The word, "bee," would be written /bi/ in phonetics. Knowing this symbol, you can easily pronounce these words written in phonetics: /ti/, /ki/, /mit/, /lin/ (tea, key, meet, lean).

The advantages of using the IPA are that it is easy to learn and to remember, it is easy to write on your copy, and it is the only acceptable international set of symbols used for pronunciation. You will find that most speech and linguistics books use the IPA, as do many foreign-language dictionaries. The *NBC Handbook of Pronunciation* (Harper and Row) adapts the IPA and has been a standard reference book for broadcasters for many years. Because the IPA uses most of the letters of our alphabet, it is easy to remember. Words you write in phonetics in your copy are easy to see and pronounce. As a broadcaster, it is well worth the effort to commit the symbols to memory and begin using them. Once you have mastered the symbols, you will have a tool you can use the rest of your career.

Kenyon and Knott's *A Pronouncing Dictionary of American English* (Merriam-Webster) is considered the bible of pronunciation by most speech and linguist professionals. It is also an excellent pronunciation reference guide for broadcasters. There is a key to the IPA in the front of this dictionary, which makes it a handy reference guide whether you know the IPA or not. Kenyon and Knott's dictionary lists only the pronunciations of words, in all three of the accepted dialects in this country: General American, Eastern, and Southern. (A word like "fare," for example, is listed as /fɛr/ for General American, /fɛə/ without the /r/ for Eastern, and /fæə/ without the /r/ and using the vowel as in "at" for Southern.) The only shortcoming of this dictionary is that it was published in 1953. Pronunciations change fairly slowly in this country, but it is a good idea to check any confusing pronunciations in a more current dictionary.

The IPA is divided into consonants and vowels just like our alphabet. These categories are then classified by the method of production. (See Appendix C for more practice words and a comparison of AP, IPA, & dictionary symbols.)

## Vowels

Vowels in our language are all voiced, meaning that the vocal folds vibrate for their production. Vowels are formed by changes in resonance and are classified as pure vowels or diphthongs. Pure vowels can be extended indefinitely when produced. You can say /i/ ("ee"), for example, until you run out of air. Diphthongs, on the other hand, change articulation during pronunciation. They require movement of the mouth for their production since they are composed of two vowel sounds coming together. Say the vowel in "toy," and you will feel your mouth moving for its production.

### Figure 11
### The Complete International Phonetic Alphabet for American English

| | |
|---|---|
| **VOICED** | |
| **Vowels** | |
| /i/ | bee |
| /ɪ/ | bit |
| /e/ | say |
| /ɛ/ | bet |
| /æ/ | at |
| /ɑ/ | spa |
| /ɔ/ | caw |
| /o/ | oak |
| /u/ | two |
| /ʊ/ | put |
| /ə/ | above |
| /ɚ/ | father |
| **Diphthongs** | |
| /ju/ | use |
| /aɪ/ | eye |
| /aʊ/ | cow |
| /ɔɪ/ | toy |

**Consonants**

| VOICELESS | | VOICED | |
|---|---|---|---|
| /t/ | to | /d/ | do |
| /p/ | pop | /b/ | boy |
| /k/ | key | /g/ | got |
| /f/ | fit | /v/ | van |
| /θ/ | thin | /ð/ | them |
| /s/ | say | /z/ | zip |
| /ʃ/ | she | /ʒ/ | casual |
| /h/ | hit | | |
| /tʃ/ | chip | /dʒ/ | Jim |
| | | /w/ | was |
| | | /j/ | yet |
| | | /r/ | run |
| | | /l/ | love |
| | | /m/ | miss |
| | | /n/ | now |
| | | /ŋ/ | sing |

Our usual a-e-i-o-u symbols are inadequate when it comes to representing the sixteen vowel sounds in our language. The IPA uses these symbols for the vowel phonemes (see Appendix C for more practice words):

Pure Vowels
| /i/ | as in bee |
|---|---|
| /ɪ/ | bit |
| /e/ | say |
| /ɛ/ | bet |
| /æ/ | at |
| /ɑ/ | spa |
| /ɔ/ | caw |
| /o/ | oak |
| /u/ | two |
| /ʊ/ | put |
| /ə/ | above |
| /ɚ/ | father |

Diphthongs
| /ju/ | use |
|---|---|
| /aɪ/ | eye |
| /aʊ/ | cow |
| /ɔɪ/ | toy |

## Consonants

To produce consonants in English we either stop or partially stop the air as it comes from the mouth. Consonants are, therefore, classified by the method of releasing the air, the position of the articulators when they are produced, and whether they are voiced or not.

Voicing is perhaps the easiest distinguishing factor of consonants. To understand the difference in voicing, put your fingers on your larynx and begin to say the word "to." Stop after you have made the /t/ sound and repeat the /t/ several times. Next make a /d/ sound as in the word "do." You should feel vibrations in your larynx for the /d/, but none for the /t/. These particular consonants are called **cognates** because they are articulated in the same manner, but one sound is voiced and one is voiceless. There are eight cognate pairs in our language:

| Voiceless | | Voiced | |
|-----------|------|--------|--------|
| /t/ | to | /d/ | do |
| /p/ | pop | /b/ | boy |
| /k/ | key | /g/ | got |
| /f/ | fit | /v/ | van |
| /θ/ | "th" thin | /ð/ | them |
| /s/ | say | /z/ | zip |
| /ʃ/ | "sh" she | /ʒ/ | casual |
| /tʃ/ | "ch" chip | /dʒ/ | Jim |

Using the classifying method of where the air is released and the position of the articulators, the consonants are grouped in the following manner:

*-Stops or Plosives-*

These sounds are formed by stopping the air and letting it explode out to produce the phoneme. For the /t/ and /d/ sounds, the tongue goes to the alveolar ridge to stop the air. The /p/ and /b/ are formed by the lips closing to block the air. The /k/ and /g/ involve the back of the tongue coming up to the soft palate to block the air (see Figure 9).

| Voiceless | | Voiced | |
|---|---|---|---|
| /t/ | to | /d/ | do |
| /p/ | pop | /b/ | boy |
| /k/ | key | /g/ | got |

## -Fricatives-

Fricatives result from friction created by forcing air through a small opening between the articulators. These sounds can be extended until all air has been exhausted.

| Voiceless | | Voiced | |
|---|---|---|---|
| /f/ | fit | /v/ | van |
| /θ/ | thin | /ð/ | them |
| /s/ | say | /z/ | zip |
| /ʃ/ | she | /ʒ/ | casual |
| /h/ | hit | | |

## -Affricates-

These two sounds are similar to fricatives, but they include a plosive. Unlike the fricatives, their production cannot be extended because of the plosive included in each phoneme.

| Voiceless | | Voiced | |
|---|---|---|---|
| /tʃ/ | chip | /dʒ/ | Jim |

## -Glides-

The movement of the tongue during formation distinguishes glides. They are also affected by vowel sounds and are sometimes called semivowels. The /w/ sound is the only glide that can be voiced or voiceless, but the voicing is difficult to distinguish.

### Voiced

/w/ was
/j/ yet
/r/ run

*-Lateral-*

The /l/ sound is unique in our language. All our phonemes are produced by sending the sound straight out of the mouth or up through the nose except for the /l/ sound. Putting the tip of the tongue on the alveolar ridge (see Figure 9) and holding it there while the sides of the tongue drop produce this phoneme. The sound is then allowed to escape from the mouth over the edges of the tongue.

### Voiced

/l/ love

*-Nasals-*

These sounds are produced by closing off the oral cavity and allowing the sound waves to enter the nasal cavity. For the /m/ the lips come together to block the air. The /n/ is formed by the tongue rising to make contact with the side teeth and the alveolar ridge to block the air. For the /ŋ/ sound, the back of the tongue and the soft palate come together to block the air, forcing it to escape through the nose.

### Voiced

/m/ miss
/n/ now
/ŋ/ sing

# Articulation Problems

There are three basic ways in which our articulation can be faulty: we can omit necessary sounds, substitute or add sounds, or produce sounds incorrectly.

## Omissions

Consonants cause the most problems involving omissions of sounds. This is unfortunate for broadcasters because consonants are so important to intelligibility and credibility. Broadcasting makes the omission problem worse because consonants often lose strength when sent through electronic media (see Figure 8).

Consonants add clarity to our language. If you say the word "oil" so that it sounds like "all," most people still know what you mean even though you are saying the vowel incorrectly. If you omit the /l/, however, you are no longer clear to your listener even if the vowel is perfectly pronounced. Without proper consonant articulation, meaning may suffer. If you say "last," for instance, and do not let the air explode out for the /t/, you have said "lass." Similarly, if you say "ass" for "ask," you have pronounced a different word. Remember that a phoneme is the smallest segment of spoken sound that signals meaning. If you leave out a phoneme, which you would be doing if you did not complete the plosive sound of the /k/ in "ask," you may be saying a different word.

One of the biggest challenges of articulation is to say your consonant phonemes correctly without sounding overpronounced. When you first begin working on pronouncing your consonants, you will most likely sound overpronounced. Only practice will eliminate the overly precise sound.

The plosive consonant phonemes cause the most omission problems. The six plosive consonant phonemes are cognates.

These plosives require a burst of air for their production. If you hold your hand in front of your mouth, you should feel a puff of air as you say each of these phonemes.

PLOSIVE CONSONANT PHONEMES:

| Voiceless | | Voiced | |
|---|---|---|---|
| /t/ | to | /d/ | do |
| /p/ | pop | /b/ | boy |
| /k/ | key | /g/ | got |

The sentence, *"Last winter the lists show it snowed two feet,"* requires the production of initial, medial, and final plosives. Say this sentence out loud. If it sounds like, *"Lass winner the lis show i snow two fee,"* you know you have not pronounced your consonant plosive phonemes, and you have lost the intelligibility of the sentence. Everyone needs to pronounce the consonant plosives in the words "last," "two," and "feet" to achieve the *least* precise end of the continuum of articulation. For a more precise sound, one should pronounce the consonant plosives in "winter" and "it." The *most* precise delivery would require correct pronunciation of the plosives in "lists" and "snowed." Pronouncing these last two words correctly requires very flexible articulators and practice to make it sound natural.

I advise my clients to decide how precise they want their delivery to sound. Once they have decided if they want a relaxed, very conversational sound or a more credible, precise delivery, they can begin to work on consonant plosives. Remember the continuum of consonant plosive articulation as you listen to other broadcasters. Some will have very precise deliveries while others omit most plosives. Ed Bliss remembers Lowell Thomas telling him he grew up hearing his father shout, "Articulate, son!" Thomas's delivery reflected this precision of articulation. You will notice that intelligibility, credibility, and precision of pronunciation are all linked. In Appendix A, you will see that twenty-four percent of news directors say they like a precise delivery. For this reason, working to pronounce ending and medial consonant plosives can be helpful.

Keep in mind, however, that overpronouncing these endings can make you sound pedantic. This is especially true if you stress consonant plosives in nonessential words. Say, "The gunman

Lowell Thomas anchored the first regularly scheduled radio network news report in 1930, and his career continued for 45 years.
Courtesy of CBS News.

ran, but the county police captured him." If you overpronounce the
/t/ sounds in "but" and "county," you have taken away from the
meaning of the sentence. You need to produce these /t/ sounds correctly, but you should not stress them. You may find you are overpronouncing when you first begin to work on your consonant plosive production. The example sentence, "Last winter the lists show it
snowed two feet," may require a great deal of practice to pronounce
correctly. At first, you may sound like Eliza Doolittle in *My Fair
Lady*, as you work to hit every plosive sound. The goal is for the
production to be correct without drawing attention to the phonemes.
This takes practice. For assistance, see Articulation Warm-Ups.

Another problem associated with plosives is the popping
sound that sometimes results from these phonemes. This is most
noticeable on the /p/ and /b/ sounds. Popping is usually a problem
of microphone placement. No one pops /p/ or /b/ sounds in conversation. If you have a popping problem, try speaking across the microphone instead of directly into it. You might also find that lowering the microphone away from your mouth helps. Most of the time,
changing the position of the microphone will eliminate the popping. If not, discuss it with your engineer. Certain microphones are
more sensitive to popping, and a change in microphones or a windscreen may be needed.

## Substitutions

There are many possibilities for substitutions of one phoneme for
another in our pronunciations. Foreign speakers, for example, often
have substitution problems with five or ten different phonemes. A
French speaker, for example, might say "sink" for "think." Broadcasters tend to have three substitutions that are most common.

### 1) /t/ and /d/ for /θ/ and /ð/

Working in the Washington, D.C., area, I have found the
substitution of /t/ or /d/ for the "th" sounds to be a problem for
many of my clients. This substitution has become part of a generalized speech pattern called the "Big City Dialect." If you are from
D.C., L.A., New York City, or any big American city, this substitution may be part of your dialect. One explanation of this dialect is

the fact that many foreign languages like French, German, and Spanish do not use the phonemes /θ/ and /ð/. Non-native speakers have difficulty forming the "th" sound; the /t/ and /d/ are easier for them to use. If you live in a city with a large non-native speaking population, you hear this substitution being made around you all the time, and you may begin to use it yourself.

This speech pattern is often associated with the stereotypical athlete who might say, "De coach put de tickets in dere." Few broadcasters would be this far off in the correct pronunciation of "th," but even a few substitutions can hurt your credibility. It is important to form these sounds correctly (see Articulation Warm-Ups).

### 2) /w/ for /l/

The /w/-/l/ substitution is a frequent problem among speakers. This substitution affects pronunciations of words like "bottle," "table," and "pull." Instead of producing the /l/ phoneme in these words, a /w/ is substituted. The words then sound like, "bottw," "tabw," and "puw." With this substitution, clarity is lost, and a childish sound results.

### 3) /w/ for /r/

The /w/ phoneme is an easy one to produce, so it is often substituted for the /r/ sound, in addition to the /l/. The /r/ is a difficult phoneme requiring a tense, high tongue and a gliding motion of the tongue and lips. It is easier to relax the tongue and substitute a /w/ for the /r/. When this happens, a sentence like, "The rough road was dry," becomes "The wough woad was dwy." The result again is a childish, almost cartoonish voice.

## Additions

Additions also cause problems with pronunciation. Easterners, for example, may suffer from an intrusive /r/ sound. When this happens, "wash" becomes "warsh" and "America" becomes "Americur." Southerners may extend vowel sounds by adding an additional phoneme. One syllable words like "pen," "men," and "an," become two syllables with this addition.

## Faulty Articulation

Incorrect production of phonemes is most often associated with a regional accent. Many factors contribute to a regional accent, such as where you spent your formative speech years and where your parents are from. If you produce a flat "i" sound by failing to complete the production of the diphthong /aɪ/ in the phrase, "right nice, bright night," for example, you or your language role models may be from certain parts of the South. A nasal /æ/ sound as in "back" (produced by the tongue being too high and tense) will identify you as a Midwesterner or a New Yorker.

In casual speech, regional pronunciations are not incorrect as long as they are within our two accepted regional dialects, Eastern and Southern. As a broadcaster, however, you should adhere to General American pronunciations unless your news director advises otherwise. Most news directors prefer General American speech—twenty-four percent of our survey respondents consider regional accents a problem (see Appendix A).

To the contrary, some stations, such as country music radio stations, may *want* a regional sound. There are times when a station will actually train you to speak the dialect of their region. This happened to a friend from Long Island who went to a Texas station. Her first few weeks there were spent learning a Texas accent and eliminating her Long Island sound. If you find yourself in a situation like this, Kenyon and Knott's dictionary, which lists all three accepted dialects, can help you learn a regional accent.

Faulty articulation also involves lisps and excessive sibilance, characterized by a hissing sound. These problems occur on fricative phonemes like /s/ and /z/, and /ʃ/ and /ʒ/. These phonemes give speakers more trouble with production than any others do. A lisp results from improper placement of the tongue for /s/ and /z/. A frontal lisp produces a "th" sound for /s/ and /z/. Instead of "Suzy sat in the swing," a frontal lisper would say, "Thuzy that in the thwing." Pulling the tongue back will usually alleviate the problem of a frontal lisp. A bilateral lisp is a harder problem to describe and correct. In its production, the tip of the tongue makes contact with the alveolar ridge (see Figure 9) and the /s/ or /z/ is produced by the sound going over the sides of the tongue. This is similar to the production of an /l/ phoneme. To correct this, make certain that the sides of the tongue hug the teeth, and that the phoneme is produced by friction in the front of the mouth.

Whistling "s" sounds are occasionally a problem for broadcasters. This results from a narrowing of the groove in the tongue through which the air is to escape. Shortening the duration of the /s/ and /z/ phonemes will usually correct this problem. Excessive sibilance in general can be corrected by shortening the duration of the /s/ and /z/ phonemes. If you feel your sibilant sounds distract from your delivery, try keeping their production light and short.

If you suffer from a lisp, a whistling "s", or excessive sibilance, you might want to see a speech pathologist to correct these problems. They can be difficult to correct on your own.

# Focus on Articulation

A) Poor articulation results from omissions, substitutions, and additions. To understand the effect of omissions, say the following word pairs and note the phoneme omitted in the second word:

| center | sinner | /t/ |
| ask | ass | /k/ |
| winter | winner | /t/ |
| picture | pitcher | /k/ |
| field | feel | /d/ |
| painting | paining | /t/ |
| crash | cash | /r/ |

Notice that omitting the consonant phonemes results in a different word being produced in column two.

To experience the /w/-/r/ substitution, say these word pairs:

| | |
|---|---|
| rag | wag |
| rate | wait |
| rock | wok |
| run | won |

B) The tongue plays an important role in the production of vowel phonemes. Say these phonemes and feel the tongue dropping progressively and the mouth opening as you move down the list (try putting your finger lightly on your tongue to feel this movement):

/i/ as in bee
/ɪ/ as in bit or /u/ as in two
/ɛ/ as in bet or /ʊ/ as in put
/æ/ as in at
/ɑ/ as in spa

C) The /t/ phoneme is produced with no voicing and an explosion of air, with one exception. In our language, it often sounds overpronounced to use a full /t/ phoneme before a syllabic /l/, /m/, or /ŋ/. Syllabic sounds are produced when consonants form syllables without a full vowel. In these instances, the /t/ may become imploded or it may sound more like a /d/. This is true of many medial /t/ sounds in our language, even if they are not syllabic. Some examples of syllabic sounds preceded by /t/ are:

little
rattle
cattle
kettle
bottle
bottom
button

mitten

kitten

cotton

# Articulation Warm-Ups

If you were training to be a ballet dancer, you would recognize the importance of exercising your body to make it flexible. Warm-ups and stretches would be part of your everyday life. You would also find you needed to practice your movements in front of a mirror to continue to improve. As a broadcaster, you should think of your voice in the same way. You are working with muscles, tissue, and ligaments when you are speaking. Your articulators must be as agile as a dancer's body in order to produce good speech. In addition, just as a dancer practices in front of a mirror, you must monitor your pronunciations to keep them correct.

Forming and shaping sound requires agile articulators and a good ear to monitor pronunciations. Warming-up our articulators before speech is imperative. Not many of us would walk out our front door and try to run a marathon without stretching our muscles. Stretching brings blood into the muscles which helps them work more efficiently. Vocal warm-ups do this for the muscles of the vocal tract.

Do not be embarrassed doing warm-up exercises. Professional singers and actors know the importance of warm-ups. As a broadcaster, your voice should be prepared prior to on-air work, just like other vocal professionals prepare. By warming up, you are showing your professionalism.

1) Say these phonemes, exaggerating the mouth positions:

- /ɑ/ as in spa
- /ɔ/ as in caw
- /u/ as in two
- /i/ as in bee

Open the mouth wide for /ɑ/, round the lips for /ɔ/, pull the lips forward in a pucker for the /u/ phoneme, and smile widely for /i/. Continue to say these phonemes in an exaggerated manner, gliding from one to the next. After repeating them a dozen times or more in an exaggerated manner, you should feel your mouth becoming more flexible. Use this series of phonemes as a warm-up before going on air.

2) Continuing with the exaggerated stretching of the last Warm-Up, repeat this sentence extending the vowel phonemes:

- You see Oz.

Pucker the lips tightly for "you." Pull the lips back in a wide smile for "see," and drop the jaw and open wide for "Oz." Repeat this sentence with these exaggerated lip positions as many times as you need to in order to warm up your articulators.

3) Repeat the following words as fast as you can while preserving the consonant plosive formations:

- Put a cup. Put a cup. Put a cup. Put a cup.
- Drink buttermilk. Drink buttermilk. Drink buttermilk.
- Fat lazy cat. Fat lazy cat. Fat lazy cat.
- Baby powder. Baby powder. Baby powder.
- Tea leaves. Tea leaves. Tea leaves.

Now say this sentence, exaggerating the plosive sounds:

- I need to get ready to articulate.

Rapid repetition of this sentence and the words above will help warm up your tongue and lips. Be sure you feel air exploding out on the plosive sounds. Say these rapidly before on-air work.

4) Chewing and talking at the same time has been used extensively to improve articulation because chewing loosens the jaw and tongue. To practice this, pretend you have just taken a big bite from an apple and count while you chew. You can also say the months of the year, days of the week, or the alphabet. You should exaggerate your chewing while you speak.

5) Ending consonant plosives are difficult to articulate properly. Use the following word lists to practice plosive endings. Hold your hand in front of your mouth and try to feel a burst of air at the end of each word:

## Practice on Ending Consonant Plosives

| /t/ | /d/ |
|---|---|
| hit | had |
| mitt | lad |
| sit | fad |
| last | tried |
| fast | fried |
| past | filled |
| laughed | bend |
| craft | bird |

| /p/ | /b/ |
|---|---|
| top | Bob |
| flop | sob |
| hop | lob |
| pipe | web |
| ripe | grab |
| deep | curb |
| seep | stab |
| leap | tab |

| /k/ | /g/ |
|-----|-----|
| peak | lag |
| sneak | hog |
| freak | frog |
| slick | log |
| talk | jog |
| make | drug |
| pick | snug |

6) For precise broadcast speech, ending consonant plosives must also be formed correctly in sentences. This involves the same burst of air for each ending consonant plosive that you experienced when you practiced Warm-Up # 5. Use the following practice sentences and news copy to improve your ending consonant plosives. Before you begin, mark each ending consonant plosive by underlining, circling, or highlighting. Tape-record your reading. Exaggerate the sounds as you say them if you need to. You may sound over-pronounced and technical at first. Since these are exercises, do not worry about the technical sound. Continue to practice the sentences and news copy until you can make the delivery more natural while preserving the correct production of the ending consonant plosives.

### /t/ /d/

1. West Grand Junction will be hot instead of mild next week.
2. The reporter missed the fight when he jumped from the boat.
3. Word of the shot was called into the station by Rod.
4. The ride was a bad one for the East Coast bird group.
5. In the last game, just one score, Maryland eighty and Washington one hundred.

/p/ /b/

1. A gunman tried to rob the Jog Shop on Curb Street.
2. Pop culture is booming in Deep Creek.
3. Bob will keep a tab on the shop next week.
4. The mob pushed off the curb and top-pled the cab.
5. The dog will jump in your lap but the cat will not.

/k/ /g/

1. The West league hit their peak in Lake Placid.
2. Smog will clog the roadways as we dig out from under the snow.
3. The dark will make a rescue effort diffi-cult.
4. The guard will pick up the sleek car at the yard.
5. He will jog the last leg of the race in the dark.

## Broadcast Copy to Practice for Ending Plosives

Gunfire shattered the quiet town of Grand Junction in Montgomery County last night. Two men were dead at the scene; another hospitalized following what police suspect was a domestic dispute.

Amtrak officials suspect a faulty rod on the rail line may have made a difficult commute for westbound passengers. Bob Bennett reported that the stop in Westchester County was the result of a break in the rail rod.

> In basketball this evening, first in
> the NBA, it was the Atlanta Hawks
> over the Washington Wizards one-
> twenty to one-thirteen. College
> scores were not as close. It was
> Louisville over the University of
> Memphis ninety-eight to eighty-eight
> and Stanford beat Georgia Tech in a
> rout—ninety to forty-eight.

7) Consonant clusters are the most difficult consonants to pronounce. They are like the final exam of consonant production. They can be learned by practicing the production of the cluster alone before attempting to incorporate it into words. Repeat clusters alone until you can say them easily and then try the words. This requires very facile articulators. Here are the most common clusters:

| **Voiceless** | | **Voiced** | |
|---|---|---|---|
| /ts/ | as in bats | /dz/ | as in rods |
| /pt/ | as in wrapped | /bd/ | as in robbed |
| /kt/ | as in talked | /gd/ | as in lagged |
| /θs/ | as in fifths | /ðz/ | as in breathes |
| /sks/ | as in desks | | |
| /sts/ | as in lists | | |
| /kθ/ | as in length and strength | | |

8) Substitutions often involve the use of /w/ instead of /l/ or /r/. Use these word lists to practice your production of these phonemes. The /w/ is formed by pursing the lips and relaxing the tongue. The /l/ sound requires the tip of the tongue to make contact with the alveolar ridge or the front teeth. The sound is then allowed to escape from the mouth by dropping the sides of the tongue. The lips can be pulled back for the /l/ sound in practice to make certain they are not pursed as for /w/. Watch your production of these two phonemes in the mirror and be certain the lips are pulled back for /l/. You can force a smile by pulling the lips back for the /l/ in practice to exaggerate the production. You can also say the word "love" after each word, blending the "l" from the word into "love". Prac-

tice "pu - love" until you can merge the /l/ with "pu" and drop the "ove". This will result in proper articulation of the /l/.

| | |
|---|---|
| pull | chill |
| sail | mail |
| meal | spool |
| roll | fail |

The /r/ requires a gliding movement of the tongue and lips. The lips are pursed at first and then they relax. The tongue is more tense for the production of /r/ than for /w/.

| | |
|---|---|
| rock | dry |
| room | pretend |
| report | travel |
| dream | around |

9) The /t/ /d/ substitution for /θ/ /ð/, involves the tongue being pulled too far back in the mouth. To produce a correct "th" sound, let the tongue tip come under the upper front teeth, making light contact. Forcing air through the space between the front teeth and the tongue should produce friction. To test your production of this, say the following words while watching your mouth in a mirror. You should be able to see your tongue each time you make the "th" phoneme. You might want to begin by lightly biting your tongue tip to position it under your teeth.

| Voiceless | Voiced |
|---|---|
| thank | them |
| thick | the |
| thigh | than |
| thorn | they |
| thrill | that |
| think | those |
| ether | then |
| wealthy | though |
| nothing | seething |
| birthday | lather |

| | |
|---|---|
| bath | worthy |
| path | breathe |
| mouth | soothe |
| south | teethe |
| worth | loathe |
| faith | weather |

10) There are a few specific words that people with a Southern accent often have difficulty pronouncing correctly. These words are "any," "again," "just," and "get." The list below links these words with rhyming words that will help produce the correct articulation. Concentrate on relaxing your tongue and jaw slightly to avoid the /i/ sound that will produce "iny," "agin," "jist," and "git."

| | |
|---|---|
| penny | any |
| pen | again |
| bust | just |
| bet | get |

Now, try this humorous sentence that allows you to practice all the words:

If you bust just one bank, I bet you will not get a penny again from any of them.

*Good anchors know their copy and relate that knowledge to the listener by using proper inflection. It also is important to realize that the job of a good anchor is not to fill every moment with the sound of their voice. A well-placed pause can be very effective.*

**Brian Gann**
**Program Director, KVOO-AM/KCKI-FM**
**Tulsa, Oklahoma**

*Don't broadcast! Don't read individual words. Write in a conversational style, so you can deliver in a conversational style.*

**John Tracy**
**News Director, KTUU-TV**
**Anchorage, Alaska**

*Don't read me a story, "tell" me a story—if you can write in a conversational style you must be able to read that way too. Good writing can be ruined by a poor delivery.*

**Doug Long**
**News Director, WGXA-TV**
**Macon, Georgia**

# Enhancing Meaning through Stress and Intonation

Style of delivery is one of the few topics upon which news directors almost unanimously agree. Appendix A shows that ninety percent of those who responded to the survey marked "Conversational" as the preferred style of delivery. News directors also responded that "Monotone" is a major vocal problem. They emphasized their choice with comments like these:

"Relax and talk *to* viewers not *at* them."

"The key to good delivery is to make the broadcast sound like a conversation."

"We want natural-sounding people."

"Talk to us as if you are telling a story to a friend."

"Most listeners want people who sound real."

"Be natural."

"My best advice is simply to relax and tell a story."

Unfortunately, relaxing and telling a story is not the easiest thing to do. For many broadcasters, no matter how much they relax, they still sound stiff in the sound booth. It is difficult to read and not sound like you are reading.

# A Broadcasting Communication Model

One of the reasons for this difficulty is that most broadcast work is an unnatural communication event. We all know how to use stress and intonation to tell a good story to a friend. Recall the last time you told a colleague about the traffic jam you encountered or an exciting event from your last vacation. Your pitch, no doubt, went up and down as you talked, and you may have stretched words out to build suspense. You probably got louder to emphasize words, and you may have talked faster to hold interest. In conversation, all of this comes naturally to most of us.

When we talk to someone in conversation, we participate in a communication loop (see Figure 12) that involves sending out a message and receiving feedback from the listener. The feedback that we receive may be verbal, with comments like "Really?" or "I see," or it may be a nonverbal nod of the head or a puzzled look. This feedback helps us adjust our delivery to hold the interest of our listener.

Broadcasters in a sound booth, or talking to a camera, work without the help of feedback. The communication loop is truncated. Messages are sent out, but no feedback returns to help the broadcaster make the subtle adjustments needed in stress and intonation to make the delivery interesting. This is why a monotone or an overdone delivery may happen in the sound booth or when talking to the camera. If you are looking at your printed copy or the wall in the sound booth, it is difficult to sound natural. Likewise, with the camera as your focal point, the communication loop is not complete.

There are two effective ways I have found to help clients

Figure 12
**Communication Models**

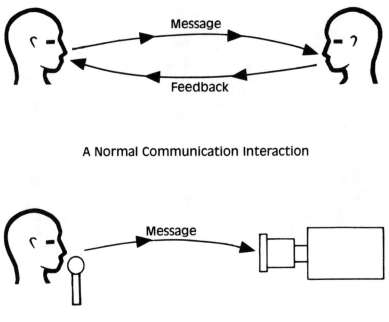

**A Normal Communication Interaction**

**A Broadcasting Interaction**

sound comfortable and conversational while they stress the proper words. Both of these methods involve creating a way to superimpose a conversational delivery on a written text. A marking system can recreate a conversational style, and this system is explained in the remainder of this chapter. Another method that stresses an interpersonal communication approach is presented in Chapter 6. This involves recreating the feedback that is missing when you read a script. One or both of these methods can be used to develop a natural-sounding delivery.

Much of a correspondent's time on-air is spent talking to a camera or a sound booth wall.

Courtesy of Michael Freedman, General Manager, CBS News, Radio.

# Developing a Broadcast Delivery Style

To compensate for the lack of natural feedback, many broadcasters develop a pattern that they think sounds conversational. They realize they sound like they are reading, so they make an arbitrary choice to stress every third word or every noun or verb. This results in a singsong delivery pattern. News directors responded in our survey that one of the main delivery problems they hear is the singsong pattern (see Appendix A).

Any predictable delivery pattern can distract from the meaning of your copy. If the audience begins to notice your delivery pattern, they have shifted their focus from content to style. Your manner of speaking should never draw more attention than the ideas you are trying to get across to your listener. In addition, a set delivery style restricts the variation that is needed for different types of stories. Within one news report, an anchor may go from a serious opening story that calls for credibility and concern to a kicker that requires a light delivery. Set delivery patterns do not allow for this kind of variety.

A client of mine recently complained that when she does serious stories she sounds credible, but occasionally she fears she is dull and uninteresting. For a recent Christmas special, her news director told her to "jazz up" her delivery to fit the mood of the show. Not knowing how to do this, she forced an artificial delivery that she said sounded like a used car commercial. She was changing pitch and rate so much she lost all her credibility and sounded foolish. Without any training in how to change stress and intonation effectively, this can be the result.

## Finding Meaning-Laden Words

An important step in developing a process to use stress and intonation correctly is to find the **meaning-laden words** in your copy. This assumes, of course, that you do not plan to commit the greatest sin of broadcast delivery, which is to "rip and read" your copy on the air without a practice read-through. Unless you are on the air live during a disaster or a rapidly changing news event, no story should ever be read cold off the news wire or straight from your computer printer. To rip and read shows a lack of respect for your professional craft and for your audience. Even if a quick read-through is all you have time for before you go on the air, you owe that to your listeners.

Read through your copy out loud (you never help your delivery by reading broadcast copy silently) and look for meaning. On the first read-through you should use a pencil to mark the meaning-laden words. You might want to underline them or circle each one. Meaning-laden words are exactly what the name implies. They are words that carry meaning. In the sentence, "The quick, brown fox jumped over the fence," the words "fox" and "jumped" and "fence" carry the meaning. It is nice to know that the fox was quick and brown, but it is not imperative to the meaning. If you read this sen-

Reading copy aloud and marking it should become routine for all broadcasters.

Courtesy of Bruce Whiteaker, News Director, KXAN-TV, Austin, Texas

tence with your stress on "quick," "brown," and "over," your listener would no doubt be confused.

I use several examples to illustrate the idea of meaning-laden words for my clients. One example happens in thousands of homes each night. If I go into my living room at six o'clock and switch on the television for the evening news, I will most likely go into the kitchen next and begin dinner. I cannot hear every word of the news, but I want to hear the meaning-laden words. If I hear "accident," "Gaithersburg," and "two injured," my interest will be piqued because I live in the area mentioned. I will go to the television to see the rest of the story.

Meaning-laden words are also important to me when I am driving and listening to the radio. Any number of things may distract me, but as a broadcaster, you need to pull me into your story by stressing the meaning-laden words.

Another way to think of this concept is to visualize lighting in a television studio. "Fill" and "key" lighting are two main types used in television. While the fill gives general illumination, the key lighting emphasizes certain people. It pulls those people out from the rest of the set, just as stressing certain words pulls them out from the rest of the sentence.

The meaning-laden words are not always the nouns and verbs. In the sentence, "Another attack by a pit bull dog has sent an elderly woman to the hospital," the modifiers "pit bull" are important to the meaning. You could find that an adverb is important, such as "continuously" in this sentence: "The gunman was continuously shooting, which made any rescue operation impossible." You will usually find that function words, including prepositions, pronouns, conjunctions, and articles do not receive stress. This is not a hard and fast rule, however. Consider this sentence: "The boy was found in the hole and not beside it." The prepositions "in" and "beside" are important. Likewise, in this sentence "in" and "on" are important: "The basketball star appeared in court today instead of on one."

A close reading of your copy is the only way to seek out the meaning-laden words. Once you have marked your copy for these words you should have an outline of your story. A robbery story, for example, might give you these meaning-laden words: teenager, shotgun, fast-food restaurant, suburban Detroit. Without reading the entire story, you have a good sense of what it says when you read the meaning-laden words.

You can also think of a mountain range. When looking at the range, certain peaks stand out above the rest. You see a fairly solid line of mountains with a few peaks standing out. As you read copy and stress the meaning-laden words, you are pulling them out just like the mountain peaks. You are making them stand above the rest by stressing them in a certain way.

## Pausing for Breath and Meaning

Another initial step in creating a conversational delivery by marking your script involves deciding where you plan to pause. We have all heard broadcasters who pause at inappropriate places. If the sentence above were divided in this manner, it would lose meaning: "Another attack by a pit / bull dog has sent an elderly woman to the hospital." Many times inappropriate pauses come from the "rip and read" problem. If you have not read over your copy out loud, you are using guesswork when it comes to pausing. Other times, broadcasters pause inappropriately because they run out of air (see Chapter 1). You should mark your breath pauses so that you do not deplete your air supply as you are reading.

When marking your copy, use a double slash mark to designate a longer pause and a single slash mark for a short catch-breath and also for a quick pause with no intake of air (see Chapter 1, Breathing Warm-Ups). Double slash marks are often found at periods and when you go to a sound bite or actuality. This is a time when you can take a fairly deep breath. Single slash marks might be found at commas, dashes, ellipses, or at any point where meaning would be helped by a pause.

Marking these pauses before you mark meaning-laden words is preferable. This allows you to work with phrases, instead of entire sentences, when you are looking for meaning. A phrase is a group of words between two slash marks. You might have two phrases in this sentence: "Another attack by a pit bull dog / has sent an elderly woman to the hospital." At the slash mark, you would take a catch-breath.

If your copy is written well, you will generally have at least one meaning-laden word in each phrase. In the sentence above you might pull out "attack," "pit bull dog," "woman," and "hospital." Those words carry the essential meaning of the sentence. It is easier to find these words when you work with the short phrases between slash marks.

# Ways to Stress Words

Once you have decided where you want to pause and what words carry meaning, you are ready to make some choices about what you plan to do with your voice to pull out your meaning-laden words and verbally underline them for your listener. You will look at each meaning-laden word and decide how you will use your voice to stress each word.

You may have heard broadcasters talk about "punching" words to emphasize them. When my clients say they punch words, they usually mean they get louder on those words and possibly go up or down in pitch. Using this method alone causes problems, however, because it sets up a predictable, singsong delivery. In conversation, we do more with our voices than increase volume and change pitch. Incorporating a variety of stress and intonation methods will make your delivery sound more natural and conversational.

## Intonation

Use of changes in our pitch in speech is called intonation. We use pitch changes within entire sentences to signal certain meanings, and within words to give them individual significance.

There are two basic patterns of intonation we use for sentences. Our normal intonation pattern calls for us to go down in pitch at the ends of sentences. This includes questions that begin with an interrogative (how, when, where, which, what, who, whose, whom, why). If you say, "How are you?" you go down in pitch at the end of the question. Try saying this sentence and listen to your pitch: "I'm going to town." If you said it as a statement, you went down in pitch on "town" to indicate a complete sentence. Now say it as a question: "I'm going to town?" You should notice that since there was no interrogative to indicate a question, you went up in pitch on "town." Rising intonation indicates a yes-no question or suggests uncertainty, insecurity, doubt, hesitancy, or an incomplete thought.

We also use pitch changes within sentences on certain words, and this is what is important for the process you will use to mark your script. In our language, for the most emphasized word in any phrase, our voices generally go up in pitch. Once you know your meaning-laden words, you should look at each one and decide if a pitch change would be an appropriate way to stress that word and what pitch change is best.

There are three ways to use pitch for specific words. You can go up in pitch as you did in the above question without an interrogative, and you can go down in pitch as you do at the end of most sentences. Going down in pitch usually indicates finality or seriousness. If you say, "Three persons were killed in the accident," you would most likely go down in pitch on "killed." A sentence such as, "There were two survivors of the accident," would require a choice on your part. "Two survivors" could either go up or down in pitch and either would be effective.

You can also use a *circumflex intonation*, which means you go up-down-up on a word or down-up-down. In our language, this intonation pattern indicates doubt or suspicion. Say this sentence and practice the circumflex intonation on the word "refused": "The CEO refused to be interviewed by our reporter." By alternating your pitch on "refused" you can indicate that something suspicious is going on with this executive.

When using a pitch change, you can glide up in pitch or you can step up. A glide up means that you begin the word at the same pitch as the previous word, but you go up in pitch as you say the word. A step up involves a clean pitch change from one word to the next (see Phonation Warm-Ups #7–10 in Chapter 2).

## Duration

We also vary the length of words and syllables to stress them. If you said, "It was the biggest ice cream sundae I ever ate," you probably stretched out the word "biggest." Stretching words out gives them more significance. This technique is very effective for numbers and figures. If a huge crowd turned out for a rally, you might say, "There was a record attendance of twenty-thousand people." Saying "twenty-thousand" slowly will impress the listener with the number.

Speeding up our speech can be effective as well. In the sentence, "The trial suffered still another set-back," it would be effective to speed up "still another set-back." You could also slow it down to make a point that the trial is dragging on. The choice would be up to you. Try saying this sentence both ways and see which sounds better to you.

Using variations in duration to emphasize words can be just as effective as variations in pitch. Changes in pitch or duration make your meaning-laden words stand out from the rest, which helps your listener understand your story.

## Volume

If you remember the last time you were angry about something, it may be easy to recall what an increase in volume is like. You may have said, "I said no!" On the word "no," you probably raised your volume. For some broadcasters, increasing volume is their primary way of stressing words. These are the broadcasters who are difficult to listen to for any length of time. You feel as if you are being shouted at instead of reported to when this becomes a pattern. Increasing volume is a legitimate way to stress words, but it should be used judiciously. It puts stress on your listener and on your throat. To increase your volume, you may use more tension in the larynx. And this tension can lead to any number of vocal problems (see Chapter 2).

## Pausing for Stress

In addition to pausing for meaning, you can also use pauses for stress. Pausing before and after a word or phrase pulls out an idea for the listener. It is as if the idea is suspended from the rest of the sentence. This might be used for a parenthetical phrase or clause such as, "The defendant, who is accused on ten counts, was not in the courtroom." It is natural to pause before "who" and after "counts."

You can use this method of pausing in other instances as well. You might say, "The county has a / restrictive limit / on new construction." By pausing in this way, the phrase "restrictive limit" is stressed.

# A Method for Marking Scripts

Using the techniques described above—pitch, duration, volume changes, and pauses—you now have a basic method to improve

Marking your copy of any script, even if your marking does not appear on the TelePrompTer, will help your vocal expressiveness.
Courtesy of Bloomberg Television.

stress and intonation in your broadcast copy. These techniques provide a way to superimpose a natural, conversational delivery on a very artificial process. You will be able to verbally underline your meaning-laden words for your listener just as you do in normal conversation. Much like a musical score, the marking will aid you in this process.

This process can be used as a method with every piece of copy you are given to read. Figure 13 outlines how the method can be used. The method as presented here is only a starting point, however, for what should become a personal shorthand for you. In Figure 14, you see how this method looks when used on copy. I tell clients I hope that if I saw their copy a year after they worked through this method with me I would not recognize their markings. You should streamline the method to fit your needs.

It is important to remember as you go through the marking process that any story can be marked in a number of different ways and still be effective. There is no set way to mark each story. While I might choose to stretch out the phrase "Ten Most Wanted" in the last sentence in Figure 14, you might want to go down in pitch. The choice is a personal one, but the important thing is to verbally underline the meaning-laden words by using a stress and intonation technique.

## BROADCAST COPY PREPARATION METHOD FOR STRESS & INTONATION

Always perform the following procedure *in pencil* on your copy since you may find that you want to change markings:

1. Read through the copy out loud to check for difficult words.

   A. Look up the pronunciation of any difficult words.

   B. Write the phonetic transcription of difficult words on your copy.

2. Mark major breath pauses with // and minor breath pauses or pauses without an air intake with /.

3. Select the **meaning-laden** words to stress. Mark stressed words (usually at least one in each phrase) with the appropriate symbol given in Figure 13. (A phrase is a group of words between breath pauses.)

4. Re-read copy out loud to check stress pattern.

5. Practice copy out loud as many times as possible.

Figure 13
**Vocal Methods for Stressing Words**

| | |
|---|---|
| 1. Inflection up | The court has refused ↗ to vote. |
| 2. Inflection down | The court has refused ↘ to vote. |
| 3. Circumflex inflection* | The court has refused to vote. |
| 4. Increase in volume | The court has <u>refused</u> to vote. |
| 5. Pausing before & after words or phrases | The court has /refused/ to vote. |
| 6. Stretching words out** | The court has refused to vote. ⟵⟶ |
| 7. Saying words faster | The court has refused to vote. |

*In American speech, circumflex inflection indicates doubt or suspicion.
**This is especially effective for numbers to give them added significance.

It is easy to use this method with copy for the sound booth as well as for the hard copy you might work with as an anchor. Unfortunately, the method cannot be used with most computer-generated TelePrompTer copy. I have not found a computer program that allows for this marking system. Hopefully, in the future such a program will be developed. Clients tell me, however, that if they mark

Figure 14
**Sample Broadcast Copy Marked for Delivery**

Three-thousand people in the Washington,
D.C., area were notified they had won two
free tickets to the Redskins' football
game. // About 100 of them showed up today
at the Convention Center for the tickets
and a pre-game brunch, / but they were
thrown for a loss: // U.S. marshals and
police sprang their trap and arrested
them all as fugitives. // Some were wanted
for burglary, robbery or murder. // Two of
those caught in the sting were on the
local list of / Ten Most Wanted. //

Reprinted with permission from *Writing Broadcast News,* Mervin Block, Bonus Books, Inc., 1987.

their hard copy for the desk and rehearse with it, they can usually remember what their stressing should be. With computer-generated TelePrompTer copy, you can also experiment with creating a marking system using spaces, underlines, ellipses, bold case, and slash marks.

When you begin marking, it might take you thirty minutes to mark one page of copy. The usual response I get from clients is that there is no way this can ever work with the deadlines of a normal day. You will reach a point where you will be able to mark your copy as fast as you can read it. When you begin working with this method, you should stick to the approach given here. As you progress with it, you will develop your personal marking method that will be much faster.

Any new process is very technical at first. Remember when you first learned to drive a car? You may have thought that process would never be comfortable. What my clients find is that the more they practice this method of marking their script for meaning, the faster it becomes. Practice should be done initially in your non-work hours (see Stress and Intonation Warm-Ups). Do not expect to be able to read through this chapter and begin marking your on-air copy the same day. I always caution my clients against trying to use a marking method immediately. One anchor at a top market did not listen to my warning and almost lost her job when she tried to learn the method on the air. Her news director called her in and wanted to know what had happened. She was stumbling over words and sounded awful. This may be the result if you rush this process.

You should spend weeks, even months, getting comfortable with a marking process. Once you are comfortable, you will hear tremendous improvement. The client whose delivery for a Christmas special sounded like a used car commercial found that this method gave her the confidence to abandon her monotone. She could use her voice to enhance meaning with the knowledge that she was emphasizing the correct words. For her, the method became part of her routine very quickly, and she was using it on the air after practicing only a few weeks.

## Script-Marking Methods

Both novice and veteran broadcasters have used personalized marking methods for years. Edward R. Murrow had a personal marking style, which is illustrated in the news lead below, provided by one of his former writers, Ed Bliss (see Figure 15). Bliss relates how Murrow always used a #2 yellow pencil to mark his script before each radio broadcast of "Edward R. Murrow—The News" (1947–1959). Murrow would spend around ten minutes marking and rehearsing a six-minute news summary. Bliss explains that

Edward R. Murrow in wartime London where his coverage began with the effective use of a pause: "This . . . is London."
Courtesy of CBS News.

Murrow used the exaggerated commas shown in Figure 15 as slash marks ". . . to feed the people a fact at a time." Regular commas indicated a slight pause. Murrow also often used a pause before verbs that he wished to emphasize. He used parentheses to set off phrases for meaning as well as underlining for emphasis. Murrow made few editorial changes in his scripts according to Bliss, but he spent his preparation time deciding how to use his voice to enhance the meaning of the copy.

Figure 15
**Edward R. Murrow Copy**

*Wednesday – February 6, 1952*

*This is the News —*

The British have a new Queen.  King George the Sixth died in his sleep

last night at the age of 56.  His daughter, Queen Elizabeth, is due in

London tomorrow, (flying back from Kenya.)  Here is a recorded report from

Howard K. Smith in London, telling us how Her Majesty's subjects reacted

to the news.

TAPE:

Courtesy of Ed Bliss and Mrs. Edward R. Murrow

# Effective Use of Rate for Broadcast Delivery

Rate is an area that many broadcasters find confusing. They feel they deliver their copy too slowly and when they speed up they get too fast. This is a common area of concern, because rate is very difficult to monitor on your own. I recently told a client of mine to double her rate as she read a story for me. She thought that was ridiculous advice until she listened to the recording of her delivery at a faster rate. What had been a plodding delivery and a dull story suddenly became interesting.

Our rate of speaking is determined in many ways by our speech models. If your parents talk rapidly, you will most likely talk rapidly. If you come from a large family where you had to talk fast to be heard, you will have a rapid rate. On the other hand, a quiet, calm childhood may have produced a slow rate of speaking. Certain dialects, such as the Southern dialect, may also produce slower speech.

In broadcasting, control of rate is important and reveals your sense of involvement and interest in a story. In your private life, it is acceptable to answer the phone with a slow, low-energy voice if you feel bad. For broadcasting you must not let your moods show in your delivery. If you feel bad, you have to cover it up with a consistent rate and the sense of involvement that comes through marking your copy for meaning.

Many broadcasters think vocal energy is created by increasing rate, and possibly an increase in volume and a higher pitch. Vocal energy is not tied to a rapid rate, a loud volume, or a higher pitch. If you have heard the voice of the actor James Earl Jones, think of how his voice sounds. It is very low in pitch, often very low in volume, and never rushed. And yet, there are few voices that project more vocal energy. Remember that vocal energy is created by proper use of your breathing and your focus (see Chapters 1 & 7).

## Appropriate Rates

Normally we read out loud at between 145 and 180 words per minute (wpm). The most comfortable speed would be around 150 to 175 wpm. To learn your rate see Focus on Stress and Intonation. Our speaking rate is somewhat slower than our reading rate. Most of us speak at around 160 wpm or less. This is probably because we use more pauses and stretch words out more when we are talking. Certain radio formats call for very rapid-fire, extemporaneous delivery. In these instances, radio deejays may talk at 200 wpm or more.

When broadcasting, you can use rate to help verbally emphasize the mood of your story (see Table 3). A serious, sad story would be read more slowly than a kicker. Adjusting your rate makes the mood of the piece clearer for your listener.

It is often helpful to make a note in the margin of your copy that indicates the mood of each story (see Chapter 6). One client told me she likes to put the mood at the bottom of the page preceding each story. In this way, she can adjust her mood and rate as she turns her page of copy. It is all too easy to begin a sad story with a rapid rate before you realize the gravity of the piece. It is hard to adjust your rate and mood after you have begun the story.

Table 3
**Rate Continuum**

| 145 wpm | 160 wpm | 180 wpm |
| --- | --- | --- |
| *Material that is* | | |
| SAD | EXPOSITORY | LIGHT |
| SERIOUS | DESCRIPTIVE | HAPPY |
| GRAVE | UNEMOTIONAL | HUMOROUS |
| TECHNICAL | | |
| COMPLICATED | | |

## Components of Rate

Pauses have a great deal to do with overall rate. Two important components of rate are the number of pauses and the length of pauses. If you mark your pauses with slash marks, you will be able to gauge the number of pauses. The more you pause, the slower your delivery rate will be.

Another factor that is more difficult to monitor is the duration of syllables. We vary the rate of syllable production based on the importance of the word and our natural speech pattern. Speech in a Southern accent is considered slow because Southerners tend to give more duration to their vowel sounds. By stretching out the vowels, the rate slows down. A Northerner or Midwesterner might clip the vowel sounds, which would speed up their speech. Tape-recording your delivery and monitoring the duration of syllables will help you become aware of your syllable production.

By marking your script, you can also monitor the words and phrases that you have decided to stretch out for meaning. If you find in a page of copy you are stretching out six or eight words, you will know that the delivery rate will be slow.

# Focus on Stress and Intonation

---

### STRESS AND INTONATION SUMMARY

1. Most broadcast delivery is done in an artificial environment that eliminates feedback as in a normal communication situation.

2. In normal speech, we use variations in pitch, rate, duration, and pauses to make our speech interesting, natural, and to reinforce meaning.

3. Our pitch goes down at the ends of sentences that are statements and in questions that begin with interrogatives.

4. Our pitch goes up at the ends of yes-no questions because there is no interrogative to signal the question. Going up in pitch also suggests uncertainty, insecurity, doubt, hesitancy, or an incomplete thought.

5. Normal broadcast speech rate when reading copy ranges from 145 to 180 wpm. Rate should be adjusted to reinforce mood.

---

A) It is sometimes difficult for an individual to gauge the amount of stress and intonation used in broadcast work. For this reason, it is a good idea to tape-record yourself reading some copy and ask a friend, a voice coach or teacher, or your news director to review the tape with you. Often when we think our pitch is rising, it is too subtle for others to detect. If this is the case, refer to the Phonation Warm-ups for ways to improve your pitch variation (see Chapter 2). Likewise, a loud volume to us may seem soft to someone else. A listener must judge volume. Tape-record a story using your normal broadcast delivery and review it with a critic you have selected.

B) Rate is also a difficult component of delivery to monitor without a conscious effort. The AP wire copy given below has a double slash mark at 150 words. Single slash marks indicate groups of ten words before and after the 150 mark. Read this section at your normal rate, timing your delivery. Mark the point you reach after reading for exactly sixty seconds. Next, count up or back from the 150 mark to where you stopped reading to calculate how many words per minute you read. If you find you were reading as slowly as 140 wpm, reread the section trying to speed up. If you read above 180 wpm, try to slow down. This is an unemotional story that should be read with a normal delivery of around 150 to 175 wpm.

A prisoner being taken by federal marshals from Alabama to California, bolted out of a moving plane's emergency exit after landing on Saturday and fled into the darkness, authorities said.

U.S. Marshal Stuart Earnest said the escapee, 44-year-old Reginald D. Still, was en route from a federal hospital in Talladega, Alabama, to Sacramento, California, where he was scheduled to go on trial on a charge of interstate transportation of a stolen motor vehicle.

Ernest said the plane contained 44 prisoners when it touched down at Will Rogers World Airport. No other prisoners tried to escape, he said.

Still wearing handcuffs and shackles, he leaped out of the plane's emergency exit, onto a wing and then the tarmac as the plane was braking,/ the marshal said.

One of the eight security people on / the plane jumped out to chase the escapee, Earnest said.//

```
Federal marshals and local,
county and state authorities fanned
out / across the airport property,
southwest of Oklahoma City, in the /
search.
    Prisoners are normally
transported by a Boeing 727, but a
backup, a Convair 580 propeller,
was being used Saturday because the
jet was being repaired, authorities
said.
    The U.S. marshal's service
routinely transports prisoners
every other day to courts and
penitentiaries around the country.
The transportation program is based
in Oklahoma City, and prisoners on
overnight trips often are housed
overnight at a federal correctional
facility in El Reno, 30 miles west
of here.
```

Reprinted with permission from *Writing Broadcast News—Shorter, Sharper, Stronger*, Mervin Block, Bonus Books, Inc., 1997.

C) To feel the effect of no feedback on communication, look just above someone's head when you are talking or turn and face the wall. Ask the person not to respond verbally while you try to tell them about an interesting event. You will notice that without feedback, natural conversational delivery is impaired. Many people feel the same way when talking on the telephone because they are not making eye contact with their listener.

D) Monitor your pitch when you first begin to speak, whether in a live shot, stand-up or package. Many reporters begin with a very high pitch on the first word, and it takes several words before they are in their normal pitch range. I call this the "ski slope approach" because they sound like they are beginning at the top of the slope and coming down. Try to reverse this and begin down in pitch when you are coming out of a sound bite in a package as well. Remember not to begin high in pitch.

# Stress and Intonation Warm-Ups

Discovering that your stress and intonation is not appropriate and deciding to change it is not always enough. You must know how to change stress and intonation to enhance meaning. The method described in Figure 13 gives you a way to do this.

When you first begin practicing this method, it will seem time-consuming and technical. For the method to work, you must continue to practice until you feel comfortable using the method and your delivery sounds natural and conversational. Practice every day marking copy and tape-recording your delivery.

Keep in mind that this method is based on meaning and is not simply a technique or a delivery trick. If you have decided where your meaning-laden words are, you need not fear that you will fall into a set delivery pattern. Every story will be different based on the meaning. You will be reading for sense and not for sound. You should be able to develop a delivery that does not sound forced or insincere.

Remember also that there are many ways each sentence can be marked. The important thing is to pull out the meaning-laden words for your listener. Where you decide to pause and how you decide to stress a word or phrase is a personal decision that should be based on meaning and your delivery style.

1) In each of the following sentences, go through the marking method as described in Figure 13. First mark pauses if there are any, and then find the meaning-laden words. Once you have selected the words, decide how you plan to stress each one and mark each with the appropriate symbol.

- Two men are dead and a third in stable condition after a multiple shooting in Gainesville last night.

- Authorities are still investigating a robbery in the southeast part of the city this morning.

• The Shelby County Mental Health Association will provide trained counselors to help locate available housing for the homeless this winter.

• 19 of 30 people sought in connection with the large scale cocaine ring, which operated out of the Pizza Shop on west Main, were arrested last night.

• A commuter aircraft on final approach and a private plane collided over the Knoxville airport this afternoon injuring ten people.

2) Once you have practiced the marking method on sentences, expand your practice to include complete stories.

A new study says the people more likely to get heart attacks are short. That applies, apparently, to men and women. In the study, men under five-foot-seven had about 70 percent more heart attacks than those over six-one. The study was done at a Boston hospital. But researchers warn that being tall is no guarantee of escaping heart trouble—and urge people to exercise and watch their cholesterol.

A Jeep flipped over on Interstate 90 in Harborcreek Township today, and a passenger was thrown out. A Life Star helicopter flew him to Saint Vincent's Hospital, where he's listed in good condition. He's a tourist from Rome, Italy: Robert Amirian, 32 years old. A state trooper says the Jeep was going too fast for the slippery pavement.

Two men jailed in Chicago on a murder charge for more than a year have been freed, and a man already in prison has been indicted for murder. The victim was robbed and shot last year on the Granville El platform. Today, charges against Derrick Hamilton and Eugene Williams were dropped.

A U-S Navy plane caught fire over the Mediterranean today, and the five-man crew bailed out. Navy helicopters rescued them—unhurt— from the sea near Cyprus. But the burning plane, an E-two-C Hawkeye, kept going. So for safety—or security—a Navy fighter plane shot it down. The Hawkeye had been on early-warning duty supporting Allied relief work for the Kurds in northern Iraq.

A fire in a home at 2220 Perkins, Saginaw, has caused heavy damage. The owner, Ernest Belford, and his family were not home. Fire officials say some clothing had been too close to a water heater and was set on fire. It took firefighters two hours to put the fire out. No estimate yet on damage.

Reprinted with permission from *Broadcast Newswriting: The RTNDA Reference Guide*, Mervin Block, Bonus Books, Inc., 1994.

*Stop talking to microphones, start talking to people. Imagine telling your story to a friend.*

**Kevin Benz**
**News Director, News 8 Austin**
**Austin, Texas**

*I tell our staff to imagine they're telling the news to a close, personal friend or relative. It sounds silly to some, but it's served as a sure-fire way to enhance our product. Our listeners feel as though they're hearing what they need to know from a trusted, compassionate friend!*

**Dan Shelley**
**News Director, WTMJ Radio**
**Milwaukee, Wisconsin**

*Try to be conversational, like you are relating a story to your mother, not "announcing" the news to the masses.*

**Richard Scott**
**News Director, WPHL-TV**
**Philadelphia, Pennsylvania**

# Soundin
# Conversati⎵

For some broadcasters, the method of marking scripts that was discussed in the last chapter offers a starting point to sounding more conversational. For others, marking scripts may seem too technical. You may find that you want to augment the marking system or use a technique that will put you more in touch with talking with a person. My advice to broadcasters is to take a few seconds to "**PREP**" before each story. Using the mnemonic of **PREP** (see Figure 16) you can follow a step-by-step process that helps you talk with a person in a conversational style.

## Developing an
## Interpersonal Style

All on-air people have been given the age-old advice to imagine they are talking to someone in order to improve their conversational

Figure 16
An Interpersonal Communication Approach to
Broadcast Delivery

**P**ERSON

**R**OOM

**E**MOTIONS

**P**LACE

quality. The problem is that it is hard to conjure up an image when you are facing a camera or the wall in a sound booth. It is not easy to hallucinate on command. Not many of us can turn a camera lens into someone's face without doing some preliminary work to make this possible. And even if we can, just seeing the face is not enough.

What is really needed is the active feedback that is an integral part of normal conversation (see Figure 12, Chapter 5).

When I ask clients to tell me whom they imagine they are talking with, I get very nebulous images such as "a young woman" or "someone sort of like my sister." I have also gotten very concrete images like "five hundred community leaders" or "all the people in the newsroom." These choices do not create the intimacy that is needed to develop an interpersonal communication event. What is needed is the well-developed image of a partner for communication.

## P=Person

The first "P" in the word **PREP** stands for "Person." Like that age-old advice, the first step is to imagine a person. But this is not a vague image. Pick a real person with whom you are comfortable talking and can imagine vividly—a friend, neighbor, cousin, etc. The demographics of your station should help in this selection. Choosing an eighty-year-old grandmother does not fit most demographics. A thirty-five-year-old housewife might be more accurate. At the end of this chapter in Focus on Sounding Conversational you will find a checklist to help you select your Person.

Once you have made your choice, this is the Person with whom you will always speak when on the air. You may at some point want to select another Person if you move to another station or want a new approach, but it is important to be consistent. Changing your Person for each story or every few days will make it hard for you to create rapport instantly in your mind.

Once you have established rapport with your Person, you will be able to use interpersonal skills when reading from a script. You will be able to come through the electronic wall and really reach your listener. We all know how to talk to a friend, neighbor, or cousin. Our pitch might go up when we want to stress a word, and we might stretch some words out and say others faster. We do this naturally because of the feedback we get from our friend when we are talking. The listener may be nodding, smiling, or looking puzzled which helps us vary our delivery. Creating a Person to talk with helps these same qualities become part of broadcast delivery.

Television and radio are very intimate communication encounters. Many people spend more time with their television or radio than they do with other people. They may even get physically closer to their television and radio than other people. The listeners must be talked with in a comfortable, conversational way. People do not want an announcer who sounds like he is talking to five hundred people. An important thing to remember is that in broadcasting you are always talking with one person as several thousands, or millions, of others eavesdrop. Good interpersonal communication sounds like you are talking with just one person in an enlarged conversational style. It is enlarged because you are more conscious of your breathing, resonance, and articulation, but it should still be conversational.

To enhance this feeling of talking with one person, you might even take a photograph of the person into the sound booth and talk to the photograph. This can help you keep the listener in mind. One of my clients imagined that the sound booth console was a breakfast bar and his Person was sitting on the other side of the bar. Whatever works to help you envision the listener can be helpful. The listener is always the most important person in the broadcasting encounter. Vividly creating this Person in your mind creates a sense of interpersonal communication.

## R=Room

The "R" in **PREP** will also help in this process. Once the Person has been selected, put that Person in a room—"R" stands for "Room." Selecting a friend or neighbor makes it easy to remember that Person in the Room where they would be watching television or listening to the radio. I know, for example, that my friend's television is in her kitchen. I can imagine what the Room looks like. I can see her sitting at the table, and I can even smell the coffee. All these sensual factors help me bring this Person to life.

We all do this every day when we talk on the telephone. If we call for airline reservations, for example, we imagine the office the agent is sitting in. We even imagine what the person looks like. Using our imaginations is something we all do well.

It will help you to use this skill in the sound booth. You

will be able to really see the Person and imagine him or her in the Room where that Person would be listening or watching. This visualization may only take a few seconds, but it will help create a sense of talking with someone. This sense may also give new life to your work if you have been on-air for a while. One client who had been a radio announcer for over twenty years said that this technique helped him change what had been routine into something with more intimacy. Thinking of his Person and putting that Person in a Room he could imagine, added a new dimension to his on-air work.

Visualization or creative imagery like this has been used in sports and theatre for years (see Chapter 9). Many sports figures spend time imagining they are hitting home runs or making three-pointers. Dancers see themselves leaping effortlessly across the stage. Broadcasters can use the same skill to create a Person with whom they can share their stories. Delivery should sound like a broadcaster is talking *with* this person instead of *at* a camera or microphone. Creating a vivid sense of the Person and putting him or her in a Room, can make this possible.

## E=Emotion

Another factor in interpersonal communication is emotion, which is what the "E" in PREP stands for. Using emotion in the news is a controversial subject, but I find *there is a difference between being impartial and being insensitive*. I hear too many anchors and reporters who have become so distanced from emotion they sound like robots.

It is never appropriate for a reporter or anchor to editorialize during a straight newscast. Showing emotion in a news story applies only to **universal emotions** and not controversial stories. A court case that is unresolved would not involve any emotion in the delivery. Likewise, a story about a possible scandal or alleged misconduct by an authority should be read without any emotional involvement.

An emotional delivery is appropriate, however, for a story about children suffering, a family killed in a fire, a plane crash, or people starving. If no emotion is felt while delivering stories such

Despite the surroundings of a studio, broadcasters must create the sense that they are talking with a person.

Courtesy of Army Broadcasting Service.

as these, the broadcaster will sound cold and insensitive. Universal emotions refer to emotions that all of us feel.

When I talk about portraying emotion, I mean a subtle feeling of emotion. In a sad story, tears or a break in the voice would not be appropriate. Portraying emotion in this situation might simply mean a slower rate and a softer tone of voice. A carefully placed pause can indicate a sense of emotion. Generally, for example, we talk faster, louder, and with a higher pitch when we are happy. We speak slower with more pauses, softer and with a lower pitch when we are sad.

Broadcasters have a greater responsibility to be aware of the meaning and emotion of stories because there is more of an archival quality to news stories now than ever before. A story about a tragic death or a lottery winner may be taped and viewed many times by the families and friends touched by the story. Before home VCRs were commonplace, news stories were not studied in detail.

Now almost every family has some news story they are saving to show others.

Even what may appear to be a routine statement often sounds more effective if it reflects some emotion. Consider the line, "We'll continue hourly updates on the progression of the hurricane throughout the evening." For a listener sitting in a beach house in the path of this hurricane, this is a very emotion-laden statement. Delivering this statement with a sense of concern will project the feeling that your station cares about its listeners.

I often hear anchors in the Washington, D.C. area reporting on another drug-related shooting death in the city as if it were a stock market report. Even if this is the 500th shooting of the year, it is still a death, and it deserves a delivery that shows that the on-air person understands the tragedy. This does not mean the anchor should become an actor. If you are going to reflect emotion in your delivery you really have to feel it. Audiences are very sensitive to forced emotion or fake sincerity. Putting emotion into stories means getting in touch with the universal emotion of the story and reflecting that with your voice.

Emotions run the gamut from joyful to tragic, happy to sad. It is important to analyze carefully the emotion of each story. I have clients who say all their stories are "serious." Using an umbrella term like this limits the possibilities for recognizing the subtle emotions in a story. You need to peel away the layers of emotion. There is a difference between a fire story where no one was killed, for example, and one with deaths. They are both serious, but the first is somber or grave, and the second is tragic or sad.

It is helpful to write the emotion of the story in the margin on the copy as a reminder. Stories may change emotion as they progress. Careful analysis is the only way to trace the progression of emotions. Listening to news headlines illustrates this. The first headline might deal with a tragic plane crash, followed by a frustrating traffic tie-up, and finishing with a joyful lottery winner headline. The anchor reading this would need to reflect these changes vocally (see Sounding Conversational Warm-Ups).

There are some techniques that will help integrate emotion into delivery. You can precede your countdown with a phrase

Prepare for stand-ups by talking with your PERSON for a few seconds about the story before you begin.

Courtesy of WWCP-TV, Johnstown, Pennsylvania.

like, "Jim, I have a really sad story to tell you. Three, two, one. . . ." This simple sentence directed at your Person will help capture the emotion before voicing. You can also talk to your Person for a few seconds about the upcoming story before you begin to record or to go live. Tell them what the emotion is and how it affected you to report on it. After doing this, you will be in the emotion when you read the story.

Using emotion can add a human quality to delivery, but remember that it needs to be sincere. Faking emotion or editorializing with your delivery is never appropriate. It is as unethical to fake emotion as it is to fake an event for the news. In order to relate to stories with emotion, you have to let your human sensitivity come into play. This is not easy considering the tragic quality of many news events. But it is a necessity if you want to be a broadcaster who has rapport with the listeners.

## P=Place

The final "P" in **PREP** stands for "Place," which refers to the place in which the listener imagines the reporter to be. This only applies to sound booth work, not to anchoring.

When most of us listen to television packages or radio stories, we imagine the reporter is on the scene. Most listeners have no idea that the reporter is really speaking to them from inside a foam-covered closet. Even though I know voicing is done in a sound booth, my immediate reaction is that the reporter is on the scene. The more a reporter can portray this feeling vocally, the more effective the voicing will be. There should be a "live" quality about the story.

The reporter is the listener's ears and eyes on the scene. The listener wants to feel there is an immediacy to the story, and that the reporter is watching it unfold. Listeners create this image just like we imagine the room in which the airline agent is seated when we talk on the telephone.

One of the best examples of this was told to me by Mike Freedman, General Manager of CBS Radio and former managing editor for the broadcast division of United Press International. Mike said that for years UPI opened its newscasts with the phrase, "From the World Desk of United Press International. . . ." When people toured the UPI headquarters, they always wanted to see the "World Desk" where they thought the newscasts were done. Bill Ferguson, a veteran UPI executive, had to have a set built that was the "World Desk" so people could see it. Even though the news was never delivered from this desk, it created the reality the listener imagined. Visitors often commented that it looked exactly as they imagined it.

A reporter's job is to create the feeling that he or she is on the scene. This is not easy to do and there are no real guidelines to help achieve this. In Focus on Sounding Conversational, you will find a checklist to help. Broadcasters have to see past the foam-covered walls of the sound booth and remember what it felt like, smelled like, and sounded like on the scene.

When this sense of imagining works, the scene comes to life for the broadcaster and for the listener. It is like the difference between standing on the stage in the middle of an event instead of looking down from the balcony and reporting on it.

## Being a Comfortable Communicator

Taking a few minutes to go through the steps of **PREP** before voicing can help create a sense of interpersonal communication with the listener. If broadcasters know to whom they are talking, and can bring that Person to life in their minds, they can reach out to that listener. Feeling universal emotions and having a sense of where the listener imagines the broadcaster to be will complete a sense of communication.

In broadcasting today, the best newscasters are not necessarily the ones with the booming, deep voices. The best newscasters are the ones who communicate with their listener. Using **PREP** before voicing can help achieve a sense of being a comfortable communicator.

# Focus on Sounding Conversational

A) Here are checklists to follow to help you select the Person with whom you wish to speak:

### P=Person
1. Find out about the demographics of your audience. Who is your primary audience? Who is a typical listener?
2. Select a person who fits into your key demographic category.
   a. This person should *not* be a parent or your child or anyone with whom you might use a different vocal style.
   b. Select someone you know very well and with whom you feel comfortable talking.
3. Write the answers to these questions about your Person:
   a. How old is your Person?
   b. How interested is the Person in listening to the news?
   c. What type of feedback does the Person give you when you speak with him or her in person? Visualize the feedback.

4. Arrange to talk with your Person if possible and observe their feedback as you talk.
5. If you want, get a photograph of your Person to help bring the Person to life in your mind.

---

**R=Room**

1. Find out where your Person usually watches or listens to the news.
2. Visit the Room if possible. This Room might be a living room, kitchen, office, or even a car.
3. Create a visual image of your Person in the Room. Take a photograph of the room if you find this helpful.
4. Get a sensual image of the Room.
   a. What smells are present?
   b. What is the temperature?
   c. What other noises are there?
   d. What lighting is used?
   e. Is your Person alone in the room? Are there other people? pets?
5. Write a visual and sensual image description of your image of the room so that you can use it for reference.

---

B) **E=Emotions.** Here are some possible emotions to consider when you analyze the *universal emotions* of what you are reading. This is only a partial list to give you an idea of the different levels of emotions:

| HAPPY | SAD | INTERESTED | ENCOURAGING |
|---|---|---|---|
| excited | sorrowful | intrigued | confident |
| inspired | tragic | curious | proud |
| optimistic | somber | fascinated | awed |
| joyful | disappointed | inquisitive | hopeful |

C)  **P=Place.** Use this checklist to establish a sense of the Place when you come back into the newsroom to voice a story:
    1. What time of day was it?
    2. What were the sensual feelings at the scene?
        a. What was the temperature?
        b. What smells were in the air?
        c. What sounds were there?
        d. Were many people around or was it isolated?
        e. How were the people feeling who were there (e.g., panicked, happy, sad, afraid)?
    3. What was the weather like?

# Sounding Conversational Warm-Ups

1. If you find it is really difficult for you to portray any emotion with your voice, try reading children's stories aloud. Some good choices are *The Three Little Pigs*, *Cinderella*, *Snow White*, or *Bambi*. Really exaggerate the emotion. Better yet, read to a child. The child will let you know right away if you are not reading with enough emotion. A child wants to hear the fear in your voice when the story is scary and experience the joy of a happy ending.

2. You can practice emotion reading news copy. Take copy home and exaggerate the emotions. Let yourself laugh in a happy story and sound overly distraught in a sad one. This is for practice only, but it will help you push the parameters of what you can do with your voice in terms of emotion. You will want to pull back from the exaggeration in your on-air delivery.

3. When you are in someone's home, observe how they watch the news. Do they look at the screen of the television? Most studies indicate that viewers look at the screen less than 50 percent of the time. What makes a person look at the screen? Become

aware of all the distractions broadcasters have to contend with when delivering a newscast.

4. Practice these headlines until you can distinguish the emotion of each one with your voice:

```
Topping the news headlines this
hour....

A commuter plane crashes into a
Birmingham neighborhood. Dozens are
believed dead...

The state school superintendent
unveils a new math program...

And a heaven-sent gift...it's the
day of the solar eclipse.
```

5. Aircheck yourself at least once a week and listen to your use of emotion. Also gauge your connection with the listener. Have you created an intimate encounter? Have you come through the electronic wall? Weekly airchecks should be part of your professional routine.

*You are an eyewitness to something people want or need to know about. Just tell it in a conversational manner with energy and enthusiasm that's appropriate to the event.*

**Dave Ettl**
**News Director, KNDO-TV**
**Yakima, Washington**

*Try to show me something rather than just stand there. Don't say, "As you can see behind me." Don't walk and talk without motivation—if you walk and talk make sure there is a "pay-off" to viewers. Surprise me by revealing something I can't see until you show me. Plan live shots carefully with help from the photographer.*

**Mike Rindo**
**Director of News and Production, WQOW-TV**
**Eau Claire, Wisconsin**

*Don't try to memorize or rehearse. Just talk. Tell the viewer what is happening naturally and normally. As Sam Donaldson said, "Put the mouth in gear and hope the brain follows."*

**Ray Frostenson**
**Station Manager, KNOE-TV**
**Monroe, Louisiana**

# Going Live

If you ask broadcasters to tell you stories about embarrassing on-air experiences, what they will most often tell you about are live shots gone awry. Live shots challenge broadcasters in ways that no other on-air work does. Live work offers one of the best opportunities to use your voice in a relaxed way that will add energy and intimacy to a newscast. But live work also can cause more anxiety than scripted work.

It is difficult to concentrate on your delivery when live because there are so many other things to consider—the weather, your appearance, your roll cues, the people around you, and your cameraman. All these elements make live shots one of the most challenging jobs a reporter faces. I find that clients often have more vocal problems in these situations because of the stress involved. News directors tell me that when viewers and listeners write or call the station with complaints or praise, it usually has to do with live work. This is an area that can literally make or break a newscast and a career.

To have a good live shot you must be able to talk easily and comfortably to the camera. This is true whether you are voicing a straight live where you are just describing the scene (this may be called a ROSR in radio: "Reporter On Scene Report"), doing a live voice-over video (VO), or a voice-over video with a sound bite (VO SOT). If you are doing a donut or wraparound, you not only have to talk live to the camera, but you have to lead into and out of a package. And any of these experiences may include a Q&A with the anchor.

Why do news directors and producers demand so many live shots if they are such a challenge? The reason is that live gives you an opportunity like no other to tell the viewer or listener what you know from the scene. You can report the very latest and paint the scene for the audience so that they can feel what it is like to be there. I often tell clients that they are my eyes and ears on the scene. I get paid to sit and be a voice coach all day, and I depend on them to go where I cannot go and tell me what is happening. It is really very simple, but it is often not easy.

Live shots become especially difficult when they are long, continuous lives or when you are called to do many of them in one day. Some CNN clients I see may do as many as 15 live shots in one day. One of my clients told me she had done nine live shots before nine a.m. This kind of schedule puts enormous pressure on the correspondent to be fresh and informative. The dancer Rudolph Nureyev made a comment about ballet that could apply to live shots: "It never becomes easy. It does become possible." Fortunately, there are some tools that help make it possible.

# Face

Four main areas need attention each time you prepare for a live shot of any kind. To make these easy to remember, think of your live experiences as "Face Time." These are the times when your face is live in front of the viewer if you are on television. For radio, you might think of "facing" the microphone. Using the mnemonic of **FACE** will help you move through the steps to prepare your live work. Think of **FACE** before every live shot you do.

(Photograph courtesy of Jeff Alan, News Director, KDNL, St. Louis, Missouri)

**F**OCUS **A**PPEARANCE **C**LARITY **E**CONOMY

## FOCUS

Nothing is more important in a live shot than focus. Focus means keeping your attention completely on what you are saying and to whom you are saying it. Focus will affect how fluid your delivery is and how smoothly you can talk about the most important points in your live situation.

When the questionnaire was mailed to news directors for this edition of this book (see Appendix A), a question about live shots was included for the first time: "What brief advice would you give a new reporter about how to do good live shots?" We received almost 200 responses to that question. When reading all of them, there are two main themes that predominate. They both involve the need to focus. The first theme is to relax, and the other is to just talk and tell a story. (You can read some of the responses in the Focus on Going Live section at the end of this chapter.)

So what is focus? In sports they often call it "the zone." It involves focusing your energy and your thoughts and screening out all distractions. Live shots always happen in places that are full of distractions. You may be reporting from a county fair, a rally, or a busy street corner. Or you may be at an accident, a fire, or a shoot-out. The locations are endless and so are the distractions.

**PREP** should be your first step in gaining focus. You always want to think about the Person to whom you are speaking and imagine that Person in a Room listening to you (see Chapter 6).

## Notes

Next, you should decide how you want to draw this Person into your live shot. One way to do this is to develop a simple sentence in your head that will summarize the live shot. This might be something like, "To show Jim how much fun he could have at the county fair this week." Or it could be, "To give Jim information and show him the severity of the tornado damage on West Grand Avenue." Once you have developed this **summary sentence**, it is easy to construct two or three main points that relate to this sentence. In the first example, you might choose the fun things to see and do at the fair: seeing the baby pigs, buying crafts, and riding the new Ferris wheel. You also might want to think of a couple of optional points to use in case you are asked to "fill" (make your live shot longer).

Once you select these main points to cover, you should write down talking points or key words for each one. These talking points are only a word or two on each point that will trigger your memory if needed. For live shots, it is not advisable to write a complete script. When you try to memorize a script, you set yourself up for failure. Ed Pearce, News Director at KOLO in Reno, Nevada, calls it trying to follow a TelePrompTer in your head. This is always apparent to the audience. It also makes you more likely to stumble, or crash and burn completely if you forget what you memorized at some point in the delivery.

You want to be able to speak in what is called **extemporaneous speaking style**, which means thinking up the words that you want to say as you say them. You will have a map to follow with your talking points, but basically you will be just talking with

### Figure 18
### Notes for a Short Live Shot Using
### Extemporaneous Speaking Style

(Here, the introduction, body, and conclusion are separated by boxes. Using boxes can help you find your place easily.)

> The county fair is serving up fun and games for the whole family this week.

> Baby pigs
> Craft's Sale
> New Ferris Wheel
> Demotion Derby (optional point)

> There's fun for young and old alike this year at the county fair

your Person. In order to do this well, however, you must have good focus.

There are a few times when you *should* memorize in a live shot. It is always a good idea to memorize your exit line. If you are doing your live from the county fair, and the demolition derby begins right behind you, the chances of finishing your live shot and being heard are slim. If you know your exit line, you can go to that at a moment's notice. That line might be something like, "There's fun for young and old alike this year at the county fair." You can use this exit line whenever you realize you need to end your live shot.

Another time to memorize is when you are giving your roll cue. A roll cue is the last three or four words before your video begins. It is important that this cue be given verbatim so that the studio will know when to roll the video. It is also a good idea to memorize the first line of the VO that goes with the video. This is because the video may not roll immediately, and you do not want your viewers to see you reading from a script. Some reporters also like to memorize their opening line so that they will feel secure at the top of the live shot.

## Delivery

Once you have your notes written on your pad, it is time to think about your delivery. Focus is very important to good delivery in a live shot. You need to have your thoughts totally present at the event so that you can talk to your Person in a conversational style about what is happening. There are some exercises you can use to improve your ability to focus (see Going Live Warm-Ups). It is helpful to work on improving focus every day when you first begin as a broadcaster. Focus can be improved dramatically with practice. One client told me she had gotten so good at focusing that she was unaware of a jackhammer nearby during her live shot. It was not until the anchor asked her about it that she even heard it.

Focus also helps you stay aware of your role as a live reporter. This includes remembering that you do not want to become part of the crisis that might be happening around you. You should be reporting on the crisis and not contributing to it. Adrenaline can be your friend when you are gathering the information for the story, but it can turn into your enemy when you go on air. Your energy should not be raw energy in a live shot. If there has been a disaster, for example, you do not want to add to the feeling of panic that may exist in the minds of your audience. You should appear poised, professional, and credible.

The wrong vocal delivery in a live experience can hurt your credibility and sabotage what could be a good live shot. One goal to have in your delivery is to reach a point where the style of all your voicing is seamless from live shots to packages to stand-ups. I often tell clients that if I am not looking at the screen, I should not be able to tell if what I am hearing is live or taped.

Often in live shots the reporter begins to shout. If you have extra adrenaline surging through your body because of the live event, you may feel that the urgency of the situation requires a loud voice. This is not the case. Even in a noisy live location, your microphone is only six inches away from your mouth, which means the listener's ear is six inches away from your mouth as well. It may be difficult for you to hear yourself, however, and this may cause you to talk loudly. Try to position yourself for your live shot away from excessive noise and speak at a conversational volume. Shouting makes a broadcaster appear to be insecure, unsure and uneasy. It is also harmful to your vocal folds (see Chapter 2). Remember that you do not have to *make* your listener pay attention. You only have to give them the information. Use good projection (see Chapter 3) and proper microphone placement to be heard—not excessive volume.

## Mental Green Room

Creating your own "mental green room" will help you achieve the focus needed for good live shots. A green room is where guests go prior to an on-air appearance to prepare to go on air. Develop this room in your mind. Always carve out a few minutes (or a few seconds if that is all you have) to go to this "mental green room" even in the most hectic of circumstances. Let it be a time when you breathe deeply, stretch your body, and do any other of the relaxation techniques in Chapter 9 that help you focus. Once you begin preparing in this way, you will notice how your live shots suffer if you fail to make this time for yourself.

## NO FREAKING OUT

Staying focused in live shots is a must.

Artwork courtesy of Alaska Public Radio Network.

A client told me about covering a funeral where over 700 press people were crammed into a small space. It was sunny and hot, which made it feel claustrophobic. She found she relied on relaxation techniques to help her avoid reflecting this situation in her live shots. Breathing deeply was a great help. Often in stressful situations it feels as if we are only inhaling. By concentrating on exhaling during breaks between live shots, this correspondent was able to refresh herself. She could escape to her "mental green room" even amidst all the chaos.

## Technical Problems

Broadcasters often lose focus in live shots because technical problems occur. Every reporter has to survive some technical glitches in live work. Having a plan to survive these glitches is important.

The IFB (Interruptible Foldback device) is often the cause of problems in live work. An IFB enables you to hear what the anchors and producer are saying, but often, you hear yourself as well. When this happens, there is a slight delay in what you hear because it goes through the system and comes back into your ear, creating an echo that can be very distracting. Unfortunately, the first time you hear it may be at the top of your live shot. This may cause you to stumble or slow down. It is often good to have a mock live practice with this feedback occurring so that you will know how to deal with this distraction. Once you know what to expect, it is not so disconcerting.

The biggest complaint I hear about IFBs is that producers talk too much during lives. This is a problem to work out with the producer if you have a difficult time concentrating because of excessive talk. The reverse of this is when the IFB does not work at all. This happens quite often. Pulling the IFB out of your ear can be a very effective, nonverbal cue to the producer that your IFB is not working. If you are expecting questions from the anchor at the end of your live, the best approach is to acknowledge that you cannot hear the question and then give additional information that you think is important.

Another technical problem that often happens in live work when you are doing a donut or wraparound is that the package does not roll. This could happen in a VO as well. In these cases, it is best to acknowledge that the video is not there and tell the viewer what the package is about.

One technical point to always remember is that you should consider your microphone to be live all the time. Always assume the audience is hearing you. It is never safe to assume you are off-mic. Many broadcasting careers have ended because of something inappropriate that was said when the reporter thought the mic was not live.

Other problems with focus can be caused by your surroundings. One client told me she was staked out for several days doing live shots, and she was positioned next to a reporter who had an excessively loud voice. So loud, in fact, that the producer told her it could be heard through her microphone. A similar problem can come from hecklers. Problems such as these are a true test of your ability to focus. My advice is not to apologize or even acknowledge the noise unless it is so bad you feel you have to end the live shot. Many times it will not be as apparent to the listener. If you apologize, you will be calling their attention to it.

Increasing your ability to focus will enable you to deal with any situation that occurs when you are going live. By having your talking points written out, you will have a map that will guide you as you talk extemporaneously about the event you are covering in a relaxed and comfortable manner.

# APPEARANCE

Live shots provide the biggest challenge for television reporters in terms of appearance. Because a reporter never knows where he or she will be sent for a live shot, it is difficult to be prepared for all the possibilities. There are two aspects of appearance to always keep in mind: wardrobe and hair. This may seem to have little to do with your delivery, but, in fact, I have had many clients tell me that it is difficult to stay focused when they are freezing or their hair is blowing across their face. What may seem superficial can actually affect your delivery. (For more on appearance, see Suggested Readings: *Sound and Look Professional on Television and the Internet*.) Having a "Go Bag" will help you be prepared with the right clothes for any live shot. Your clothes need to be adaptable. You do not want to find yourself doing a live shot from the beach in a business suit. Look at the suggestions for a "Go Bag" described in Focus on Going Live at the end of this chapter. Finally, it also helps to consider a simple hairstyle that adapts to different conditions. You will be out in the rain, snow, wind, and humidity. You do not want your unmanageable hair to ruin a perfectly good live shot.

## Movement for Meaning

What you do with your body also affects live shots. Many reporters find the need to gesture continuously during live shots. This may not present a problem for radio, but it can be distracting for the television viewer. When a hand or finger flies through the screen, or the reporter's pad or clipboard pops into the picture, the viewer does not know what they saw because it moves so quickly, and the movement only detracts from what you are saying. This is what I call "flying body parts." If you plan to gesture in your live shot, you must make your gesture fairly high—at shoulder level—and it should enhance the meaning of what you are saying.

The primary thing to remember about movement in television is to **move only for meaning**. Otherwise, the movement is there only to help you burn off some energy, which should not be your only reason to move. This applies to gesturing as well as walking.

There is a great desire on the part of news directors and producers to have moving stand-ups and live shots simply to add interest. Viewers, however, often wonder why reporters are walking toward the camera or moving for no reason. Many times the movement is distracting. I watched one live shot, for example, in which a reporter was on a tarmac taking steps backward toward a plane. The propeller of the plane began turning during the live shot, and anyone watching worried about the safety of the reporter's head. He was so intent on moving that he was unaware of the danger. Remember that you should *move only for meaning*—if there is no justification to move, you should avoid it. Natural, meaningful movement, on the other hand, will enhance your delivery.

Movement for meaning will also help you establish the feeling that you are comfortable in the space. This is true whether you are in the field or at the anchor desk. You want to look like you *own the space* you are in. This increases your credibility and shows the viewer your confidence level.

When you are in the field, you should work closely with your photographer to plan some movement that will add to the live shot. This might be taking a few steps to reveal an important aspect of the surroundings, walking along a street and gesturing at the buildings involved in the story, or moving up to a prop you might use in the live shot. Any movement you can justify in terms of meaning has a good chance of working. Remember also that if your photographer is not aware of your plan to move, you may move out of the shot. It is important to always work together.

## Using Notes

How you use your notes is important when you are in the field. Because it may be windy, dark, or raining, make certain that your notes are readable. When you write your talking points, make them bold and limit them to one sheet. If you find a reporter's notebook does not give you enough space, use a legal pad. Have something with a hard back so that the paper does not blow around. In more than one live shot a reporter's notes have "gone with the wind." This can leave a novice reporter stammering in shock and unable to finish the live shot. Plan what you want to use for your pad, and always have it with you along with some bold, waterproof markers or pens. It also is a good idea to have a plastic bag with you to protect your notes if it is raining or snowing and your live shot is delayed.

Thinking of FACE will help you communicate with your audience in any setting such as this correspondent experiences in front of the White House.

Courtesy of Chris Black, CNN.

When you need to look at your notes in the live shot, do so with confidence. If you try to sneak a peek at your notes, you will simply look insecure. It is better to look down at your notes with confidence than stumble through the live shot. Do not be afraid of a short pause while you look down. It may seem like an eternity of silence to you, but the pause gives your viewer a chance to digest what you have said. When you have numbers or quotes to relay, you may want to actually bring your pad into the shot so that your audience will see that you are reading *because* of your desire for accuracy.

## Facial Expressions

As explained in Chapter 3, a big smile causes an erosion of good resonance. Though you may feel you should smile during some live shots, if you do, you will not be able to have a rich, fully resonant voice.

The final thing to consider about appearance in live shots is your reaction face. In each live shot, at some point, you will be looking at the camera while someone else is talking. It helps to remember your Person (see Chapter 6) and focus your attention on looking into the face of your Person. This will help you have a natural-looking expression on your face. If the anchor is talking to you, you may also imagine the anchor's face. You need to nod or look questioning or whatever you would be doing if you were looking at the anchor or your Person in conversation. Begin this expression as soon as the anchor begins to "toss" to you in the field. You never know when the camera will be on you, so have your reaction face ready.

## CLARITY

Developing your summary sentence and your two or three main talking points will give your live shot clarity. Your main goal in a live shot is to take a very complex event and boil it down to clear and understandable information. You want to distill the important facts for your audience. See Going Live Warm-Ups for ways to practice this distilling process.

You may also want to paint the scene in your live shot. This is the primary goal of a ROSR for radio (which may be live or taped). These are in first-person and are used to paint word pictures. Think of using this approach in your live shots for television as well. Even though the viewer will have video to look at, it is often a good idea to be clear in your description of other senses like the temperature, the emotions of the people around you, and the overall feeling of the place. This is not necessary in all live shots, but always consider it as a possible element. Describing the scene can be especially helpful when the lead-in from the anchor covers most of the main points you planned to cover. In this situation, you can revert to a scene description for your live.

Clarity in live shots also involves being factual. Bruce Whiteaker, News Director at KXAN in Austin, Texas, offers excellent advice: "Be careful about reporting unconfirmed information and scanner traffic. Go with what you know, but only with what you can confirm." It is often tempting when you are on the scene to report information you have not fully verified. But remember that there is no editing of a live shot, and what you say is what the audience gets. You must filter what is coming out of your mouth not only for clarity, but for accuracy and appropriateness as well. Many libel cases have involved comments during live shots.

## ECONOMY

Steve Boyer, Assistant News Director at WPBF in West Palm Beach, Florida, sums up the idea of economy nicely when he says, "Keep it shorter than you might think. Less said well is better than more said rambling." Economy means keeping it short, precise, and unembroidered. You want to encapsulate the information in a few sentences. Limit each sentence to one idea.

One way to achieve economy is to avoid fillers in your live shots. These might be verbal fillers such as "uh," "okay," or "um," or they could be sentences you include just to fill up the live shot. You might also use verbal fillers to begin sentences like "Now. . . . " or "As you can see. . . . " Every word in a live shot should be a carefully crafted diamond. Verbal fillers may help you, but they distract the audience from what you are saying.

There are times, however, when it is difficult to be economical in your word use. If you are doing a live shot from a natural disaster where the emotion is running high, the tendency is to embellish your live shot because you are feeling so many emotions yourself. This is a time when focus is crucial. Again, remember that you do not want to be part of the crisis. You want to report on the story in a clear and economical way so that your audience will be able to understand what is happening.

Economy is an important concept to use when you are first beginning to do live shots. Go for short sentences and short live shots at first. It is much easier to answer questions from an anchor than to talk live. Use the Q&A to get some of the information across so you do not have to talk as long in the straight live. Give the anchor your questions ahead of time so you will know what to expect, and, again, keep your answers short. This holds true for donuts or wraparounds as well—when you first begin doing these, keep them short.

Live shots offer one of the biggest challenges in broadcasting. Becoming accomplished at live shots is a goal most veteran reporters will tell you they still have. If you remember the concepts of **FACE** you will have some guidelines to use in your process of becoming an excellent live reporter. Your delivery will improve, and the information you give your audience will be clear and helpful.

# Focus on Going Live

A) Here are selected comments from the almost 200 responses received in answer to the question, "What brief advice would you give a new reporter about how to do good live shots?" These responses are from television and radio news directors from the United States and Canada.

> The purpose in doing a live shot is to give the listener or viewer "inside" or first-hand information of a kind the anchor cannot provide . . . so do it! Ask the questions, get the info that an interested citizen would want to know if he or she stumbled upon the scene or event. You must be curious if you want to be a reporter.

> Think about what you're saying and paint a "word picture."

> Explain it to me like you would explain it to your mom.

> Don't memorize. Know your subject. Think who, what, where, why, and how in your mind. Make bullet points for your live shot and deliver the information around the bullet points. Practice before you go on. When a reporter is new, it's much easier to break them in live with Q&A rather than to ad lib for two minutes!

> Be natural. Know your material. Drop the notes. Tell me; do not broadcast to me!

> Stop memorizing every word. It shows! Gather three main thoughts and group them in order of importance then talk in conversational form.

> Relax. Do not rely on notes. Notes should be bullet points, not written out. Refer to surroundings (tell why you are there). Voice should be comfortable, not shouting. Focus!

Obviously you need to be precise with roll cues, but trying to completely memorize a live shot is a bad idea. Respond to what's going on! (That's why you're live.)

Report only the facts. Do not become involved in a story to the point that you take sides. Give only the facts. Don't speculate on a story.

Organize your thoughts. Know where you're going and try not to repeat yourself. Describe what you're seeing around you if you're in radio news. Paint a word picture.

Keep it tight and don't be afraid to say, "I don't know . . . I will check" when asked a question for which you don't have an answer.

Tell people where you are, and why, at the beginning.

Listen to what officials and others have said to you when you have/had the mic in your hand.

Tell me what you'd ask out of curiosity! What does the average Joe want to know?

Every great live shot can be prefaced with the words, "Let me show you something." Take me there. Be my tour guide. Lead me. Show me. Give me the same feeling I'd have if I were there myself.

Be active! Give the viewer a reason for you to be live. You will be much more conversational if you're active than if you're standing stiffly in front of some building.

Remember, you're telling a story, not just imparting facts. Tell the story but never forget the facts.

Don't be a statue. Movement is good, especially when you have good reason to move. Don't walk if you're not taking the viewer somewhere!

Look for ways to make it interesting. Work with your photographer to be creative.

Know your story. Stand and tell it. Trying to follow a "TelePrompTer" in your head will usually lead to stumbles.

Preparation: Know as much about the situation and your whereabouts as possible. Concentrate on telling the story simply—one fact leading to another—so you accomplish communication with the viewer.

Have a basic idea of your opening sentence and have your ending outlined. Live shots die when talent doesn't know how to stop talking.

First, know your story. Don't read from notes unless it's a name or you're quoting someone or some fact. Ad lib around two or three main bullet points. Keep it SIMPLE. Don't try to overload the viewers with information.

Slow down. Organize your thoughts. Speak to ME! It's also critical not to try and deliver too much! Accuracy and confidence are keys to credibility.

Use the space around you. Move the camera. Act as a tour guide and visually explore the space you are working in.

There is nothing more important in this business today than an ability to ad lib on any topic, and there is nothing that is so often painful to hear and see than a reporter trying to ad lib.

Keep the material tight. Trying to "bite off" more than you feel comfortable with causes nervousness. Nerves cause errors.

B) **David Steck, Senior Producer & National Remotes Producer for CNN America, Inc.,** knows what it takes to do live shots from remote locations. He has been on the front lines of CNN newsgathering for over a decade. Because lives shots know no boundaries in the news business today, his checklists will help you be prepared:

---

## REPORTING LIVE: ADVANCE PLANNING

### 1. *CALL YOUR ASSIGNMENT DESK AND/OR SHOW PRODUCER*

❏ Find out which satellite truck you'll be working out of at the live site.

❏ Get your on-site contact's name, pager/cell number and exact truck location.

❏ Get the satellite coordinates for your live shot and/or tape feed.

❏ Get IFB phone number. Get back-up IFB line in case your IFB phone is busy.

❏ Get engineering dept's direct phone in case live truck op has tech questions.

❏ Get your exact live shot "hit" time in the show.

❏ Find out which anchor(s) will toss to your live shot.

❏ Discuss with your show producer the elements in your live shot.

❏ Discuss any "roll cues" for your live shot's elements (i.e. donut, VO, SOT).

❏ Determine if you'll toss back OR the anchor(s) will ask follow-up questions of you when your live report is finished.

### 2. *ARRIVE AT LIVE LOCATION WELL IN ADVANCE*

❏ Show up at least 90 minutes before your live report/tape feed is to begin.

---

❏ If you aren't using your station's sat truck, find your network's truck. Often networks use rental sat trucks with unfamiliar exterior lettering.

❏ Say hello to your on-site contact and/or truck engineer.

❏ Make sure your on-site contact knows about all your live shot and feed plans.

❏ Confirm that your format tape (SX, BETA, DVC-PRO, S-VHS) can be fed.

❏ If feeding, ask which tape deck & coord phone you'll use for your sots/b-roll.

❏ Reconfirm your satellite coordinates with your on-site contact.

❏ Provide station IFB line, back-up IFB number and engineering direct line.

❏ Let your contact know where you'll be working/waiting while at the site.

❏ Walk around and get acquainted with the remote site.

## 3. DETERMINE WHO SHOOTS . . . YOUR PHOTOGRAPHER OR NETWORK'S

*If your STATION'S photographer is shooting:*

❏ Photographer and on-site contact discuss the IFB set-up. Adapters needed?

❏ Have your shooter determine camera location, lighting, available AC power.

❏ If not firmed up, consider backdrops no more than 200 feet from the truck.

*If your NETWORK'S photographer is shooting:*

❏ Discuss w/your on-site contact the IFB set-up. Adapters needed?

❏ In advance of the live shot, get together with the shooter and discuss your elements along with any preferred live camera moves.

### 4. *LIVE SITE BASICS*

❏ Control your stress if there is a production failure during your live shot.

❏ Make sure your station's control room clears you before you leave your live position or your photographer begins to break down gear.

❏ Space is at a premium, never overstay your welcome in a satellite truck.

❏ Don't leave the remote site for the day without checking out with your station.

❏ Following your live/tape-feed, thank everyone on-site including your truck-op . . . do this no matter how good or bad your live shot/feed goes.

## BROADCASTER'S WORKBAG

Each TV job carries different responsibilities, but you may want to consider cramming your workbag with many of the key items compiled in the list below. Remember, your "stocked-up" workbag needs to go to each in-town and out-of-region assignment.

❏ Cell Phone, plus an extra "fully charged" cell phone battery or two.
❏ Cell Phone DC "cigarette lighter" adapter.
❏ Cell Phone AC "wall" adapter/charger.
❏ Extra batteries for your pager.
❏ Big bunch of pens, a highlighter marker, small stapler.
❏ Extra pile of your business cards.
❏ Tape recorder, plus extra recorder batteries and micro-cassettes.
❏ Pocket "AM/FM/TV" radio.

❑ Copy of personal sources "black book" if it usually sits back at your office.

❑ 1-800 numbers to your station's preferred hotel chains and car rental firms.

❑ Long distance calling card.

❑ List of all station personnel work, home, pager and cell phone numbers.

❑ IFB kit: Complete with assortment of IFB cord "jack" adapters.

❑ Small dictionary and thesaurus.

❑ Small packaged food items for instant energy after the usual missed meals.

❑ Bottled water.

❑ Personal remedy for headaches.

❑ Regional state highway maps; include your state & surrounding states.

❑ Small compass, binoculars and a penlight sized flashlight.

❑ Small calculator.

## BROADCASTER'S GO BAG

Keep a three day "Go Bag" under your desk at work.

❑ Pack clothing for both dress-up/dress-down news stories. Include in that bag clothing that can be worn in layers so you are ready for out-of-town assignments on warm days and/or cool late evenings.

❑ Bring a nondescript baseball hat for windy, humid, sunny or long workdays.

❑ Toiletries, sunscreen and rain gear are musts.

❑ Pack boots so you can safely walk through locales where it may be dark or Mother Nature might have just left a ton of debris or water.

❑ Don't forget to pack an alarm clock.

# Going Live Warm-Ups

1. There is no better way to improve your ability to do good live shots than to become your own voice and talent coach. In order to do this, look at a tape of every live shot you do or listen to a tape if you are on radio. Study your live shots just as a coach would. Use **FACE** to help you. When I study television live shots, I always watch first with sound and video. Then I look away from the screen and just listen. Finally, I turn the sound down and just watch.

Without the video, you will be able to study your delivery. Listen to your level of vocal energy. Listen to the resonance of your voice, the richness and fullness of the sound. Listen to your volume. Also, listen to what you are saying. Is it clear? Is it economical? Does each sentence need to be there? Are there too many verbal fillers?

When you are just watching without sound, watch your gestures. Look for any tension in your body. Notice how focused you appear. Watch how you are breathing. I can often notice rapid breathing and/or blinking when I fast-forward a client's tape. Also look for your connection with the audience. If some of these areas seem weak, go back to the chapters in this book that offer tips on how to improve them.

2. The idea of analyzing live shots does not have to be limited to your own. Watch and listen to other broadcasters going live. For television, take notes on what you see that works well and what you see that you would change. Use the same process given above for listening to live radio pieces or to television with and without pictures.

3. Pay attention to what your nonverbal responses are when you are in a conversation. This will help you with your reaction face for live shots on television. Also practice having a "poker face" or "stance" so that you can hold an expression if you need to in a live shot.

4. To improve your ability to stay focused, pick a busy place like a shopping mall or the lobby of a movie theater. Lock your

focus on one thing such as a plant or a poster and see if you can stay totally focused on that object. You will need to erase all the distractions from your mind. If your mind wanders, keep bringing your focus back to your object. This practice will help you stay focused in live shots. Actors and athletes often use this technique backstage or prior to a game to attain the focus they need to succeed.

5. Economy and clarity can be improved by distilling a story to two or three main points much like you would for a live shot. You can do this by taking a newspaper or magazine story you have read and first developing a summary sentence for it. Next write your talking points. Then actually do the live shot. Audio- or video-tape yourself if possible, and critique this as suggested in the Warm-Up #1.

6. You can use the practice of coming up with a summary sentence and three main points in just about any situation. Do it while driving when you see something interesting or when you are walking somewhere. The practice possibilities are limitless and each time you practice, you will improve your ability to focus and think in clear and economical ways.

7. The beginning of a live shot is often a difficult time to maintain your focus. Try taking a slight pause at the beginning and thinking of a word to help you focus. That word might be "focus" or it could be "contact" or the name of your Person. Remember that you do not have to start talking immediately. It is better to take a second to get connected with the listener and begin with composure.

It is important to prepare for your live shots by relaxing prior to them when possible. If you are at the site of your live shot and it is not coming up for a few minutes, step away. Create your own "mental green room." Find a place away from everyone and take a few deep, abdominal-diaphragmatic breaths. Think about your Person and what this live shot will mean to him or her. Compose yourself as much as possible before going live. Let your mind catch up with your body, which may have been running all day, and calm your mind if it is caught up in the chaotic energy at the scene (see Chapter 9, Coping With Stress).

*Remember that you want the listener to think you're speaking to them. Work in the "you" leads whenever possible. Also, keep the pace up—this will keep the listener's interest.*

**Jack W. Miller**
**News Director, WWNY-TV**
**Watertown, New York**

*Be natural. Viewers are sophisticated enough to know when you're not being yourself.*

**Bruce Whiteaker**
**News Director, KXAN-TV**
**Austin, Texas**

*Speak to the viewer as you like to be spoken to; be clear, conversational, and say it "like you mean it."*

**Desirée Landers**
**News Director, WVLT-TV**
**Knoxville, Tennessee**

# Other Live Experiences

Live shots are not the only time when you will be called upon to go live on the air as a broadcaster. Other types of live interactions present special challenges in terms of stress that can affect your delivery: cross-talk and tosses at the anchor desk, and interviewing, which may be in the field or in the studio. In any of these situations, if your stress level is high, it will affect your performance. Broadcasters' voices often go up in pitch, deliveries may be rushed, and there may be misplaced emphasis on words. And perhaps most damaging to both the broadcaster and the station are the inappropriate things that may be said on the air. Thinking of your listener is of paramount importance in these live situations.

# Cross-Talk and Tosses:
# A Party of Three

Nobody likes the feeling of being left out at a party. We have all had that awful feeling of sitting alone while others are laughing and having a good time. That is exactly how many viewers and listeners tell me they feel when radio or television anchors are chatting at the desk. The listener feels like he or she is the outsider watching a group of people have a good time. What creates this feeling? It has to do with a basic communication theory of *dyads* versus *triads*.

A *dyad* is an intimate relationship between two communicators much like two friends would have if they were involved in an intense interaction. You can think of this dyad as creating a protective shell that encloses these two people so that others do not try to intercede. You have encountered this at parties or in the newsroom. A nonverbal message is sent out that says, "Do not bother us. We are involved in our own discussion right now." Unfortunately, when a dyad exists at the anchor desk, the audience is left out. No matter how "chatty" the conversation is, the listener is still a third wheel. It may result from the tendency to try to personalize the news by making anchors more human and personable, but if you are instructed to do this, you are receiving misguided advice. The goal is admirable, but the implementation of it is not working. The listener needs to be *pulled into* the discussion. When you create a *triad* with three people involved, cross-talk can work well. Your listener becomes the additional person at the anchor desk. In tosses when the anchors talk with the sports or weather person, also called "cross-overs," the listener or viewer feels like they are in the studio as well.

One news director explained good cross-talk by saying that it is like you are in a discussion with three people and one of the people is remarkably quiet. You continue to attempt to draw them into the conversation with your voice and eye contact anyway. Another way to think of this is to focus on making cross-talk more journalistic and less personal. No one likes to have to listen to others' small talk. The "happy talk" idea that was popular several years ago is not the goal. "Happy talk" is so personal it alienates the listener. Instead, use "we" statements, not "I" statements, and say something meaningful. Cross-talk and tosses should have the dual goal of progressing the newscast and building the credibility of the news team. There will always be some difference between the cross-talk used in a morning news show versus the late night news, but it is important to remember the goal of progressing the show and increasing credibility.

For any news show, when talking with the weather person, for example, you might say, "We sure need more rain for the gardens in this area. This has been the driest year in the last ten years." With the sports anchor you might say, "We all watched the Olympics last night. Can we expect to see three more gold medals won tonight?" This use of "we" works to create a *triad* as opposed to saying, "My garden is so dry. I wish it would rain" or "I watched the Olympics last night." These are simple examples that illustrate how you can pull the listener or viewer into the scene.

An even more obvious way to draw the audience in is to speak to them directly. You could look at the camera and see your Person (see Chapter 6) and say; "I don't know about you, but we all loved seeing the U.S. win all that gold at the Olympics last night." Then you can turn to the sports person and ask, "Can we expect more tonight?" A direct interaction with the listener makes them part of the interaction.

## Problems in Cross-Talk and Tosses

Not only can you alienate your listener as an anchor, but you can also alienate your co-anchor in your cross-talk. Clients tell me that the hardest thing to handle is when cross-talk falls flat because the other anchor does not respond appropriately. Or, conversely, when the toss is one that nobody could catch. This should not be verbal sparring.

It is important to remember that these interactions are not just verbal. Facial expressions can create the same effect. A cold smile following a comment from one anchor to another creates an icy atmosphere that any viewer can sense. Unfortunately, this is sometimes a result of animosity at the desk. I have been in studios where as soon as there is a break for commercial, the anchors begin

Cross-talk and tosses offer an opportunity to create a good relationship with the listener and with the other anchor or reporter.

Courtesy of Bruce Whiteaker, News Director, KXAN-TV, Austin, Texas

shouting at each other in anger. The stress this creates is obvious,
and it is easily heard in the voices of the anchors when they are
back on air. It also results in cross-talk that falls flat because of the
tension between the two people. This is not only unprofessional behavior, it is career threatening. Avoid this kind of atmosphere at all
costs. (See Other Live Experiences Warm-Ups for guidelines on
how to deal with a difficult co-anchor situation.)

Some anchors attempt to script their cross-talk to avoid
problems, but this is rarely successful. It takes great skill to be able
to read chatter from a TelePrompTer and make it sound like conversation. Even the best actors cannot make this work. Think of any
awards show presenters, and you can remember the stilted chatter
they go through. It never sounds natural and conversational because
it is scripted, and they are attempting to read from the
TelePrompTer. The only ways to accomplish appropriate and spon-

taneous cross-talk are to think before you speak and always concentrate on making your talk journalistic and relevant.

It is beneficial at times for a reporter to give the basic idea for a question to be asked to the anchor before the toss (see Chapter 7). This can assure that the question is relevant and answerable. Sports and weather anchors can do the same with their tosses. You will get more spontaneity if the questions are not written out but are only talking points.

But even in a good-natured relationship, a bad toss can happen. One client told me of a reporter who tossed back to her with a no-win line during breaking news. It was at the end of a very contentious trial and the verdict had just come in. The toss was, "Tomorrow the jury who convicted him will decide if he lives or dies and tomorrow happens to be his birthday as well." This anchor responded, "That will be a tough day for him, I am sure." This resulted in an onslaught of viewer calls saying she was sympathetic to this accused killer. This reporter needed to anticipate what responses the anchor would have to the toss. Thinking of her possible responses, the reporter would probably have dropped the line about the birthday.

Anchors can also toss badly to reporters. This happens in live shots quite often. If the anchor tells all the facts in the toss, it leaves the reporter with little to say. In this situation, one solution is to reiterate what the anchor has said. Another approach is to simply describe the scene around you. Often this is a valuable contribution a live reporter can make (see Chapter 7).

## Watch What You Say

As mentioned earlier, cross-talk and tosses also offer an opportunity for inappropriate things to be said. Anchors have been fired for making a racially or ethnically charged comment. One client told me that after a weather report her co-anchor began a discussion of how it always rains on Good Friday because of the crucifixion. This left her with no idea how to respond. A comment like this is inappropriate.

It is important to remember that you always represent the station when you are on the air. Your personal beliefs and opinions have no place on the station's airtime. Unless you are giving a clearly identified editorial, stay away from stating opinions. If you are caught in a situation where an inappropriate comment is made, the best idea is to ignore it and continue on as if it were not said. Getting into a discussion or trying to correct it will most likely make it worse and draw you into the discussion.

One anchor explained to me that he has multiple filters in his head that he puts any comment through before he says it. He thinks about the implications in terms of the diversity of his audience and their sensitivities. He tries to use a filter for each area he can define, including racial and ethnic groups, sexual differences, age, body shape and size, and religious affiliations. He tries not to say something until it passes through all his filters.

# Q&A: The Art of Interviewing

Gathering information is a basic component of broadcasting, and interviews are a part of that. Whether you are an anchor or reporter, there will be times when you have to ask questions of a person during a live broadcast. This is a bit more challenging than cross-talk and tosses because you are usually talking to someone you just met. Remember in these situations that you are still in a triad that includes you, the interviewee, and the audience member who is listening.

Live interviews may originate in the field or they may be done in a studio. An entire book could be written on this topic, but there are some basic guidelines that will help you sound well-prepared and skilled in the delivery of your questions. Being prepared will reduce the stress involved in interviewing, which will help you use your voice effectively in these situations. These guidelines apply to interviews of all sorts as well as talk show formats.

In live interviews, it is important to be an active listener. Pay close attention to what your interviewee is saying.

Courtesy of Desirée Berenguer.

## Basic Guidelines for Interviewing

*Prior to the interview. . . .*

- Do your homework. One of the best ways to be a good interviewer with a credible delivery is to be a knowledgeable interviewer. Know as much as you can about the person and the topic. Personalize the interview by becoming an expert on the person and/or business you will be discussing.
- Have achievable goals that relate to your audience. Think about why you are interviewing this person and what the audience would like to ask. Ask yourself what about this person will be of interest? How does this topic affect the lives of the audience members?
- Chat with your interviewee prior to the interview to establish rapport and break the ice. If needed, tell them approximately how long you want their answers to be. You may also give them an idea of the slant you plan to take in the interview. Avoid submit-

ting questions to interviewees in advance since this will make their answers sound prepared and will limit your ability to control the interview as it is taking place.

*In the opening of the interview. . . .*

- Establish the credentials of the interviewee at the start of the interview and do this indirectly again if the interview is lengthy.
- If you thank your interviewee at the beginning of the interview, make your thanks sincere. Do not rush this part of the interview—it helps establish your authority and your level of confidence as the interviewer. Make eye contact with the interviewee while thanking him or her.

*In the body of the interview. . . .*

- Make sure that the interviewee keeps eye contact with you during the interview. The best television interviews give the impression that the people are involved in an active discussion with one another with no thought of the camera. The format of your interview may require that you look at the camera at times, but during the active interviewing you and your interviewee should have good eye contact.
- Be an active listener. Pay attention while the other person is talking. Let your nonverbal feedback be genuine and spontaneous, growing out of your active listening. Never "act" interested in an interview.
- Remember that you are an important component of the interview. There should be a balance between your vocal energy and involvement, and the interviewee's. Your questions provide half of the product that is the interview.
- Your interviewee will often mirror your energy level in an interview. Be sure you keep your energy level high throughout the interview.
- If you need to look at your notes, do so confidently. Sneaking a look at your notes hurts your credibility.
- Never refer to something said in your conversation with the inter-

viewee off air. To get that information, ask a question in the interview that will elicit the same information from the interviewee on air so that the audience feels they are part of the interview.

- Do not attempt to use the interview to show off how much you know about the topic. You are not the interviewee. You are the person asking questions. Make your questions simple and short. The listener wants to hear what the interviewee knows and not what you know. Get out of the way and let the interviewee talk.

*In the closing of the interview. . . .*

- If appropriate at the end of the interview, ask the interviewee if he or she has anything else they would like to add.
- Thank your interviewee at the conclusion of the interview with sincerity. Do not rush your thanks or do it in a perfunctory manner. Remember that the audience is observing your sincerity.

*Delivery considerations. . . .*

- Think of how a Q&A looks in a print format or on the Internet. Questions are often printed in bold type. The print does not fade out toward the end of each question. Do not let your voice do this either.
- Ask your questions at a conversational rate. Do not rush your questions—they provide balance in the interview. If you think your questions are not important enough to take any time, then you should just ask the person to talk without any Q&A.
- Avoid verbal fillers like "uh," "okay," and "um" in your questions. Do not begin your questions with "Well" or "So." Verbal fillers only help *you*. They do not contribute to the meaning of your questions. Remember, this is enlarged conversation, not sloppy, casual conversation.
- Do not interject verbal feedback responses when the interviewee is talking such as "I see," or "Uh huh," or "Okay." These responses are distracting and may cause editing problems if parts of the interview are used without your questions. Learn to give the interviewee only nonverbal feedback such as smiling or nodding.

- Make the interview as conversational as possible by using the interviewee's name at times. Write the name in large print on a card or your notepad to have in front of you during the interview.
- In longer interviews, avoid using cliches like "Stay with us . . . ," "That's interesting . . . ," and "Well, I see we're out of time. . . . " Your responses should be conversation-based so that they are fresh and spontaneous.
- Vary your use of question lead-ins like, "Let me ask you. . . . " Put several of these phrases on a note card and use a different one each time. Do not repeat the same lead-in in an interview.

*Question structure in the interview. . . .*

- Ask only one question at a time. Your interviewee may be able to answer several questions at once, but it will be confusing for the audience.
- Use the interviewee's last statement as a springboard to your next question, but avoid repeating word-for-word what the interviewee just said as the start of your next question.
- Use simple, understandable English in your questions. Remember that your audience is made up of people with different levels of knowledge about the topic. Do not use jargon or acronyms.
- Avoid technical questions unless you can explain them completely. Remember the demographics of your audience. Ask questions that the layperson would want answered, as well as more advanced questions that are easy to understand. Be conversational but not condescending.
- Ask open-ended questions. The last thing you want is for your interviewee to answer with "Yes" or "No."
- Do not ask leading questions or provide choices. For example, avoid a question like, "Will the school board provide more money for teachers or equipment or . . ." This leads the interviewee in the answer. A better question would be, "What will the school board provide more money for?"
- If you want to get more than just the "company line" from an interviewee, you have to ask the **second-level questions.** These are the kinds of questions that break news. They go below the surface to the next level of information. These are the "Why?" and

"How?" questions. In the school board example, you could follow-up by asking, "How will these new teachers be used by the city?" Or you might hear something in the answer that signals your second-level question. But you must be an active listener to hear this. If you go into the interview with an agenda and never vary from it, you will miss these opportunities. It is much like a jockey who knows how he plans to run a race and never looks up during the race. He might miss the one opportunity to change lanes and win the race. Listening is imperative for a good interview.

## Safety Issues with Live Broadcasting

Whether in an interview or doing cross-talk, anchors and reporters can put themselves at great risk by revealing too much personal information. When the "happy talk" days began in broadcasting some years back, anchors and reporters were given the advice to make their live work personal, especially at the anchor desk, so that they would be more human to the audience. That advice has backfired for more and more broadcasters who are finding themselves the targets of fans who crossover into the realm of stalkers. This creates the most stressful situation that can exist for a broadcaster and the effect it has on voice and delivery is profound. It is difficult to concentrate on anything else when you fear for your life.

What begins as a nuisance can escalate into a threat. A stalker is defined as a person who intentionally and repeatedly harasses or follows another person causing that person fear. This unwanted contact can be in the form of phone calls, letters, gifts, or personal contact. The Justice Department estimates that more than one million women are pursued and harassed by stalkers every year. Dr. Park Dietz, one of the country's foremost forensic psychiatrists, says that the perceived approachability and the high visibility of broadcasters make them prime targets for stalkers. His company sees a couple of dozen cases of stalking involving broadcasters every year.

I have had many clients tell me about being stalked. Although most are female, several male clients have revealed this to me as well. Most of these clients came to me because they were

Spontaneous, unscripted cross-talk can be effective, but it holds the potential for problems.

Courtesy of Jeff Alan, News Director, KDNL-TV, St. Louis, Missouri.

suffering from vocal problems because of the stress of an overly aggressive fan. Stress affects the voice in many ways (see Chapter 9), and there is nothing more stressful than thinking your life is in danger. The mental anguish this creates can be paralyzing.

One client came to me because she had been experiencing anxiety attacks while anchoring. She thought it was because her breathing was shallow and voice work would correct that. As I talked with her, I learned that she was in a frightening situation relating to a viewer. She told me that when the situation began, the same man would approach her when she left the station every night and ask her how the show went. He would always make a comment about something that she had said during the show. She had perceived him as a friendly viewer out for a walk. But when he began sending her flowers at the station she began to worry. Then he told the station receptionist one day that he was her boyfriend and asked why she had not come out to meet him. This terrified her, and she reported his activity to the police. But every night when she anchored she was aware that he was watching her. This became very stressful for her and severely affected her delivery.

This stalker fit the category of a love obsessive stalker with a mental disorder called erotomania. This type of stalker develops a love obsession or fixation on a person with whom he has no personal relationship. Many of these stalkers are delusional, which can make them very dangerous. Both women and men can become targets of love obsessive stalkers. David Letterman had to deal with a love obsessive stalker who actually broke into his home. Many male anchors have told me that they have had experiences with love obsessive viewers.

When dealing with a love obsessive stalker, it is important to take action immediately (see Other Live Experiences Warm-Up #4). My client should have been on the alert when she was approached the first time walking to her car. This type of encounter is very different than a fan who approaches you in a restaurant or a grocery store. The very fact that he was waiting outside the station was enough to cause alarm. Clients who have been stalked tell me that you should not be afraid to get aggressive immediately when a person or a situation feels inappropriate. By waiting until he had given her flowers, she caused herself more stress and put herself in potential danger.

Almost anything might attract a love-obsessive stalker, and the person being stalked is never at fault. But a potentially dangerous situation occurs when an anchor is told to make her cross-talk and tosses personal to show the audience how human she is. When this advice is followed, anchors often reveal personal information like their birthday or their hometown. I have even heard potentially dangerous information being given. I recently heard one anchor say in a toss to the weatherman, "Well, it really rained out our way in the Shady Grove apartments. And there was lots of wind damage on Chelsea Drive. In fact, right next door to my apartment a tree hit the carport of a house." This anchor practically drew a map to her apartment with this statement, and she said everything except that she sleeps with her windows open. Anyone interested in finding her apartment would have no trouble doing it.

In another instance, when asked by a co-anchor what she did on the weekend, one anchor responded, "I had a birthday party for my twins, who turned six years old. And afterwards I took them to ice skating practice like I do every Saturday." Considering there was only one ice rink in this town, this anchor made it very easy to find her and her children.

If you remember to make your cross-talk and tosses journalistic, you should be able to avoid these pitfalls. It is often personal opinion or personal information that makes stalkers feel they know you. In the last example this anchor could have answered by saying, "Well, like most of you out there, we shoveled snow this weekend. In fact, I saw lots of you at the hardware store buying snow shovels and salt. Can we expect more snow?" This progresses the newscast and keeps the toss friendly while involving the audience. It also protects the anchor's privacy.

Stalkers often feel that a newsperson is talking just to them. Another client of mine had a stalker who made persistent calls to her saying things like, "You, Goddess of Dawn, and I are briefly alone each morning you appear in my room." She also had a caller who called saying he wanted to hear her gargle for him. This progressed to him saying he wanted to drown her in her bathtub. She was terrified for months, and this fear affected all aspects of her life. She said, "When a person is making death threats, every man who looked at me, I wondered, Is that him? They don't tell you about that in journalism school."

There are other mistakes you can make that will make you more vulnerable to overly interested fans. A reporter told me she paid with a check at a video rental store and received flowers the next day at her home from "A Secret Admirer." By having her home address on her checks, she had left herself open to unwanted attention. Another television anchor took her vacation photos to a one-hour photo shop. She later found out that pictures of her on the beach had been copied by the developer at the photo shop and distributed to all his friends. This was not only humiliating, but frightening to her as well. She realized she should have sent the photos to a national lab to protect her privacy in the community.

In addition to remembering to consider your safety whenever you are involved in cross-talk, tosses, or any type of on-air chatter, it is important to think about safety measures you can take.

You will find some additional simple guidelines to help create a safe environment at the end of this chapter (see Warm-Up #4). But it is also important to remember that not all fans are stalkers. You need to be mindful of your safety but not obsessed by it. Dave Cupp, a news director and veteran television anchor, offers this advice about being on the air:

> You have to understand that being on air is a very public profession, and your life changes. The key is to surrender your anonymity, which is unavoidable, while preserving a zone of privacy and safety. But do not become paranoid. Most of the time a fan is just a fan.

> Being instantly recognizable can be great. It can also be annoying. You will be more likely to get a good table, even in a crowded restaurant. But you will also be more likely to have your dinner at that restaurant interrupted by a viewer. It all gets old very quickly, but it comes with the territory.

> During your broadcasting career you will undoubtedly have a handful of experiences with disturbing people who might fall into the potential stalker category. But for every scary interaction, you will have scores of encounters with perfectly normal, friendly folks. This can feel strange when viewers talk to you as if you are actually a friend, but it is exactly the sort of bonding with the audience you want to achieve. So do not be surprised or frightened by strangers coming up to talk to you. It is the dynamic that is strange and not necessarily the people. Be pleasant but remain reserved. You will naturally be on the lookout for any tips that a person is acting inappropriately, but remember that most folks are just trying to be friendly. It is important to keep this in mind when you are trying to figure out what you do need to worry about. Take steps to keep yourself safe on a daily basis but allow yourself to be accessible to your audience.

# Focus on Other Live Experiences

A) Become aware of cross-talk and how it is used on newscasts. Listen to a news program in each time slot (morning, noon, afternoon, and evening) and observe the cross-talk. Was it different in each show? What made you feel part of a *triad* with the anchors? Which anchor used cross-talk in a journalistic way to progress the newscast? Watch this anchor more and observe how this is done.

B) Listen to anchors at your station (if you are working in television or radio) and observe their cross-talk. Alert them if they are revealing too much personal information. Check out the station website as well and warn colleagues about the importance of not revealing personal data.

C) Listen to interviews on radio and television and become aware of interviewers who pursue second-level questions. Notice how these probing questions affect the interview. Think of second-level questions you could ask in the interview.

# Other Live Experiences Warm-Ups

1) Watch the news and turn down the volume after a block of news. Imagine you are at the anchor desk and respond with appropriate cross-talk to the anchor. Create cross-talk that relates to the previous story and is journalistic, meaning it advances the newscast. Practice will help you be spontaneous and avoid making personal statements. You can practice tossing to sports and weather in this way as well.

2) If there is any animosity in the newsroom or between anchors, it is a good idea to create a time-out policy with the person with whom you are having difficulty. Agree that five minutes before the newscast, you will put your conflict on hold until the newscast is over. Find a quiet location like the restroom and focus on deep

breathing to let go of the conflict. Go to your "mental green room" (see Chapter 7). Once you are relaxed, focus on the newscast. Remember that your most important responsibility is to convey the news to your audience. Do not let newsroom conflicts get in the way of that.

3) Being a knowledgeable interviewer is one of the best ways to lower your stress level in an interview. Practice completing this "Research Preparation Form" so you will be prepared to do it quickly before an interview. Read an article about an author who has a new book out or a corporate executive. Prepare by doing your research just as if you plan to interview this person on live television later in the day.

---

**RESEARCH PREPARATION FORM**

**Thesis Statement:**
(What's the main topic of the interview, e.g., XYZ Corporation has a new president.)


**Definitions of Important Terms:**


**Brief History:**


**Information About the Interviewee:**


**Current Situation or Proposed Outcome:**


**Important Points to Consider for Questions:**

---

4) It is important to think about ways to make yourself safe so that you do not increase your stress level. Remember that increased stress affects your delivery. Use this Safety Checklist to help ensure your personal safety:

# Safety Checklist

## If You Begin to Feel Uncomfortable—

Contact the police if you receive two or three calls, letters, or gifts from the same person that seem suspicious or if the same person approaches you on several different occasions. No threats need to have been made.

Do not talk to the person yourself to try to clarify things or make them understand your feelings.

Do not return gifts or letters. Save these and any telephone messages for the police. Document any contact with the person. Do not eat any food items sent from a stranger.

To educate yourself more about stalkers, go to The National Center for Victims of Crime website at www.ncvc.org for helpful information.

## When You Move To A New City—

An on-air name that is different from your real name makes security and safety much easier. Many broadcasters use on-air names. If you choose to use your own name on the air, consider the suggestions that follow:

Request an unlisted and unpublished telephone number.

Consider using a private mail box service to receive all personal mail. Make certain that they will not release your address to anyone other than law enforcement personnel.

Avoid putting your home address on personal checks or business cards. Use the station's address.

Pay with a credit card in your community to avoid showing your ID.

File for confidential voter status and request that your motor vehicle information have a privacy or record restriction status. In many states, without this restriction status, any person who knows your license plate number will be given your name, address, and telephone number upon request.

If renting an apartment, place the rental agreement in another person's name. If you must use your name, ask the landlord not to give your name to the city directories. Do not rent an apartment on the ground floor or one that has easy access through windows or balconies.

Have a friend or reputable locksmith install dead bolt locks on all doors. Secure all sliding glass doors and windows with locks. Keep all doors and windows locked.

Demand identification from all repairmen and salesmen prior to entry. Even ask the police for identification prior to entry. Ask neighbors not to give out any information about you to anyone.

Do not put personal information on the station's website. Imagine what goes on the website is the same as a chat room where you are corresponding with someone who seems too interested in your personal life. Keep your comments very general.

Ask that your name and address be left off any address list made up for station employees. Alert the station employees (especially the receptionist, assignment desk, and camera people) not to give out personal information about you such as your birthday, address, or marital status. If you are single, you might consider wearing a wedding ring on the air to give the impression that you are married.

## When You Are Commuting to Work—

Be alert! Many attacks happen in cars going or coming from home or work. Watch for vehicles that might be following you. Always keep at least half of a tank of gasoline in your car.

Have an exact time you are to arrive at work and check in with the same person every day when you arrive. This is especially important if you work an early morning shift. If you are driving in the early morning hours, use a cell phone or radio to talk to someone at the station while you drive in.

Park in a different place everyday both at home and at work and vary the route you drive to work. If you will be leaving after dark, park in a well-lit area. Get someone from security or master control to walk you to your car.

Avoid driving an easily recognizable car and do not use a vanity license plate. Keep your car doors locked at all times both when unattended and when you are driving. Look into the front and rear of your car before entering the vehicle.

Notice where police stations, hospitals, fire stations, and other public places are on your driving route. If you are being followed, drive to a well-populated place like a hospital or fire station and sound your horn to attract attention. Remain in your locked car. Use your cell phone to call for help.

*Stress can be your worst enemy when it comes to on-air performance. It's impossible to remain conversational if your stress level is high. Relating to the viewer on a conversational level is the most important thing you can do.*

**Jeff Alan**
**News Director, KDNL-TV**
**St. Louis, Missouri**

*Relax! Relax! Relax! It's only TV. Develop your own best broadcast voice—be the best you. Don't try to imitate someone else's voice.*

**Bob Walters**
**News Director, WBOY-TV**
**Clarksburg, West Virginia**

*One challenge many on-air people face is caused by the stress involved in the job. For some, it results in poor breath control or an unnatural voice; for others, the stress causes physical tension that interferes with articulation by stiffening the jaw or hampering the flexibility of the tongue. Stress control is a real, ongoing issue in our newsroom and studios.*

**John Erickson**
**News Director, KKCW-FM**
**Portland, Oregon**

# Coping with Stress

*"Without rest, we respond from a survival mode, where everything we meet assumes a terrifying prominence. When we are driving a motorcycle at high speed, even a small stone in the road can be a deadly threat. So, when we are moving faster and faster, every encounter, every detail inflates in importance, everything seems more urgent than it really is, and we react with sloppy desperation."*

—Wayne Muller

Live work is not the only stressful activity in the news business. In fact, if you work in television or radio news these days, it is very hard NOT to be tense no matter what job you have.

There is no profession more demanding than being on-air. Even a brain surgeon can take a break during surgery, but an anchor or reporter doing live work does not have that option. If a television or radio anchor begins getting tense during a newscast, that person has to be able to deal with it on live television or radio. There is no walking off the set or asking for a time-out.

A tense body means a tense voice. It is possible to learn every muscle in the throat and all the information available on how to improve vocal delivery, but nothing will help if you are tense. I have seen this problem with many clients. One international network correspondent told me she suffered so severely from stress that she barely slept at night, ate no more than a few rushed bites of

---

For more detailed information on coping with stress, see *Broadcaster's Survival Guide: Staying Alive in the Business* by Ann S. Utterback, Ph.D., Bonus Books, Inc. 1997.

The stressful demands of a live broadcast are a part of most broadcasters' workdays.

Courtesy of KTTS AM/FM, Springfield, Missouri

food a day, and used caffeine and sugar to keep going. Not surprisingly, she suffered headaches, had trouble breathing, and had repeated bouts of hoarseness. She was not even able to take a deep abdominal-diaphragmatic breath and was on the verge of hyperventilating all the time. Before any vocal progress could be made, she had to work on the chronic stress her body was experiencing.

# The Importance of Coping with Stress

Like vocal exercises, stress control techniques should be part of every broadcaster's day. Other professionals, like actors, dancers, and singers, know the value of keeping their body fit and relaxed, and it is equally important for broadcasters.

News directors and general managers should recognize the effect of stress in the workplace as well. It is estimated that stress-related diseases account for seventy-five to ninety percent of visits to primary care doctors. Job stress is believed by many to be the *number one* adult health problem in this country. And these statistics are drawn from a cross-section of jobs. If we consider the unrelenting stress of working in broadcast news, with hourly deadlines and split-second timing, we begin to get an idea of how stress affects newsroom personnel.

## The Physiological Response

Let's look at what stress really is. Basically, it is a feeling of being out of control—a feeling that at a particular moment you do not have control of your life. I think that this is often the result of having too much to do in too little time.

What produces what we feel as stress? It is the flight or fight response, which is a chain reaction of automatic bodily processes. The same reflexes that allowed our ancestors to run from attacking animals and fight to defend their tribes allow us to deal with deadlines and get interviews. Our body does not know the difference between an irate congressman and a saber-toothed tiger. Stress is stress.

When faced with stress our brain releases a surge of adrenaline. This increases our blood pressure, makes our heart beat faster, and ups our oxygen intake. Blood rushes to our muscles, which makes the digestive system shut down. We begin to sweat, and our muscles tense. All of this increases our strength, gives us more energy, and makes our thinking clearer.

But this response is meant to protect us in an emergency. The adrenaline is supposed to be used up by the stressful event. There should be a healthy cycle of arousal which leads to increased performance followed by fatigue, which forces us to rest and restore the body. We have all experienced this when we play a heated game of tennis or swim laps. We feel lots of energy, which gets

Figure 19
**Stress Patterns**

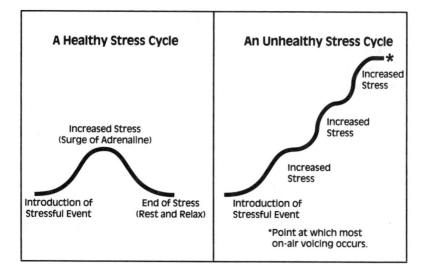

burned off, and then the body wants to rest to regenerate (see Figure 19).

There is a place for healthy stress in the newsroom to help get you through a crisis, but the problem is that the hypothalamus in the brain takes all incoming messages and prepares the body for action. There is no discrimination. So a constant state of stress can develop. Even if the actual physical release never happens, our body has been prepared. And our emotional state alone may place our body on alert. Being anxious or fearful or impatient may signal the brain that we are in danger and need the burst of adrenaline.

If there is uninterrupted stress, as there often is in a newsroom, the body never has a chance to return to its relaxed state (see Figure 19). Chronic stress short-circuits the natural process. The effect is like a tape recorder stuck on fast-forward. The machine overheats and quickly burns out.

Unfortunately, the more stressed we are, the less we are likely to realize it. And many people become stress addicts and enjoy the high they get from the extra energy. But chronic stress keeps the body running at such an unnatural level that our organs cannot function normally and regenerate, as they should.

## Panic Attacks

Stress can be more than just a slight inconvenience. One of the best-kept secrets in a newsroom is panic attacks. A panic attack is the ultimate response to too much stress. Many broadcasters have them and most tell me they have never told anyone else about them. The tension of working in broadcasting can produce symptoms as severe as panic attacks.

A panic attack is like the core meltdown of stress. It feels like someone pulled the emergency brake at 80 miles per hour. The body goes into a full-scale panic very quickly. In fact, a panic attack is the fastest and most complex bodily reaction. It is one of the most distressing experiences a person can go through. Many people think they are dying when they have a panic attack.

What does this feel like? Well, it may begin with a tingling feeling in your feet and move up your body. You begin to sweat all over and breathing becomes difficult. Your body may feel really cold or hot. You feel nauseated, your heart races, and you may get dizzy or your vision may begin to go black. One television anchor felt she wanted to run off the set. Another said her mind would go blank, and she would forget where she was. Others begin sweating profusely.

Panic disorders affect three million people in this country, and most people affected are overachievers, perfectionists, and controlling individuals. Therefore, it is not surprising many broadcasters are victims of panic attacks.

Broadcasters at every level of the business have had panic attacks while on the air. These include veteran network correspondents as well as anchors. It is much more common than people realize because it is usually suffered in silence. News directors are often the last to know that someone on their staff is suffering from severe stress.

## Negative Effects of Chronic Stress

The toll chronic stress takes on the body is devastating. A stressed-out person may suffer physical symptoms, emotional symptoms, or both. The first reactions might include exhaustion, irritability, irregular breathing, sleep disturbances, or possibly nervous mannerisms like nail-biting and finger-tapping. These may progress into headaches, back pain, chronic stomach upsets, and skin rashes. As the stress continues, ulcers may develop as well as artery and heart problems.

Stress affects the voice in very significant ways. Every aspect of the voice—breathing, phonation, resonance, and articulation—suffers when a person is tense.

The first place many broadcasters feel stress is in their breathing. Stress inhibits breathing, which affects vocal production because breathing is the energy for speech (see Chapter 1). Poor breathing results in low vocal energy or a tired, monotone sound. It also limits air supply, which can make it difficult to finish sentences without lots of pauses to breathe. And you may hear audible intakes of air when the person stops to breathe. A glottal fry can also happen, which is a popping sound at the ends of sentences when the air supply is low (see Chapter 1).

I find that poor posture brought on by stress often contributes to breathing difficulties. There is a body position called the startle response, which is a posture we go into when we are startled—we pull our shoulders up toward our ears and tense our stomach and chest muscles. All of this makes comfortable abdominal-diaphragmatic breathing difficult. This posture affects breathing, which affects the voice (see Focus on Coping with Stress).

Pitch also rises when the body is tense. The voice gets higher and higher as tension increases. Resonance is restricted when the body is tense as well. If the jaw is clenched and the throat and mouth muscles are tense, the voice is more likely to sound high-pitched and thin (see Chapter 3). Holding the mouth in a tense position also limits articulation, making it harder to sound precise when speaking.

As if all these physical problems were not enough, there are also emotional reactions to tension. Chronic stress makes it

The stress of broadcasting increases in dangerous situations such as the one this Armed Forces Network correspondent faced in Sarajevo, Bosnia.

Courtesy of Army Broadcasting Service.

more difficult to think clearly. Radio and television reporters find live work difficult because they cannot focus their thinking. They have trouble making a transition from the hectic schedule of deadlines and interviews to the focused, one-on-one demands of a live broadcast (see Chapter 7). Stress affects anchors and reporters reading copy, as well. Stressed broadcasters tend to read faster and lose the vocal expressiveness needed to sound conversational. They have a difficult time focusing on the listener because they are so aware of their own stress level. Every aspect of voice is affected by the level of stress a person is experiencing. That is why it is so important to stress-proof your life as much as possible.

# How to Stress-Proof your Life

There are three aspects of life that can be adjusted to help relieve stress. The first is diet and environment. The second is exercise. And the third involves conscious relaxation. In addition to these three areas, it is important to look at the health of the work place.

## Diet

One aspect of daily life that is very controllable is what is consumed by the body (see Figure 20). Diet and smoking have a direct

Figure 20
**A quick checklist to determine if your diet or eating habits are increasing your stress level.**

1. Do you usually do polyphasic activities? Do you do two or three other things while you are eating, like reading, listening to the radio, watching television monitors, surfing the net, or editing copy?

2. Do you eat in less than thirty minutes?

3. Do you often skip meals, especially lunch, because you just do not have the time to eat?

4. Do you drink more than two cups of tea or coffee or caffinated sodas a day?

5. Do you drink more than two alcoholic beverages a day?

6. When you need an energy boost, do you grab a candy bar or something high in sugar or caffeine?

7. Do you eat foods high in fat?

*Answering YES to any of these questions means you are adding stress to what is already a stressful work day.*

affect on stress. Many of the foods we rely on in times of stress actually make the condition worse. They give an instant energy burst, but in the long run they add to chronic stress.

Caffeine has a strong effect on the amount of adrenaline in the body. It mimics stress by stimulating the adrenal glands and the heart. Add sugar to that and the problem is compounded because sugar affects the adrenal glands. Drinking coffee and sodas all day accompanied by snacks or junk food full of sugar, and the adrenaline level, which is already high, gets even higher, and the body gets even tenser (see Figure 19).

Many broadcasters do not eat enough to keep their blood sugar at a constant level. Undereating deprives the brain of essential nutrients and asks your body to function without fuel. None of us would drive our automobile with the gas tank on empty, and we should not ask our body and mind to operate without fuel. It is important to take care of your body and stay in training considering the demands of the news business.

Eating complex carbohydrates and proteins will provide the steady energy it takes to do your job well (see Figure 21). Substitute healthy snacks such as fruit and raw vegetables for junk food. Keep a supply of these snacks in your desk to avoid the run to the vending machines. Also, stay away from fatty foods, which may take five to seven hours to digest. The digestion process takes blood to the stomach and sluggishness will result. The brain can not function as efficiently when digestion has deprived it of blood. Eating fruit, which takes less than an hour to digest, or bread, which takes one to three hours, will help you stay alert.

Another diet consideration is how often you eat during the day. I have had many clients tell me they eat only one meal a day. This is usually a large dinner when they get home at night. They wonder why when they sit down to anchor at six o'clock they usually have a bad headache. Our bodies need food throughout the day to avoid the effects of low blood sugar, which can include headaches, nervousness, and dizziness. Your stress level will be higher if your body has not gotten enough food throughout the day to keep your blood sugar at an appropriate level.

Some clients like to eat small meals throughout the day to keep their energy up. This is ideal and can be done without any weight gain if you select your foods wisely. For expert advice, check with a nutritionist. With proper exercise and a good diet, you can eat what you want throughout the day and sustain your optimum energy level.

Eating a good breakfast is important to have the energy to perform well during the morning hours. It is also important to eat lunch. Reporters in the field often skip lunch. I suggest to clients that they take foods with them that are easy to eat like granola bars, fruit, and breads so that they are not tempted to skip lunch (see Figure 21). When thinking of meals or snacks, apply the two-thirds/one-third rule. Eat two-thirds carbohydrates and one-third protein whenever you eat. This will provide both the short and long-term energy that you need. And try to eat something every four hours during your workday, even if it is just a healthy snack.

Stay away from caffeine. The best alternative is water because it has no calories and keeps the vocal tract moist and healthy (see Chapter 2). For warm drinks try herbal or decaffeinated tea or, if you cannot live without your morning coffee, at least limit it to no more than two cups and then switch to decaf coffee.

The brain is 75 percent fluid, and brain function is affected by dehydration. (For the amount of water your body needs, see Chapter 2, "Vocal Hydration.") Undereating and poor hydration both affect performance. You will help your voice and your thinking ability by drinking lots of water and eating healthy foods that sustain your blood sugar level throughout the day.

## No Smoking

Cigarettes should be avoided at all costs. Nicotine stimulates the adrenal glands, which adds to stress—though that is the least of the problems with cigarettes. As explained in Chapter 2, the effects of smoking on the voice are devastating and life-threatening. In addition, the National Cancer Institute reports that smokers are absent from work fifty percent more often than nonsmokers, are fifty percent more likely to be hospitalized, and have twice as many on-the-job accidents. Smoking affects productivity, and people making their living with their voices are foolish to abuse it by smoking.

FIGURE 21
**Ingredients for Healthy Meals and Snacks**

Use this ratio when eating:
**2/3 carbohydrates with 1/3 protein**

**Carbohydrates**

*These can be stored in your desk or bag in a plastic or metal container. Check your storage items once a week to restock and dispose of old or spoiled food.*

Low-fat granola bars
Canned or dehydrated soups
Pretzels
Baked or low fat chips
Breadsticks
Low-fat microwave popcorn
Rice cakes
Oyster crackers
Small cans of fruit in light syrup
Vegetable juice in small cans
Pita bread
Animal crackers
Vegetable sticks (store in fridge)
Whole wheat bagels

Small boxes of raisins or dried fruit
Low-fat sports bars (contain protein and carbs)
Vanilla wafers
Instant Oatmeal
Individual boxes of cereal
Graham crackers
Fig bars
Juice boxes
Snack-packs of applesauce
Whole grain breads or crackers

Fruit (Oranges, pears, bananas, grapes, & apples are easy to store and travel well. You might want to keep these in a bowl on your desk as a reminder to eat!)

Baking potatoes (These make a quick meal when microwaved and topped with some protein.)

**Protein**

*These items will need to be refrigerated or kept in a lunch bag with a cold pack. Check food in the fridge once a week and discard spoiled items.*

Nonfat yogurt
Nuts (high in good fats)
Low-fat milk
Natural peanut butter
Small cans of tuna in water

Low-fat cottage cheese
Low-fat cream cheese
Individual cheese slices or sticks
Slices of turkey, ham, or chicken

## Environment

There is not a lot you can do about the general ambience of a news-room. There will always be phones ringing, television monitors and scanners blaring, and people talking.

But studies have shown that plants and pictures help create a less stressful environment. They provide something to look at besides the usual papers and printouts. Incandescent desk lamps instead of overhead fluorescent lights have also been shown to reduce stress.

Another way to improve the workspace is to post affirmations. Something simple like, "I am in control of my life," or "Life is not an emergency," may help break the tension of the newsroom. When life is at its craziest, just thinking of one of these phrases will help.

It is important to consider the stress level in the studio as well. I am amazed at the unprofessional activities that go on *during broadcasts* in television and radio studios. These run the gamut from squirting people with water guns during commercial breaks to working puzzles and telling jokes. I have seen television co-anchors engage in shouting matches every time they go to a commercial (see Chapter 8, Other Live Experiences Warm-Ups for a way to deal with this problem).

Any unprofessional activities in the studio contribute to a more stressful environment. You may think that clowning around during a break will help lessen stress, but the effect is a loss of focus. Staying focused on the newscast by reading the upcoming copy out loud during commercial breaks is the best stress reliever. It may be necessary to alert floor directors or engineers to the importance of creating a professional environment in the studio. Everyone should contribute to the quality of the newscast by concentrating on his or her job. They owe that to the listeners.

## Exercise

One thing that can help you relax is physical exercise. Adding a workout session three times a week can greatly reduce stress and relieve the pressure of the business. This can be done at home, at a spa, or some stations like WUSA in Washington, D.C. have an exercise room at the station. That is really ideal. Any exercise that increases the heart rate for at least twenty minutes and can be done three or more times a week is what is needed. Exercise will help the body stay fit, and the endorphins released in the brain will relieve stress.

Avoid highly competitive sports like racquetball and squash because these may actually make you more stressed. Exercise does not have to be aerobic to help relieve stress. Yoga, tai chi, or simple stretches can work as well (see Figure 22). These create a sense of relaxation while moving the body. Getting a massage is another excellent way to achieve a relaxed state.

## Relaxation

For most broadcasters, the most difficult time is often when they walk into the sound booth or sit down at the anchor desk (see Figure 19). Their day to that point has needed a healthy level of stress to cope with split second deadlines and the demands of their day—the telephone calls, interviews, writing, editing, and all the other pressures of the news business. But in order to sound conversational and relaxed when voicing, they have to eliminate that stress. They have to make a conscious transition from the daily routine of getting the news to the actual voicing of that news.

One way to break the cycle of stress is with a planned period of relaxation. Twenty minutes of deep relaxation have been shown to revitalize the body as well as two hours of sleep. Relaxation turns off the arousal response started by stress. It slows down the body. Just like a well-maintained computer works most effectively, a relaxed body reduces the stress on all parts of the body.

A relaxation period can be effective if it clears the mind or if it focuses the mind on something that allows the mental chatter to stop. One Zen master said the mind becomes like a glass of muddy water. What we have to do is still the mind so that the mud settles and the mind becomes clear. This type of relaxation is not some mystical Eastern technique. It simply involves sitting quietly for a few minutes and concentrating on a word, a sound, an object, or your breathing (see Chapter 1 and Coping With Stress Warm-Ups).

Figure 22
**Simple Stretching Exercises**

A relaxed upper body improves vocal delivery by making it easier to breathe correctly and by releasing tension from the laryngeal area in the throat. Simple stretching warm-ups can help prepare the body for good vocal production prior to voicing. They are also beneficial during tracking or at breaks during anchoring to ensure a relaxed upper body. This entire series of stretching exercises can be done in less than five minutes, so stretch—easily and comfortably—as often as possible. You will feel the difference in your body and hear the difference in your voice.

*NOTE: Do all these stretches in a standing position with your knees slightly flexed and your feet shoulder-width apart. Never bounce or throw your body into a stretch. If you have any pain, do not do the stretching and check with your physician.*

1. Begin with your hands at your sides. Raise your hands above your head in a slow stretch. Reach up several times as if you are trying to pick apples just above your reach. Lower your arms. Repeat four times.

2. Interlace your fingers with your hands behind your head and your elbows out to your sides. Stretch up and back, drawing your shoulder blades toward each other and gently arching your back. Stretch your elbows forward as if trying to touch them together. Let them drop down toward the floor, and gently pull your head down toward your chest. Repeat gently in a flowing manner four times.

3. Pretend you are swimming using the breaststroke. Begin with your arms straight out in front of you with the backs of your hands touching. Stroke back as far as you can comfortably with both arms. Repeat four times.

4. Pretend you are swimming using the backstroke. With the same beginning position as number two, rotate one arm back and follow your hand with your eyes. Repeat with the other arm. Begin again. Repeat four times with each arm.

Figure 22 (Continued)

5. Interlace your fingers behind you with your arms straight. Begin with your face forward and your chin level with the floor. Attempt to pull your hands apart. As you pull, let your head stretch upward. (Be careful not to let your head fall backward, since this can injure your neck.) Hold the stretch for five seconds. Repeat four times.

6. Roll your shoulders, moving both at the same time. Begin by pulling them up toward your ears. From this position, rotate them back so that your shoulder blades are coming together. Now stretch them down. Finish by rotating them forward as if trying to make your shoulders touch in front. Continue this rotating four times. Change direction and rotate four times.

The body will function better and the voice will sound better when you give yourself time to do conscious relaxation. This is not a luxury. It is a necessity.

Having a relaxation routine as part of your workday is effective in two important ways. First, it breaks the stress because the relaxation works to turn off the stress arousal response. Secondly, it provides a sense of having control over your life. Since stress is basically a feeling of not having control of your life, this is an important benefit. And it is good to remember that the busier your day is, the more important it is to relax. When it seems you have the least time to take a relaxation break is when you need it the most.

## Breathing for Stress Reduction

Breathing is a key factor when working with stress. It is one of the first bodily functions to suffer from the effects of stress. Some of the warning signs of tension that involve the breath are frequent yawning or sighing or holding your breath and then gulping in air. It is also common to hyperventilate when stressed. This is a fast, shallow breathing that gives a feeling of breathlessness. It causes the carbon dioxide level to drop, resulting in lightheadedness and dizziness. As a broadcaster, learning to use the abdominal-diaphragmatic breath is one of the best ways to maintain a healthy, relaxed voice (see Chapter 1).

## Stretching for Stress Reduction

Breathing combined with stretching is also an effective way to relax (see Figure 22). Take it slow, however. One of the quickest ways to pull a muscle is by jumping up from your desk after sitting for a while and whipping your head around in neck rolls or twisting your body to stretch it. Conscious stretching is a good relaxer but it needs to be done with care. Let the breath help coordinate any stretching. Exhale as you tense a muscle and inhale as you relax it.

## Visualization for Stress Reduction

Visualization is another relaxation technique that works very well. Everyone knows how to do this. In fact, visualization is nothing more than day-dreaming. But what it does to our minds and bodies is really very positive. You can look at the details of something like a shell for a few seconds and really concentrate on the shell. Then let yourself remember the island vacation where you picked up that shell. This short, mental vacation will relax your body and mind (see Coping with Stress Warm-Ups).

Creative visualization can also have a very positive effect on the body and on performance. This type of visualization involves closing your eyes and imagining an activity. This has been used in sports, theatre, and dance for years as a way to improve performance. Studies have shown that imagining you are completing a task well can be as effective as actual physical practice. One study of people making free throws in basketball found that the group that practiced and the group that only visualized improved at almost the exact same rate after a twenty-day period.

Creative visualization is especially helpful for people experiencing panic attacks. One anchor was having a panic attack on the set almost every night. Her heart would race, she would start sweating, and she would feel like she was going to pass out. She began taking ten minutes before each newscast to sit quietly with her eyes closed and imagine herself doing the best job she had ever done as an anchor. She remembered a specific newscast where everything went just as she wanted and she felt completely confident and in control. Each night she would go back to that experience in her mind before going on the set. She found that this greatly reduced her panicky feeling. Her overall performance improved as well because she became more centered and focused before each broadcast.

# Environmental Health and the Newsroom

Some factors related to stress are within our immediate control and some are not. One area of concern is the health of the working environment. The term "sick building syndrome" is used to designate buildings where there are unexplained respiratory problems, excessive fatigue, headaches, and/or eye irritations experienced by ten to twenty percent of a building's occupants at a given time.

This syndrome has special significance for the health of broadcasters. All of the associated symptoms can be potentially harmful to vocal production and add to a person's stress level. Nose and throat irritation and sinus discomfort affect resonance. They also cause changes in the mucosal lubrication of our vocal tract, which can cause vocal damage. Respiratory problems and lethargy affect vocal energy. Headaches and eye irritation make concentration difficult. While these problems might be uncomfortable conditions for a worker in another type of office, in a newsroom they are career damaging.

Little concern has been given to sick building syndrome in the broadcasting field. Broadcasters often work in conditions that are appalling when considering vocal health. One newsroom I visited was being completely remodeled while the on-air talent worked around the construction. The construction dust was so thick it was possible to write on most of the surfaces in the newsroom. The computers had been carefully draped with plastic, but the most expensive equipment in the newsroom, the vocal tracts of the on-air staff, was unprotected. The news director voiced concerns that so many of his people were ill, and yet no one connected the illnesses with the construction.

Another newsroom had recently completed renovation and had a beautiful working space to show for it. What had been ignored, however, was the placement of the air vents. Both the lead anchors had desks positioned directly below air conditioning vents. Again there was no association made between their bouts of hoarseness and laryngitis and this unhealthy design.

These errors are fairly major ones, but subtle building problems exist as well. Most of us know of the hazards of radon and asbestos, but sick building syndrome involves more than this. There are literally thousands of low-level pollutants that fill the air. Indoor chemical toxins include paint, cleaning and office machine chemicals, off-gassing from new rugs and upholstery, and cigarette smoke. Another culprit is negligent maintenance of heating and air conditioning systems. Dealing with these pollutants is a complex issue. Consult my book *Broadcaster's Survival Guide* for a more complete discussion of the possible solutions.

## Improving Newsroom Hygiene

To maintain a healthy environment, broadcasters also need to consider newsroom hygiene. The voice is a delicate instrument (see Chapter 2) and viruses and bacteria can cause career-threatening illnesses. I often see newsrooms where a flu virus has circulated through the entire newsroom staff. This results in absenteeism, which affects the news product and the vocal health of the staff.

Any office has common areas where germs can be transmitted, like desks that are close together and telephones that are used by more than one person. One additional area of concern for broadcasters is the sound booth. A typical sound booth is small and poorly ventilated. It also contains a microphone that is used by many people. The windscreen on a microphone is a perfect breeding ground for viruses and bacteria.

If a persistent illness plagues most of the staff in your newsroom, look at the places where it may be being transmitted. Touching infected surfaces and then touching your nose or mouth transmits viruses and bacteria. The flu is an airborne virus and can be transmitted by coughing and sneezing. Use an anti-bacterial spray on telephones. Wipe microphones with a similar solution and keep windscreens cleaned. Use an anti-bacterial soap in restrooms. These precautions can help maintain good vocal health in the newsroom.

## Caring for Colds

Poor hygiene can spread cold viruses throughout the newsroom. Colds are one illness that we all suffer, but they can be especially bad if you have to go on the air.

The symptoms you feel with a cold are a natural response to the invading virus. What makes you feel miserable are actually the symptoms associated with your body healing itself. You develop a sore throat because the virus has located itself in the tissue in your throat, therefore causing it to swell. As a consequence, you get a flood of mucus, which is the body's natural flushing agent, to move the virus out of the throat and nose and into the stomach to be killed. If you have to go on air, this mucus seems like your enemy. Mucus is actually your friend because it is trying to make you well. It even contains enzymes that kill some bacteria. But coughing may result from the excess mucus. Coughing is a vicious assault on the vocal folds with the air moving several hundred miles per hour. Your nose may also be blocked because of the swollen tissue and mucus. All of this results in vocal challenges when you have to work with a cold.

The best advice is to NOT work with a cold, especially if you are experiencing hoarseness (see Chapter 2). When you must work, take the advice of an advisory panel of the Food and Drug Administration and use single-symptom, over-the-counter medications to treat your cold symptoms as they occur. Avoid multi-symptom medications because they often contain medications you do not need. They also may not have a large enough dosage of the individual drugs you do need to get relief.

Take a simple decongestant to clear blocked nasal passages. Avoid antihistamines because they do more harm than good with their excessive drying effect that can cause hoarseness. (If you think your stuffiness may be related to allergies, see a doctor for proper medications.) The drying effect of antihistamines may also cause your mucus to become thick, which may turn a simple cold into a bacterial infection. Stick with a single-action decongestant like Sudafed.

Avoid nasal sprays, except a pure saline spray, because they can cause a rebound effect, making you even more congested. Antibiotics are not effective when you have a cold or flu because they do not kill viruses. Take antibiotics only if you have been diagnosed with a bacterial infection.

If coughing is a problem during your cold, use a single-action cough medication. Use a pain reliever to lower your temperature if necessary. Remember to drink lots of water during a cold to keep the mucus thin and to stay hydrated.

A virus also causes the flu, but it is a different virus than the common cold. The symptoms of the flu are different as well. The flu usually hits suddenly, unlike the slow progression of a cold. The flu often begins with high fever (102–104 degrees), muscle aches, and extreme fatigue. Respiratory symptoms may not be apparent until later, and they may be accompanied by intestinal distress. The flu usually keeps a person in bed for three days or more, and that may be followed by weeks of fatigue.

The flu virus is spread much more easily than a cold virus. Airborne droplets that are contaminated by the flu virus move through the air, which means it is difficult to protect yourself against infection. One cough may disperse germs as far as thirteen feet. For this reason, at the first sign of the flu, you should stay home. Fortunately, there are fewer flu viruses than the over two hundred cold viruses, and a flu vaccine can be very effective in protecting you each year against the latest flu virus.

# Focus on Coping with Stress

A) To feel the effect of stress on your vocal mechanism, pull your shoulders up toward your ears and hold them there. Feel the tightness in your throat. Relax your shoulders and feel the difference.

B) You can recreate how the startle response feels by imagining a car backfiring next to you. You may notice that this is not such a foreign feeling. Holding your muscles this way may be your common response to stress, and one that stays with you even when there is nothing startling you. Use stretching exercises to keep your shoulders relaxed (see Figure 22).

C) Lie on the floor and consciously release tension in your muscles beginning with your scalp and ending with your toes. You might want to tense the area first and then relax it. Become aware of how relaxation feels. (For more relaxation exercises, see Suggested Readings: Relaxation Practice audiotape.)

# Coping with Stress Warm-Ups

1) Taking a relaxation break can be very simple. Find a comfortable, quiet place to sit where you will not be disturbed. Close your eyes and think of the word "relax." Think "re" as you inhale and "lax" as you exhale. Be sure you are breathing in the abdominal-diaphragmatic area. Simply inhale "re" and exhale "lax." Continue doing this for at least a minute. If thoughts come into your mind, gently let them float away or say, "thinking" to yourself. Try to increase this process up to five minutes or more. Doing this simple exercise several times a day can break the stress cycle.

2) To turn off the noise of the newsroom and really focus on what you are doing, try this Countdown to Center. It can be done aloud or silently.

Sit in a comfortable position with both feet on the floor.

Close your eyes and begin with the number "5". Say the number slowly five times and as you say it try to see it behind your eyes. You might want to imagine writing the number or just allow it to be there. You may have only a vague sense of seeing it. Or you can imagine five of something. One of my clients likes to envision the statues they give for Emmy awards. That may have an added benefit! You can see five Emmy award statues or five trees or anything you want to envision. Go slowly enough that you take the time for each number or set of objects to appear. Then continue by saying "4" four times seeing the number each time or four objects. Do "3", three times, "2", two times and finally "1" —each time seeing the numbers or objects behind your eyes. This may be difficult at first and you may have to go very slowly, but as you do it more it will be easier.

3) Practice conscious relaxation when the telephone rings. Most of us have a hypervigilant response to a phone ringing on our desk. We grab it as quickly as possible. Next time, try stopping and inhaling when the phone rings before you pick it up. This takes less time than one ring of the phone, but it allows you to make a quick transition between what you are doing and what the phone call may be about. You become focused and ready to deal with the phone call, and you break the hypervigilant response.

If you feel jumpy or edgy every day, practice stopping and taking a breath before you respond to any stimulus, like a phone ringing or pager beeping. Give yourself little time-outs during the day when you take control of the event. Jumping to answer a call means the call is controlling you. You can control the call with something as simple as a breath. Remember that life is not an emergency. The news business is full of crisis situations, but the two or three seconds it takes to inhale is not going to alter a crisis. It is simply going to ensure that you are better able to deal with it.

4) Have objects on your desk that are pleasant to look at. You can use one of these objects for a short visualization exercise. You might use a shell, for instance. Looking at the details of this shell for a few seconds and concentrating your thoughts on the shell will give you a break from your workday. If you brought the shell from the seashore, you can let your mind go back and feel the sun

and the warm sand beneath your feet. Hear the ocean and really escape to the beach for a few seconds. This short, mental vacation will relax your body and mind.

You can use any object that you find interesting for the exercise. Just try to pick something that does not relate to work—a flower, picture, or an object that has meaning for you.

5) Visualization can be very effective in reducing anticipatory stress. If you want to improve your stand-ups, imagine yourself doing the best stand-up you have ever done. If you have problems with tension in the sound booth, visualize that performance being the best it can be. Create the scene in your mind and let your body relax. Take a deep breath and feel the sense of well being in your body. Visualization can be a very effective way to reduce tension and improve your performance.

6) Create a checklist for yourself to help you prepare for on-air work. Keep this list on a card or in your notebook. Here is what your list might look like:

---

# Sample

## Checklist for Preparing for On-Air Work

1) Take two abdominal-diaphragmatic breaths.

2) Relax my body.

3) Develop my focus:

> What is the main point of what I have to say?
> Why am I saying this?

4) Review any voice or presentation points I need to remember

> (e.g., place my voice correctly, monitor any phonemic problems, do not gesture with my head).

5) Take one abdominal-diaphragmatic breath and begin.

---

# 1999 News Directors Survey

Written and researched by Gary Hanson and Michelle McCoy,
Assistant Professors,
School of Journalism and Mass Communication,
Kent State University, Kent, Ohio

If you have poor or underdeveloped vocal skills or have trouble reading copy, you might have a tough time breaking into the broadcasting business as an on-air performer. The results of our 1999 News Directors Survey[1] show that news directors place a high degree of importance on voice and vocal skills, and evaluate current and potential staff members on their vocal performance. A copy of the 1999 News Directors Survey can be found on pages 247–48.

Broadcast news directors have been surveyed three times in the past decade on the importance of vocal quality for on-air radio and television professionals. Each time, the overwhelming

*The data collection was underwritten by a grant from the Cleveland Chapter of NATAS, the National Academy of Television Arts and Sciences, and from the support of the School of Journalism and Mass Communication at Kent State University. The researchers gratefully acknowledge the financial assistance of both institutions.

[1] Note that the term "news director" includes news directors and other news executives who responded to this survey

Table 4

TV News Directors Rate Importance of Voice in On-Air Talent

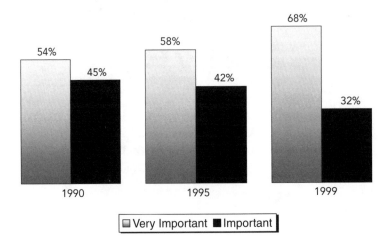

majority rated voice as an "important" or "very important" consideration in on-air performance. In fact, more television news directors rated voice as "very important" in 1999 than they did in 1990 or 1995 (see Table 4).

It is not surprising that broadcast news professionals pay close attention to vocal quality. Voice is the primary conduit of information for radio and television news broadcasts. Most of television's factual information is contained in the voice track and nearly all of it is in radio. Think of it this way—the broadcast voice in the world of electronic media is analogous to the typefaces and layouts in the print world. In fact, typefaces are often referred to as having a "voice," such as loud, bold or thin. News directors recognize the many shades of meaning and interpretation that broadcast voices can convey.

Perhaps it is for that reason that voice continued to be a factor in the hiring and/or firing of on-air talent. More than four out of every five news directors report that voice quality is an issue in the decision to hire someone, or in some cases, to keep that person on the job. This trend is reflected in the two previous *Broadcast Voice Handbook* surveys (see Table 5).

Table 5

Has voice been a factor in your hiring or
firing of on-air talent in television?

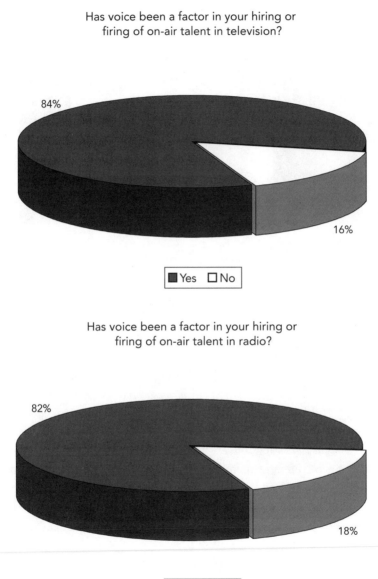

84%

16%

■ Yes  □ No

Has voice been a factor in your hiring or
firing of on-air talent in radio?

82%

18%

■ Yes  □ No

Table 6

Do you have on-air talent who could improve their vocal delivery?

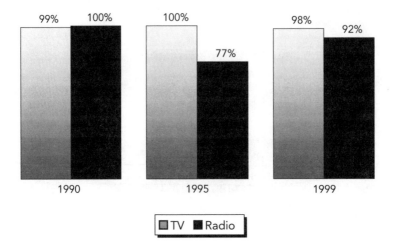

99%    100%    100%    77%    98%    92%

1990         1995         1999

TV ■ Radio

Continued voice training is also an issue for news directors. An overwhelming majority of the respondents in the current survey said they have on-air talent at their station who could improve their vocal delivery. This finding is also consistent with the two previous *Broadcast Voice Handbook* surveys (see Table 6).

Television and radio news directors look for people who can communicate conversationally and in a credible manner. The 1930's-style radio announcer who speaks in golden, round tones is not in much demand in today's broadcast and cable newsrooms. Ninety percent of the respondents said they favored a conversational delivery. The desirability of a conversational delivery has changed little over the past ten years (see Table 7).

The majority of news directors who responded to the survey said they preferred conversational or credible delivery styles over other choices, such as precise or authoritative (see Table 8).

When news directors were asked to describe their preferred choice for on-air delivery, they used terms such as: expressive, energetic, genuine, pleasant (not harsh), intelligent, believ-

Table 7

Is a conversational on-air delivery important?

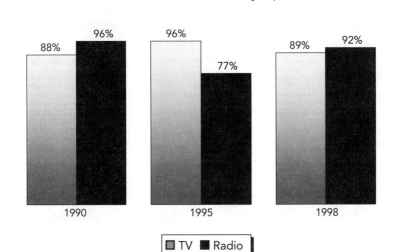

Table 8

News Directors' Preferences for Certain Types of Delivery

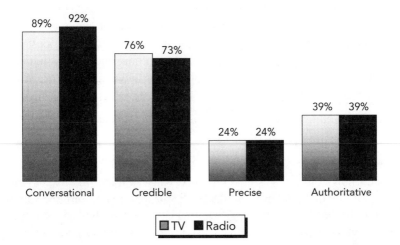

able, melodious, warm, friendly, sincere, reassuring, personable, friendly, natural, passionate and relaxed.

Others described the best on-air delivery as: variable (in that it benefits the story), clearly enunciated, easy to understand, easy to listen to, clean and natural with smooth pacing, a style where you do not shout, and having flexible range and tone.

Still other news directors described a more formal delivery style: confident, clear, well-paced, mature, resonant, distinctive, comfortable, understandable and semi-formal.

These open-ended responses all support the long-requested goal of a conversational delivery—one in which the content of the material is clearly delivered to the audience in an unaffected and naturally pleasing way.

Television and radio news directors are not shy about identifying the voice and delivery problems that they have encountered among people in their own shops. Not surprisingly, these problems reflect news directors' desire for a conversational and credible performance style. The three problems identified most often relate directly to a performer's interpretation of copy: singsong delivery, sloppy articulation, and reading in a monotone. These can be thought of as performance issues, as opposed to physiological problems with a person's voice, and are issues that can be remedied with professional coaching and exercises (see Table 9).

There are some interesting differences in the way in which radio and television news managers identify vocal problems (see Tables 10a and 10b.)

The top five concerns listed by television news directors are: singsong delivery, voices that are too high-pitched, sloppy articulation, broadcasters who speak in monotone, and voices that are nasal. The top five concerns listed by radio news directors are similar—but are listed in a different order: sloppy articulation, monotone, singsong delivery, nonauthoritative delivery, and voices that are nasal.

Radio directors see fewer vocal problems than their television counterparts. For example, the top-ranked problem for television news directors (singsong delivery) was identified by 59 percent of the respondents, while the top-ranked problem for radio news directors (sloppy articulation) was identified by only 46 percent. Moreover, nearly 68 percent of the television respondents

Table 9

Frequency of Vocal Problems dentified by News Directors

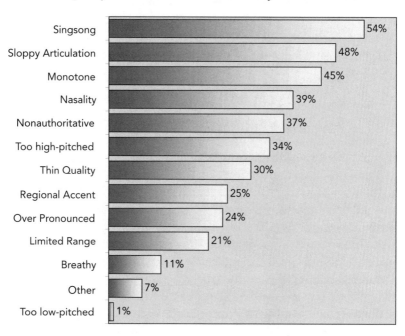

| Problem | Percentage |
|---|---|
| Singsong | 54% |
| Sloppy Articulation | 48% |
| Monotone | 45% |
| Nasality | 39% |
| Nonauthoritative | 37% |
| Too high-pitched | 34% |
| Thin Quality | 30% |
| Regional Accent | 25% |
| Over Pronounced | 24% |
| Limited Range | 21% |
| Breathy | 11% |
| Other | 7% |
| Too low-pitched | 1% |

rated voice quality as very important, while only 50 percent of radio respondents rated it in the same manner. This appears to contradict the conventional wisdom that radio, since it is an aural medium, should be *more* concerned about voice than television is. One explanation might be that radio on-air employees need to have good vocal skills to get their jobs in the first place, so voice and voice problems are seen as less serious because of the required entry-level skill. Television news directors consider other factors (appearance, story packaging ability, video skills) when making their entry-level hiring decisions. Someone starting out in television could have strengths in those areas and still lack the skills for voice work. Table 11 lists the top five voice problems identified by television and radio news directors in each of the three Broadcast Voice and Performance news director surveys.

The survey indicates some universally held perceptions

Table 10a

Frequency of Vocal Problems Identified by
Radio News Directors

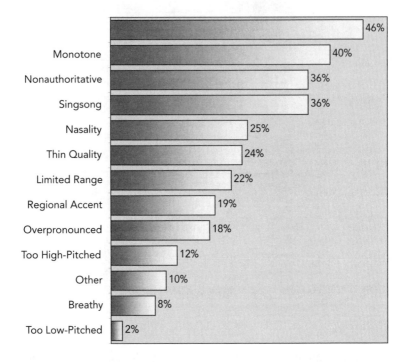

| | |
|---|---|
| | 46% |
| Monotone | 40% |
| Nonauthoritative | 36% |
| Singsong | 36% |
| Nasality | 25% |
| Thin Quality | 24% |
| Limited Range | 22% |
| Regional Accent | 19% |
| Overpronounced | 18% |
| Too High-Pitched | 12% |
| Other | 10% |
| Breathy | 8% |
| Too Low-Pitched | 2% |

on the part of radio and television news directors about industry-wide standards for vocal performance. Whether they are all trained in the same value system, or genuinely reflect the public's preferences for vocal performance, the survey found little overall significant difference in how various groups of news directors responded. Women tended to respond the same as men, large-market news directors tended to respond the same as those in smaller markets, longer-tenured news managers tended to respond the same as their younger counterparts. There are some important nuances contained in the survey. For example, small-market news directors see more voice-related problems (albeit the same ones) than their larger-mar-

Table 10b

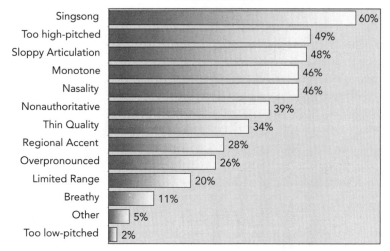

Frequency of Vocal Problems Identified by
TV News Directors

| | |
|---|---|
| Singsong | 60% |
| Too high-pitched | 49% |
| Sloppy Articulation | 48% |
| Monotone | 46% |
| Nasality | 46% |
| Nonauthoritative | 39% |
| Thin Quality | 34% |
| Regional Accent | 28% |
| Overpronounced | 26% |
| Limited Range | 20% |
| Breathy | 11% |
| Other | 5% |
| Too low-pitched | 2% |

Table 11
Voice Problems Identified by News Directors

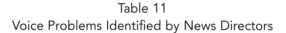

| **1990** | **1995** | **1999** |
|---|---|---|
| Nasality | Sloppy Articulation | Singsong |
| Overpronounced | Singsong | Sloppy Articulation |
| Breathy | Limited Range | Monotone |
| Nonauthoritative | Nonauthoritative | Nasality |
| Monotone | Nasality | Nonauthoritative |

ket counterparts (see Table 12). This is not surprising, since smaller markets tend to hire more entry-level workers.

The results suggest that entry-level job candidates need to hone their vocal skills. Those who do may find themselves at an advantage when it comes to finding that first job.

Table 12

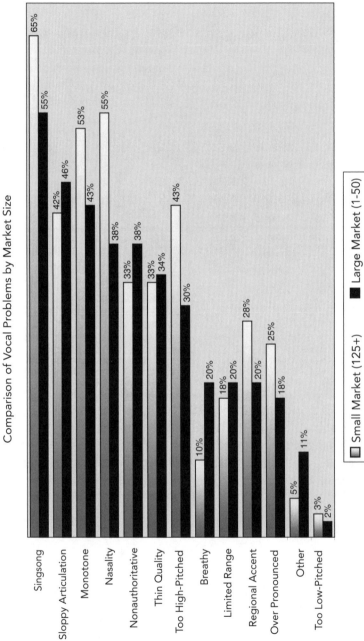

Comparison of Vocal Problems by Market Size

□ Small Market (125+)    ■ Large Market (1-50)

# 1999 NEWS DIRECTOR'S SURVEY

## BROADCAST VOICE HANDBOOK

Ann S. Utterback, Ph. D.

When evaluating on-air talent, do you consider voice to be:

(Please check one)

____ Very important

____ Important

____ Not very important

Has voice been a factor in your hiring or firing of on-air talent?

____ Yes ____ No

What type of delivery do you like? (You may check more than one.)

____ Conversational

____ Credible

____ Precise

____ Authoritative

____ Other:_____

What's the major voice or delivery problem you've encountered in your staff? (You may check more than one.)

| | |
|---|---|
| ____ Nasality | ____ Overpronounced |
| ____ Nonauthoritative | ____ Limited range |
| ____ Too high-pitched | ____ Too low-pitched |
| ____ Breathy | ____ Singsong |
| ____ Thin quality | ____ Sloppy articulation |
| ____ Monotone | ____ Regional accent |
| ____ Other (please specify): | |

**Your comments on the following questions
are extremely valuable to the readers of Broadcast Voice Handbook.**

What comments or advice concerning voice or delivery do you have ?

(If needed, please use the **back of the survey form**.)

What brief advice would you give a new reporter about how to do good live shots? (If needed, please use the **back of the survey form**.)

# 1999 NEWS DIRECTOR'S SURVEY

Please rate the importance of the following factors when evaluating on-air talent

|  | More important |  |  | Less important |  |
|---|---|---|---|---|---|
| Experience | 1 | 2 | 3 | 4 | 5 |
| Education | 1 | 2 | 3 | 4 | 5 |
| Physical appearance | 1 | 2 | 3 | 4 | 5 |
| References | 1 | 2 | 3 | 4 | 5 |
| Voice | 1 | 2 | 3 | 4 | 5 |

What is the minimum level of experience you require in hiring on-air talent?

____ 0-2 yrs.      ____ 3-5 yrs.      ____ 6-8 yrs.      ____ 8+ yrs.

How many of your on-air personnel

|  | Most of them |  |  | None of them |  |
|---|---|---|---|---|---|
| mark scripts with delivery cues | 1 | 2 | 3 | 4 | 5 |
| stand when they voice their scripts | 1 | 2 | 3 | 4 | 5 |
| complain about stress in the newsroom | 1 | 2 | 3 | 4 | 5 |
| smoke | 1 | 2 | 3 | 4 | 5 |

Do you have on-air talent at your station now who you feel could improve their vocal delivery?

____ Yes     ____ No

*Tell us about yourself (Optional)*

Name: _____

Call Letters: _____ Market Size: _____      (Circle one) **TV   Radio  Cable**
Gender: ___ Male ___ Female      Years in the business: _____

What is your job title?
____ News Director/VP News          ____ General Manager
____ Assistant News Director        ____ Reporter
____ Executive Producer             ____ Other
If you prefer your name NOT be published, please check here ___

**Please return the survey in the enclosed envelope to:**
School of Journalism and Mass Communication
Kent State University
Kent, OH 44242

Surveys were sent to approximately 1000 members of the Radio-Television News Directors Association. 244 surveys were completed and returned for tabulation. Fifty-four percent (131) of those who responded are television news directors, 28 percent (67) are radio news directors, and the remaining 18 percent (46) did not list a media type.

# Comments from News Directors

Written and researched by
Gary Hanson and Michelle McCoy, Assistant Professors,
School of Journalism and Mass Communication,
Kent State University, Kent, Ohio

Aspiring on-air broadcasters often wonder what news directors are looking for in voice quality when hiring talent. What better way to learn than directly from the source? This section allows you to develop a clearer idea of what is expected of broadcasters' voices in the profession.

One of the highlights of the first two editions of *Broadcast Voice Handbook* was the anecdotal comments from news directors at radio and TV stations throughout the United States. Note that the term "news director," as used here, includes news directors and other news executives at radio and TV stations. In addition to the new data in this edition, which includes comments in 244 questionnaires returned from news directors worldwide,[1] the section

[1]The data collection was underwritten by a grant from the Cleveland Chapter of NATAS, the National Academy of Television Arts and Sciences, and from the support of the School of Journalism and Mass Communication at Kent State University. The researchers gratefully acknowledge the financial assistance of both institutions. A copy of the survey can be found on pages 247–48.

also has some of the responses supplied by 130 the news directors in 1994 and 197 news directors in 1990. The newest comments include the respondents' names and stations, while the 1994 and 1990 responses are listed by state, city and media type only. The question asked was, "What comments or advice concerning voice or delivery do you have for the readers of *Broadcast Voice Handbook?*"

# ALABAMA

Pre-read all script out loud before air time. Mark your scripts for inflection. Project your voice and be confident in what you are reading. If you don't have a command of the material it will show on air.

**Dothan, WTVY-TV, Jeffrey S. Raker**

Don't be afraid to work to improve voice delivery. Too often, people feel their voice equals their style. I disagree. Voice can be improved and made more credible, more conversational, and more articulate. It can make the difference in some cases of moving up in your field.

**Huntsville, TV**

1. Think about how you would tell the story to a family member or friend. Then write your story that way. Then take out the slang. Then refine it.
2. If your delivery tends to be monotone, write notations on your script regarding the "tone" of the story.
3. Know your video and reference it. It will make your delivery more conversational.

**Montgomery, TV**

I like to get a TV News candidate who has had several years of Radio News background because I feel it improves their breathing, voice quality, and delivery.

**Birmingham, TV**

Good voice quality is every bit as important as a broadcaster's writing style. Even the best written copy has far less impact when the delivery isn't right.

**Huntsville, TV**

I believe the most effective human communication is "one-on-one" conversation. The effective anchor must be able to deliver the message as if he or she were talking to one person. Therefore I believe that a natural style rather than affected "deep tones" is the best way to communicate in the "one-on-one" style.

**Montgomery, TV**

# ALASKA

Don't broadcast! Don't read individual words. Write in a conversational style, so you can deliver in a conversational style.

**Anchorage, KTUU-TV, John Tracy**

# ARIZONA

Good delivery/performance starts with good writing; simple direct, active sentences.
Don't overlook the importance of pauses in an audio passage—conversation is filled with pauses, breathing space.

**Tucson, TV**

Be conversational; don't try to sound like an announcer—need to speak naturally.

**Phoenix, TV**

# ARKANSAS

Write like you talk and delivery is much easier. Any voice can be interesting to hear if inflection, pace, emphasis, etc. is present. The best way to learn to anchor is to tape a broadcast—type out the copy—and read along with the anchor—This will teach you which words receive the correct emphasis—Anyone can read—Very few can *anchor.*

**Little Rock, KATV, Bob Steel**


Practice! Learn correct pronunciations! Be conversational!

**Fort Smith, TV**


Practice reading at least ten minutes a day. Read anything you want but read it aloud.

**Jonesboro, TV**


Diaphragmatic breathing is a must in broadcasting . . . too many people come out of school and have never heard of it!

**Little Rock, TV**


# CALIFORNIA

Tell your students to be themselves. Their delivery should not be all that different on or off the air.

**Los Angeles, KTLA-TV, Jeff L. Wald**


Anchors and reporters need to speak from their diaphragms instead of their throats!

**Palm Desert, KESQ-TV, Erin Gilhuly**

Read morning newspaper aloud daily.

**Napa, KVON, Radio, Scott Craig**


Tell me the story. Don't announce it. Keep energy up!

**Sacramento, KFBK, Radio, Paul Hosley**


Sound like you know what you're talking about (by actually knowing) and you can overcome vocal shortcomings.

**San Francisco, TV/Radio, Joe McConnell**


Do *not* be just a reader—be a communicator. Have a lot of energy—sound interested.

**San Diego, KGTV-TV, Mike Stutz**


1. Be *yourself* at your best (be conversational).
2. Consider tenor/mood of the story.
3. Breathe, think, read.

**San Francisco, KQED, Radio, Raul Ramirez**


Have a coach who knows about voice and performance. Don't try to do it yourself. We are news directors, not consultants.

**Los Angeles, KMEX-TV, Jairo Marin**


Many people say that broadcasters should be relaxed and natural. That usually translates into a flat and boring delivery. Professional broadcasters have a specialized style. People entering the business need to recognize that and produce some elements of that "broadcast" style.

**Fresno, TV-Radio**

I work in an entry-level market, so I normally hire talent on their first or second professional job. I think anyone who aspires to be a television or news anchor or reporter should also aspire to be a good radio anchor or reporter. Voice is the only tool in radio, and the vocal skills are the same for television. A person with good vocal skills has a great jump on the competition for TV jobs.

**Palm Desert, TV**

My best advice: Take speech and voice and diction courses, drama classes, too, in college.

**San Diego, Radio**

The major problem with younger staff is that "somebody" tells them they need to sound "authoritative" since they look "young." Well hell, they are young! By trying to sound "authoritative" they start to strain their voice and make it thin and nasal. I have to "relax" their style back to what it was when they were hired.

**Bakersfield, TV**

Careful! Voice "quality" is highly subjective. Personality in a voice, including non-standard pacing and "regionalisms" are becoming more desirable.

**Los Angeles, Radio**

Don't try to sound like the network people. Sound like people. This is the first and greatest commandment.

**Sacramento, TV**

I try to hire reporters and anchors who talk to people in conversational style—rather than "deliver." I have worked with a dozen people over my twenty years in news, who had great voices—but bad attitudes—or lacked the intelligence, drive, and insight to do this job properly. In all but the worst cases, I'll take brains and ability over voice any time.

**San Francisco, Radio**

Voice is more than pitch and articulation. It is physical and psychological. Beginning broadcasters should work with professionals who can help in these areas as well.

**San Francisco, TV**

I'd advise your readers not to try to use a broadcast voice (or, rather, what they think is a broadcast voice) for on-air work. Unless a reporter is very talented, that kind of delivery comes off as faked and unnatural. Much better, I think, to use the natural voice as a point of departure for on-air work, and infuse it with a slightly larger quality through inflection and word emphasis.

**San Francisco, Radio**

A conversational style of storytelling is our preferred method of communicating. The most common problem seems to be reporters walking into the tracking room and *reading a script* instead of telling a story about people. Often even our best writers drag down their copy by trivializing it verbally . . . or not emphasizing the right key words to give the impact the story needs and deserves. The best communicators in our newsroom are reporters with a radio background who know how to tell stories and don't underestimate the power of their voice and delivery in getting the viewer emotionally involved or excited about the story. Ninety-five percent of TV news reporting is voice-over. Competent and compelling storytellers are the people we look for, people who can not only write to video but can hold the audience with the power of their voice.

**San Jose, TV**

# CANADA

Too many young people starting out try to copy voices they admire or try to take on a voice personality they cannot attain and so end up sounding false, phoney, insincere and sound like they are playing radio.

**Toronto, Ontario, CHUM & CHUM-FM Radio,**
**Brian D. Thomas**

I start with a program of basics. Most people don't understand the voice as an instrument. So, diaphragmatic breathing is the first step. Then delivering and understanding of sentence structure, key words, and the meaning of the story is almost the "philosophy" of being able to deliver a story. I work with an individual to develop a personalized program concentrating on projection, inflection, pausing, and emphasis. However, projection and inflection are usually the least important elements of a good delivery. Correcting improper inflection may be important, but not emphasis through inflection. But projection and inflection should flow from an understanding of how your voice works. A person's mental state is also a huge factor. This is hard to teach. On air performance is my passion and tools to help people improve are essential.

**Kingston, Ontario, CKLC/FLY-FM Radio, Tony Orr**

# COLORADO

Record yourself on the air in various segments of the programming (news/announcing music/delivering a PSA, etc.) Listen to yourself and critique what you hear. Have peers and management do the same.

**Denver, KPOF, Radio, Patricia A. La Plante**

Strong voice is one of *the* most important attributes of an on-air presentation.

**Denver, KUSA-TV, Patti Dennis**

For women—lower voice *and* speak with more whole tones. Men—more authority—strength of delivery and range of voice.

**Denver, KMGH-TV, Diane Mulligan**

Use a sense of restrained urgency in your voice. Get listeners to feel you are interested in what you have to say. It makes them interested enough to pay attention.

**Denver, Radio**

# CONNECTICUT

If someone is just getting started, such as a student, I tell them to take a speech class. I also advise (and remind) people that in broadcast journalism, you are writing for the ear, not the eye—so read it out loud to hear what it sounds like. Proper breathing is also important to a good delivery.

**New Haven, Radio**

It is more important to be understandable than to sound like "Joe anchorperson."

**West Hartford, TV**

# DELAWARE

1. More job candidates need to know how to use their diaphragm.
2. Good pipes don't mask unfamiliarity with the material.

**Wilmington, WDEL, Radio, Todd Halliday**

Don't try to make your voice something it's not. Work to improve it within its range. Be natural. The worst mistake is to put on a "radio" voice instead of a natural delivery.

**Wilmington, Radio**

The biggest concern is a voice which is too fast in delivery and "forced." Too many young reporters sound like they work too hard at making their voice sound authoritative. Also, the drop off at the end of a sentence which creates a singsong sound is prevalent in applicants.

**Wilmington, TV**

# DISTRICT OF COLUMBIA

More than anything else, reporters must learn to breathe. If necessary, even to mark places to breathe in their scripts.

**Washington, D.C., WMAL, Radio, John Matthews**

A broadcast voice should be trained, controlled and modulated to the point that you are aware not of the voice, but of the information that is being delivered.

**Washington, D.C., TV**

Voice in a news story should not be noticed. If it is, something is wrong.

**Washington, D.C., TV**

It is very difficult to improve one's delivery by reading a book. It entails reading aloud to a coach who can listen and suggest improvements.

**Washington, D.C., TV**

In certain periods of the day people watch/listen to TV news as they do something else. A strong and pleasant authoritative voice helps to keep them focused on the station and the news being delivered.

**Washington, D.C., TV**


Reporters do not place enough emphasis on the voice. Often they do not realize how much impact the voice has on the communicative ability of the story.

Students do not have a good understanding of when accents are acceptable or not acceptable. Often, they express interest in trying to get rid of an accent but don't know how to go about it or don't have the necessary dedication.

The voice is the #1 detriment to good delivery. Its effect is immediate and overpowering. No amount of excellent writing or good on-air presence can compensate for a poor voice. It is the #1 detractor of good delivery.

**Washington, D.C., TV**


We want natural-sounding people—not people stamped into a cookie-cutter style—which means every on-air reporter must develop his/her own personal flair and style—but be himself/ herself—consistently. And I respectfully suggest people listen to TV reporters with their eyes closed to appreciate the value of a strong radio presence.

**Washington, D.C., Radio**


# FLORIDA


On-air talent needs to spend more time working on his/her delivery. The best way to begin is with Ann Utterback's book.

**Pinellas Park, Bay News 9, TV, Elliott Wiser**


Talk to me, not AT me.

**Sarasota, WWSB-TV, Julie Ford**

Women in particular seem to strain their voices and lose them—perhaps voice training should be part of talent training and education.

**Tampa, WFLA-TV, Deb Halpern**

Listen to your pieces during review with eyes closed . . . this will assist in critical listening and lead towards improvement.

**Tampa, WTUT-TV, Philip Metlin**

Schools should have classes for broadcasting students on voice and delivery. I use people just out of school or with little experience. They all need voice help.

**The Villages, VNN-Cable, Ed Rose**

The biggest problems I run into among students are sloppy articulation and fast pace. I tell them to relax, slow down, and *pre-read* so they know what their copy means as well as what it says. If the words have meaning for them, they tend to be more careful how they read.

**Gainesville, WUFT, Radio, Kevin Allen**

Be yourself.

**Orlando, WDBO, Radio, Marsha Taylor**

Slow down, pauses are sometimes as important as words.

**Gainesville, WCJB-TV, Harvie Nachlinger**

You must use your voice as a tool for communication, not as a club for attention. A well-modulated conversational delivery is a much better form of communication than one which plumbs the heights and depths of vocal range and emotion.

**Bonita Springs, TV**

The most important factors are that talent needs to be understood and credible. The voice must be pleasant to listen to.

**Ft. Myers, TV**

Your voice is the delivery system by which you're able to communicate to the viewer or listener. In any endeavor, a faulty distribution system can lead to failure. If you have a weak voice or otherwise poor delivery, find coaching, etc., with which to fix it. It you have a strong voice, work just as hard to maintain and strengthen it. If the viewer or listener rejects the voice, they never get to hear the message.

**Jacksonville, TV**

On-air talent too often neglect their voices. They become overly preoccupied with how they look rather than how they look *and* sound!

**St. Petersburg, TV**

It doesn't come naturally. It takes coaching and practice, practice, practice.

**Tampa, TV**

Please, as an anchor, don't try to "sell" me on a story by overdoing. "Serve" me instead—make me comfortable with you. Make me want to invite you into my home.

**West Palm Beach, TV**

I look for reporters with a background in radio. They generally have a much better delivery because they have had to rely on their voice alone in telling their story to the viewer. People with just TV experience rely on the pictures and don't place enough emphasis on voice. A great delivery coupled with great pictures makes for a GREAT story.

**Miami, TV**

I tell beginning reporters to find a voice model . . . someone in the industry whose presentation they can learn from. Until a reporter/anchor has an idea of what they want to sound like, it's difficult for them to develop a style.

**Orlando, Radio**

The delivery must be clear, with no hurdles for the listener to overcome. A flawlessly delivered newscast is one of the only ways you have of making sure the listener hears what you are saying, instead of focusing on the mistakes, stumbles, accent, . . . etc.

**Orlando, Radio**

The notion that deep voices are better is a myth. Research clearly shows this rates very low on the list of reasons why people like announcers.

**Tampa, TV**

1. Good (proper) inflection.
2. Don't read too fast.
3. Learn how to let the listener know you're going from one thought to another without telling them.

**West Palm Beach, Radio**

# GEORGIA

Work on it—work on it—work on it—voice is so important.

**Columbus, WTVM-TV, Mark McGee**

Don't read me a story, "tell" me a story—if you can write in a conversational style you must be able to read that way too. Good writing can be ruined by a poor delivery.

**Macon, WGXA-TV, Doug Long**

*Know your subject.* Broadcast that information with authority. Your listening audience can tell when you are fluffing your way through a story.

**Augusta, WGAC, Radio, Wayne W. Roberts**

In a small market, lack of experience, at times a lack of confidence based on that inexperience, causes young reporters to mimic their favorite broadcast journalist. You just haven't lived until you've heard a young lady from Atlanta, Georgia, try to be the next Barbara Walters. Find yourself!

**Macon, TV**

Too much emphasis has been placed on "booming pipes" in radio. Radio announcers should talk like people talk.

**Atlanta, Radio**

If it appears it's unlikely that voice problems can be overcome— suggest another role in the broadcast news business.

**Macon, TV**

Don't forget to breathe! And tell the story, don't read it! Forget that you are "doing the news," and tell your story as if you were talking to one person in the listening audience—the days of stiff news delivery like Jim Dial on TV's "Murphy Brown" are over, be human when you deliver the news and use inflection to bring the story to life.

**Savannah, Radio**

The viewer decides quickly whether to accept an anchor. The appearance and vocal quality are the criteria used first to help them decide.

**Savannah, TV**

No viewer wants to be announced to—they wish to be part of a conversation. The on-air talent who can be an effective conversationalist reaps the highest rewards . . . money!

**Savannah, TV**

# HAWAII

1. Better writing makes better delivery.
2. Most unused vocal tool—pacing and pauses.
3. Beware of sounding like everyone else. Do not lose your uniqueness.
4. Don't try to sound like an anchor (man) (woman). Do try to get the viewer to remember what you said.

**Honolulu, TV**

# HONG KONG

Be yourself, be natural, don't ever try to imitate other anchors.

**Kowloon, TVB-TV, Raymond R. Wong**

# IDAHO

It's not hard to find people with good qualifications in broadcasting, even among the entry-level candidates. But their vocal quality is *often* one of the key factors I used to weed out the real contenders from the "also rans." And the frustrating thing for me in a small station is that I usually figure a person's voice and their ability to use it is pretty much a part of them that I can't fix . . . so I'll just go on to the next most qualified person who *does* have a good voice. I think most viewers would say that a person's voice (on TV) goes a long way in their opinion of the reporter or anchor. Good writing, editing and presenting can all be destroyed by the lack of a good voice and the ability to use it well.

**Twin Falls, TV**

Suggestion for work on articulation . . . read Dr. Seuss books aloud . . . he wrote some real tongue-twisters!

**Pocatello, TV**

# ILLINOIS

I can live with just about everything as long as the person can be conversational.

**East Peoria, WEEK-TV, Jim Garrott**

In a small-market station, delivery plays almost as important a part as writing, shooting, and packaging. So many audition tapes don't make it past the first minute because of poor delivery.

**Quincy, TV**

There is nothing magic about a good broadcast voice. Good vocal delivery is often as much the result of hard work and following the right advice as it is God-given talent.

The best vocal deliveries are not automatically the booming, resonant recitations that laymen often associate with the notion of good broadcast voices. In television, the medium is sufficiently multidimensional that people who make good use of average voices can do very well. In fact, I feel they make up the lion's share of the talent in this industry.

In my experience, proper breathing and phrasing are the main stumbling blocks to a good delivery. Part of this comes from not understanding the story, even if the reporter has written it. But some of it also comes from not knowing how to make the story and the individual understood. In other words, the reporter may understand the story but use of his/her voice is a roadblock to convincing the viewer of that.

One way I help young people to work around this problem is to get them to mark their copy on the words that need to be emphasized. Inflection goes a long way toward credibility.

Another think I work on with them (after the fact) is to make sure that certain words, phrases and sentences are written in such a way as to allow for best use of the voice. Eliminate certain clauses and the rest of the clutter, etc.

I do not work with people on general voice quality. I do suggest to them this is a professional coach's job, and I don't want to be party to them doing something that will screw up their voices. Bad advice can get a person sued.

**Champaign, TV**

Ann Utterback is excellent at showing young, inexperienced reporters how to improve their delivery. I use her frequently to help train my students in using their voice properly. The response has been extremely favorable. Her techniques are easy to use and practical. Long after you have heard Ann in person or read her work you can use her techniques.

**Evanston, TV**

My best advice is simply to relax and tell a story. Too often I get air-checks from people who are forcing their voices beyond their natural ranges. Simplifying writing helps make a delivery more natural as well. Think about the kind of words and phrases you use. If they would not come naturally in everyday speech—don't use them.

**Mokena, Radio**

I think voice is a very important career development issue too many broadcasters pay too little attention to.

Far too many of today's young broadcasters never get much of a chance to develop their voice or style of delivery, because they don't get the necessary practice. They graduate from college, get a job as a TV reporter, and at the most, read about a minute's worth of copy per day in a package for the evening news. Unlike most equipment a broadcaster uses, a voice gets better the more it is used. That's why those who grew up in radio and switched to television generally have much better voices (deeper, more authoritative, more relaxed and conversational) than those who have worked only for television.

A good voice does not make a good reporter, but a bad voice can ruin a good reporter's chances for success in broadcasting. I have seen very good reporters passed up for anchor jobs because no one would want to listen to them for an entire newscast.

There is also no excuse for having a bad voice, unless one has a physical impairment that affects his or her voice. With a minimal amount of expert advice and a maximum amount of use, any voice can and will improve.

For the most part, however, you will have to practice on your own time. Make copies of the day's newscast, and read it out loud into a tape recorder. Play it back. Listen for things you don't like, and read it again. Do this for half an hour a day, five days a week, for six months, and your voice (and delivery) will improve more during that time than it would over a five-year period if you do nothing more than a general assignment TV reporter is required to do.

Here's another hint. Get about five minutes of copy together, and team up with another broadcaster who is also working on developing his/her voice. Split up the copy, and take turns reading stories. (You should be taping this.) After you have read the news, discuss it for another five minutes. Play it back and critique yourself. You will probably find you were too stiff while you were reading and too sloppy with your enunciation while you were discussing it. Your goal should be to merge the two styles, so eventually you can both read and discuss the news in an articulate, but conversational, style. This will help you immeasurably in the event you one day become a TV anchorperson who is expected to have on-air conversations with your co-anchors.

If a news director tells you your voice doesn't matter much, he/she is either a bad news director or he/she wants you to remain a general assignment reporter for the rest of your professional life.

A clear, pleasant, articulate, authoritative, and conversational voice is the quickest ticket any good broadcast reporter can have to good jobs and promotions.

Bad reporters should forget everything I've said and look for another profession.

**Quincy, TV**


Do not think that you must speak like the network's Washington, D.C. correspondent—especially for local news!

**Chicago, TV**


Be "non-distracting"—don't surprise viewers. Allow them to comprehend easily.

**Peoria, TV**


Voice should be conversational. Listen to yourself (record your voice. Relax. Emphasize "power" words. Voice should reflect emotion, concern (there should be difference in your voice from reading a murder story, a fun story or a business story.

**Rockford, TV**


# INDIANA


Practice, imitation of pros.

**Evansville, WEVV-TV, Jim Hale**


I see almost no "style." There seems to be very little thought given to having a solid, distinctive delivery. Markets have many, many reporters. The best way to distinguish and set one apart from the crowd is to have some unique aspect of delivery. . . . always tied to writing!

**Evansville, WTVW-TV, Dave Smith**

Read everything you write out loud and ask yourself, is this how I would "tell" a story or am I just "reading?"

**Terre Haute, WTWO-TV, Susana Schuler**

More TV people should work in radio, at least in college.

**West Lafayette, WLFI-TV, Mike Piggott**

Practice, Practice, Practice! Using recorders and playing back is my recommendation to my reporters. Also, diction practice.

**Columbus, WCSI/WKKG, Radio, Wes Roy**

One should exercise the voice with a workout, similar to other exercises.

**Evansville, WUEV-FM, Radio, Len Clark**

Be interested in your stories and interesting in your delivery! Don't just read the story, tell it like you're talking to a friend. Exercise those vocals . . . Practice, practice, practice.

**Evansville, TV**

Don't underestimate the importance of voice. Some news shows, mornings for example, tend to be passively accepted by the viewer. That is, they might be "listened to" to a large degree because the viewer is busy doing other things. I place a great amount of emphasis on voice when hiring my morning anchors. Voice also has a tremendous influence on the anchors' authority, believability, and likability.

**South Bend, TV**

While new reporters need to work on their reporting and newswriting skills, they must not forget to work on delivery. Before I ever applied for my first radio news job, I practiced with a tape recorder. When I stopped laughing at what I heard, I went for the job.

If you haven't spent years listening to radio newscasts and watching network news on television, do that! See how the newscasters who've made it, do it. Learn from them and develop a style that is conversational.

Here's some quick advice that is not entirely my own:

1.) Write news in short, one-thought sentences.
2.) On radio, treat the mike as if it were someone's ear.
3.) On television, read as if you were speaking to one person.
4.) Don't announce. Announcer is a job title. Speak.
5.) Relax. Tension does all kinds of bad things to your voice.

**Fort Wayne, TV**


I wish anyone going to school to be an on-air personality would first have a voice instructor evaluate their voice and the use of it and give advice on what should be worked on in preparation for applying for a job in radio or television.

**Fort Wayne, TV**


Learn proper breathing (and writing that accommodates it . . . run on sentences make for bad delivery).

Delivering with authority so that the viewer believes you know what you are talking about is another problem area. I see a lot of young people here who don't quite understand this until they are worked with.

When I see a tape from an individual who has a bad voice, I ask them if this is the kind of voice and delivery they regularly hear from successful people in the business. If it's not, I tell them what to work on.

**Fort Wayne, TV**

Don't become pedantic and at the same time don't get "sloppy" with your words . . . be natural . . .be yourself . . . don't imitate . . . project . . . (that doesn't mean shout—one can project in a conversational tone).

**Indianapolis, Radio**

You only have one opportunity to get your message across to the public—if they don't understand (or get bored listening to a lackluster delivery) there are other channels to watch.

**Indianapolis, TV**

# IOWA

Practice is critical for new talent—learn to use those muscles and develop them. Good writing can help delivery problems. Listen to your copy out loud.

**Des Moines, KCCI-TV, Dave Busiek**

Read your script as you talk. Care about what you say.

**Sioux City, KTIV-TV, Dave Nixon**

Your voice is an instrument. Use it as such. If you find yourself talking in a high-pitched way, start over in a different key—just like music.

**Des Moines, IOWA, Radio, O. K. Henderson**

Don't try to sound "like a news announcer." There are too many "Ted Baxter" types out there.

**Des Moines, KIOA, Radio, Polly Carver-Kimm**

Talk to your audience, not *at* them. Picture the average audience member in your head as you deliver the news.

**Sioux City, KMNS, Radio, Mike Bailey**

Bad delivery is the biggest reason I find not to hire an applicant. The voice communicates so much, yet there's an overemphasis on appearance. I find a lot more voice problems than appearance problems.

My advice? Learn proper enunciation, inflection, flow— then *practice*. News anchors need to develop and strengthen their vocal muscles.

Practice is critical for new talent—learn to use those muscles and develop them. Good writing can help delivery problems— listen to your copy out loud.

**Des Moines, TV**

Dealing with many entry-level reporters, I find the main thing they need to do is relax and be themselves. Often they try to overdo it, trying to project false enthusiasm or energy.

**Mason City, TV**

# KANSAS

Practice listening to your voice and become comfortable with listening to it. That way you can make changes more easily.

**Wichita, KFDI-AM/FM, Dan Dillon**

If you have a regional accent, lose it.

**Pittsburg, KOAM-TV, Kristi Wilson**

Speak clearly and as you would talk to a friend, not as you think a reporter *would* talk.

**Wichita, KAKE-TV, Jim Turpin**

Tell the young would-be anchors/reporters to lose the "clipped college-speak manner." It seems to be a rather recent development and hurts an otherwise excellent candidate's chance of being hired on.

**Wichita Falls, KSWO-TV, Jan Stratton**

Many of the tips I use I read from your previous books or heard from tapes of your presentations. I would not smoke. Work in a smoke-free environment. (Our building is smoke-free.) Don't strain your voice at sporting events. (I learned the hard way too many times. I now just clap often instead of yell.) A friend of mine recently caught a chest cold that settled in his throat. He didn't treat the problem or take time off. He continued to work. The result was he sounded very hoarse for at least four weeks. I wonder if he damaged his vocal cords by doing this.

**Wichita, Radio**

If viewers don't understand your anchors, regardless of their news talents, they will tune you out.

**Topeka, TV**

I always look at reporting skills, writing technique, and ability to get along with people when I hire someone. But in radio news the most important aspect is on-air delivery. It's "the final product."

**Wichita, Radio**

Can the "Ted Baxter" technique.

**Salina, Radio**

# KENTUCKY

How to sound conversational/natural—most important.
**Highland Heights, WNKU, Radio, Maryanne Zeleznik**


Listen to yourself on tape to really hear how you sound. Get professional coaching.
**Louisville, WAVE-TV, Kathy Slaughter Beck**


Voice quality, or lack of same, is the responsibility of the talent.

FOR STUDENTS, vocal problems should be addressed early in their training. If a student has not reached an acceptable level of vocal performance by their senior year, they should be advised to follow a course that would put them off-camera (production, assignment editing, videography). I'm more than a little irritated at broadcast schools that take tuition from students and then cut them loose to be disappointed by news directors.

FOR EXISTING PROFESSIONALS looking for a job change, ask for professional advice and cure the problem before you send out the resume tapes.

No news director will hire a problem. There are too many available professionals without problems.
**Louisville, TV**


I've found from both personal experience and from hiring talent . . . especially young people . . . have not developed their own style of delivery. The most natural (and successful) announcers often come from radio where they've had the opportunity to develop their style (experiment, change, etc.). Young broadcasters should copy successful styles from solid professionals . . . then combine them into their own personal style.
**Paducah, TV**

# LOUISIANA

Be natural. I think too many young reporters try to do their "Billy Broadcast" voice instead of working to sound on air like they actually talk—to sound natural instead of like a bad Gary Owens imitation.

**Monroe, KNOE-TV, Roy Frostenson**

Adopt standard American diction. Regional identification is good only if a talent wants to remain in a specific area an entire career.

**Alexandria, TV**

As a manager in a small market, we do not have the money for coaching. And we do hire people who have potential to develop. All too often though, new graduates refuse to seek help or work to improve. I feel a lot of voice work can be done with quality advice found in books. But you need to be disciplined and work on your own along with seeking help. I can offer some advice from my own training—but I am not qualified to go beyond simple exercises. Remember that your voice does count—but nothing improves until you put forth the effort. Also, remember to be patient and don't give up.

**Monroe, TV**

The ability to develop control of one's voice is vital to becoming a success in broadcasting. I have seen many advance far beyond their other abilities simply because they learned how to use their voice, and likewise, I have seen the opposite apply. The voice is the dominant sellable commodity in broadcasting, and therefore, cannot be taken lightly.

**Alexandria, TV**

The key to good delivery is to make your broadcast sound like a conversation. This is a special mix. A delivery must be easy to listen to yet authoritative enough to be credible.

**Baton Rouge, TV**

Communication and broadcast journalism students should be required to take more speech classes.

**New Orleans, TV**

# MAINE

Listen to your story without watching—turn your back to the monitor. Does your story sound good using bites and not sound? The video is the photographer's responsibility.

**Portland, WPXT-TV, Matt Ledin**

Bring words up from the gut—take the strain off the throat. Always have good energy. Adjust tone to reflect the emotion of the piece . . . *feel* your story, tell your story.

**Bangor, TV**

# MARYLAND

Talk to one person, not the mass audience. Be sincere and sensitive.

**Westminster, PV3, Cable, Dean Minnich**

While one's voice is important, it does not have to be heavy for a male or rich for a female. A lighter voice, if presented with a credible style, can overcome most voice problems.

The proper use of the voice is paramount and is probably one of the most overlooked areas in college training.

Regional accents are the least acceptable voice/speech problem in this area of the country. "Bawlamerease" is unacceptable in this market.

**Baltimore, Radio**

Less and less often we're seeing a deep, rich voice as a primary consideration for hiring in this industry. That doesn't mean news directors take lightly the idea of voice quality—to the contrary. We're now trying to get the most out of what would have been considered "marginal" voices only a few years ago. My major obstacle in working with younger anchors and reporters has been to get them to stop "pretending" they're something or someone they're not. When one fakes or forces authority it comes off so poorly. A viewer isn't fooled—only bothered.

**Salisbury, TV**

# MASSACHUSETTS

The days of eliminating people from consideration for on-air jobs because they lack a big, booming voice are behind us. Excellent writing and a professional, personable delivery can overcome even minor voice problems. It's the total "package" that counts.

**Boston, Radio**

Proper phrasing, combined with a conversational writing style, can do more to create an authoritative, credible sound (i.e., no b-s, here's the straight story) than almost any other approach.

**Boston, Radio**

The vast majority of applicants have had little or no professional voice training. As a result, they lack proper breathing techniques, and never achieve the voice potential they have. Very few know how to breathe from the diaphragm.

As for advice, take all the journalism and related courses you want . . . but . . . take the time to learn how to use your voice properly.

**Boston, Radio**

Talk, don't speak. You're not Miss America giving a speech about saving the world—you're talking to people in their homes.

**Springfield, TV**

Words are our business. We must not only use them correctly in print, but pronounce them correctly as well. Communication is an art, if you do it properly. You have to work at it, and never take it for granted.

**Springfield, TV**

# MICHIGAN

Work with voice coach or talent coach whenever possible to be better aware of your voice delivery.

**Clio, WEYI-TV, Roger Lyons**

Voice and delivery are the two biggest problems I encounter on resume tapes. Colleges and universities pay little, if any, attention to this concern. Ninety percent of the tapes I review are rejected based on poor voice and/or delivery.

**Cadillac, TV**

Voice training is vital to broadcast communication, yet it's one of the last things many TV reporters/anchors are concerned with. Proper breathing technique, articulation and interpretation of copy can help set people apart from the pack when competing for jobs!

**Kalamazoo, TV**

Don't try to imitate "broadcast" voice. Write for the ear, not the eye. Pretend you are talking to someone when you are editing a package or doing a live shot.

**Traverse City, TV**

Many broadcast grads get little or no voice training in school. Taking some theater classes could help them.

**Negaunee, TV**

# MINNESOTA

Women especially seem to come out of school with *no* vocal training.

**Brooklyn Park, KEVN-TV, Dan Schillinger**

Just talk to me, tell me, don't "report" to me. Own your vocabulary. Be comfortable with yourself.

**Eden Prairie, KMSP-TV, Alan Beck**

Know your copy and interpret its meaning.

**Minneapolis, WMNN, Radio, Curtis Johnson**

Voice quality is less important than the talents' abilities to "tell news stories" as opposed to "reading news copy at me." Conversational, informative delivery using colloquial language.

**Minneapolis, WCCO-AM, Radio, Chuck Dickemann**

Slow down and speak from your diaphragm—not throat!

**Minneapolis, NWCT, Cable, Anne M. Angerer**

I use your book regularly in my operation. Voice is critical to a news department at this level, because it is the first indicator an audience has to gauge whether a reporter knows what he or she is talking about. If the reading is non-conversational, or insincere, or if the reporter sounds young and inexperienced, the audience is immediately put on notice.

"Does this reporter know what he or she is saying?" "Why is the reporter so tentative?" "Is there a problem with facts?" If your audience is thinking this you have lost them, and the station has lost them as well.

Today's entry-level reporters cannot afford to "sound like they don't know what they are talking about." There are far too many people in the competitive job market who already sound like they do know what they are talking about.

If coaches and college professors and short courses spent as much time telling young reporters to prepare their voices as their faces there would be a lot fewer surprised applicants visiting news directors like me. I am always amazed by the sincere reaction from people proudly showing me their tape to my criticism about voice work. Invariably in the conversation they will say something like, "Well, nobody ever told me that," as if some coach or professor failed them.

I tell interns and journalism students to explore outside their normal courses for voice help. In your college theater department you will find people to help you speak conversationally. If your mass communications department has an oral interpretation course, seek it out. Some of the best news people I've worked with, from a voice and delivery standpoint, learned early that voice work is closer to theater than journalism.

I still agonize over an applicant's writing ability and news sense, but voice is right behind in my hiring priority. I tell people all the time that I can always change their looks, but I don't have the time to make significant change in their reading style.

**Duluth, TV**

Follow the pointers on copy marking, and your delivery will be far more effective and expressive.

**St. Paul, Radio**

Broadcast journalists should realize that voice is a tool of communication. It can affect viewers' perceptions of a story. Reporters and anchors should take a much more active approach to improving their voices. It is probably the most ignored of all broadcasting tools. It shouldn't be.

**Minneapolis, TV**

Be natural.
Be believable.
Know what you are reading; don't just read words, communicate the ideas, concepts, and feelings behind the words.

**Minneapolis, Radio**

We always seek maturity in voices. Too many young candidates have "college student accents."

**Mankato, TV**

Many broadcast grads get little or no voice training in school. Taking some theatre classes could help them.

**Duluth, TV**

# MISSISSIPPI

Relax!

**Jackson, WAPT-TV, Sam Moore**

Practice voice projection from diaphragm as often as possible.

**Jackson, WLBT-TV, Dennis Smith**

Being able to project yourself without it sounding as such is very important. This requires precise breath control with the simple ability to communicate. Being able to display confidence without being pretentious, some knowledge on most subjects, hearing while listening, and the ability to convey your thoughts in an intelligent fashion and with a fluid delivery is extremely important for anyone aspiring to be the future broadcaster of tomorrow.

**Jackson, TV**

# MISSOURI

Always pre-read scripts and know the subject matter. Never put a smile in your voice during serious stories.

**St. Louis, KDNL-TV, Jeff Alan**

Enunciation, diction, articulation.

**St. Louis, KMOX, Radio, John Butler**

Just relax and be yourself. Have fun but also make sure that the message you are trying to convey gets to your audience.

**Branson, KRZK/KOMC, Radio, Brett Onstott**

Voice is very important when reviewing tape. It is normally the first thing that eliminates a candidate. I prefer a strong conversational voice, a good storytelling voice. A good voice for delivering stories need not be authoritative—an anchor's voice needs more authority.

**Columbia, TV**

Your delivery must be natural and your body relaxed because it always gets worse when you are nervous, hurried, or reading off-the-cuff.

**Jefferson City, TV**

Our changing industry requires us to change the way we present the news. No longer is it OK to "pronounce" the news; we have to deliver it in such a way that it doesn't sound like we're delivering at all. We must become more conversational without compromising our only true asset, credibility. Increasing competition from a variety of sources mandates that we compel our listeners and viewers to pay attention, and to certainly not change the dial. I tell our staff to imagine they're telling the news to a close, personal friend or relative. It sounds silly to some, but it's served as a sure-fire way to enhance our product. Our listeners feel as though they're hearing what they need to know from a trusted, compassionate friend!

**Springfield, Radio**

Be yourself and use your own voice and inflections. Too often, new people try to be someone else. They must be themselves, and talk as if they were telling the story to a friend. In this way, they will use the proper emphasis and stress the points they would want to make to a friend. Use a tape recorder to capture general conversation, then analyze the delivery of others and yourself. Use this style while on microphone.

When writing stories, write for the ear and not the eye. It may read well but sound bad.

**Jefferson City, TV**

Broadcast schools/college journalism programs should devote more time to teaching good broadcast delivery. Too many people seeking entry-level positions have inferior deliveries.

Voice instructors should *not* try to improve newscasters by trying to make their voices deeper. Credible, conversational deliveries are much more important than deep voices.

**Springfield, Radio**

The importance of voice quality cannot be overemphasized. An award-winning reporter may never get recognized if viewers can't stand to listen to more than two lines of copy!

**Springfield, TV**

Practice! Learn correct pronunciation! Be conversational! Seek help from voice coach if natural voice is too high-pitched.

**Kansas City, TV**

# MONTANA

Be conscious of it. It's easy to improve and then fall back into the predictable patterns of a personal comfort level.

**Billings, KULR-TV, Dave Rye**

Seek "optimum pitch" and then mask inflection in that arena.

**Butte, KXLF-TV, Dennisjon Nettles**

Tell the story to our viewers as you would tell it to a friend.

**Great Falls, KRTV-TV, Joel Lundstad**

It continues to amaze me that colleges and universities continue to graduate students destined for broadcast positions who have sub-standard communication and presentation skills.

Many schools offer courses in something called "Speech," but they seem to emphasize writing and preparing speeches, not delivering the final product.

As a small-market news director, I receive dozens of applications each year from young graduates looking for their first full-time reporting position. I am appalled by the number who won't make the cut because of some delivery problem . . . or a combination of delivery problems.

I don't care if a student graduated Cum Laude from an Ivy League school; if they have a thick regional or ethnic accent or a thin or plodding delivery, they won't be offered any on-air position here . . . or at most broadcast stations.

The regional or ethnic accent may be the most important to attack. Viewers and listeners will question the credibility of someone who obviously doesn't sound like they are from "around here." For example, I believe Boston, New York City, and heavy Texas accents just don't play well outside those limited geographic areas.

Less difficult to fix, and far more common in my experience, are people with underdeveloped voices. They tend to breathe in the wrong place, or have a monotone or singsong delivery. I also find most don't know how to use their vocal range effectively.

Sometimes these problems are worked out by the individual due to just time-in-grade. On occasion, they are lucky enough to find themselves in a position to get professional help from a talent coach or speech teacher. Some never overcome this handicap. It hurts their chances for promotion.

Members of my staff are able to get occasional coaching from talent specialists with our consultant. I also send a couple staff members to regular sessions with a professor from a local college, to help them hone their skills. It's that important . . . even in the 164th market.

**Billings, TV**


Beginners should do a lot of watching and listening. Pay close attention to radio and television broadcasters who are good, not to copy their particular style but to get an idea about delivery. Everyone should develop his or her own style of delivery, but individual initiative is very important, rather than waiting for a news director or voice coach to try to show you the way. This is an area that seems to be ignored, or treated too lightly at many schools.

**Great Falls, TV**

# NEBRASKA

The biggest challenge for an anchor or reporter is to make the copy "come alive" while maintaining a conversational and credible delivery. An anchor has to work to engage the viewer in each story.

**Hastings, KHAS-TV, Dennis Kellogg**


For young journalists in particular: you've spent tens of thousands of dollars on education, how about a bit more to improve your presentation? In a very competitive market, excellent delivery can give you the edge.

**Omaha, TV**


Some thoughts on "voice" . . .

1. When I put an anchor's audition tape on, the first element in my evaluation of the talent is "voice." Do they "sound right?" I am not as concerned about specific qualities as I am concerned about "distractions." Is there something about the voice that causes me to notice it and to be distracted from what they are saying?

For a reporter, I am not as concerned about voice as I am with an anchor, unless the voice is really a distraction. Maybe it is because a reporter is not on the air for as long or because I am also watching video. Or maybe it is because the reporters I have known who possessed what some might call "poor voices" were excellent storytellers and used television well.

2. A concern I have is the number of audition tapes from college students with serious voice problems. Print journalists are taught to type. Why aren't broadcast journalists taught to "speak" properly? The voice of a television journalist is a "tool" and the journalist should learn how to use it properly just like learning how to use a camera and how to edit.

3. I hear a lot of young anchors reading every story in a newscast the same way. I think every story has a mood and tone and the anchor's delivery should reflect that mood. I think it is

something young anchors should think about, and be taught; how to develop the skill of changing moods during a newscast.

**Lincoln, TV**

It seems that our education system has forgotten the power of voice. We don't teach people how to use and improve their voices in school. Often by the time they get through college and their first two jobs, it is almost too late. It's great to be a good journalist but if the voice is bad the audience won't want to listen.

**Omaha, TV**

# NEVADA

Remember to breathe, relax, try to achieve natural phrasing and pace. Hand gestures (out of frame) can help loosen you up.

**Reno, KOLO-TV, Ed Pearce**

# NEW JERSEY

Build on the basics—practice what you can through air check evaluations. Be yourself. Be relaxed. Speak with, not at, the audience. Let writing reflect your voice. Lastly, breathe!

**Asbury Park, Radio**

Don't ignore voice-impairing illnesses. This is one of the biggest problems I encounter with employees. They won't admit that they are stressing their voices, and often spreading disease to others in the newsroom. Take a day off and give everyone a chance to stay healthy.

I have found that most radio news people don't realize how fragile their voices can be, until they lose their voice. The recovery time is typically much longer than expected.

**Toms River, Radio**

# NEW MEXICO

While voice quality is no longer critically important to success in broadcast journalism, effective verbal presentation is. A person who is difficult to understand or to listen to is not an effective communicator.

**Albuquerque, TV**

# NEW YORK

*Conversational*, don't read to audience, *speak* to them.

**Middletown, Cable 6, Tracy Baxter**

Be conversational, credible, personable and friendly. Know your copy, tell me the story don't *read* it to me and have fun.

**Syracuse, WSYR, Radio, Jim Reith**

Remember that you want the listener to think you're speaking to them. Work in the "you" leads whenever possible. Also, keep the pace up which will also keep listeners' interest.

**Watertown, WWNY, Radio, Jack W. Miller**

Distinctive "voice" quality is a great asset—combine that with solid "on camera bizness"—viewers will remember you.

**Albany, WRGB-TV, Joseph Coscia**

Once your professors in school have filled you with all these bizarre styles of writing, scrap them all and speak conversationally!

**Albany, WFXL-TV, Bruce A. Layman**

Breathe from the diaphragm, not from the throat.

**Syracuse, WTVH-TV, Gary Wordlaw**

My biggest difficulty in finding good people centers on speech and writing. Three out of four applications come from people who just don't cut the grade . . . and we're talking about college grads! Better yet, we're talking about people who don't seem to understand that how they sound affects more than their singular job prospects. Voice, delivery, and writing skills are critical to a news organization's credibility and marketability.

**Albany, Cable**

Authoritative does not mean speaking in a low pitch and loud! An authoritative reporter has command of the story but still speaks conversationally.

**Rochester, TV**

Even the most brilliantly written and produced news story can be ruined by a poor delivery or an untrained voice. Likewise, a skillful, expressive delivery can liven up a mediocre package and make it seem special.

**Woodbury, TV**

I feel broadcasters take the matter of voice for granted. New people especially must work harder and with more attention to how they present their material. We must never forget that it is our voice only that gives the listener an image, if you will! We must gain the listeners' respect and trigger their imagination!

**Buffalo, Radio**

Think about what you are reading, communicate with thought and conviction.

**New York, TV**

1. Careful of "fast" delivery . . . items run together.
2. Keep it simple . . . use everyday language.
3. Air check yourself . . . I have been in broadcast 43 years—I still air check! And be yourself!

**New York, Radio**


Job applicants at my TV station need to be more concerned about using their voice as a tool. Using the dramatic pause and a wider vocal range. It is why I have always looked at applicants with some kind of experience in radio.

**Plattsburgh, TV**


I can't stress enough the importance of proper breathing to assist in supporting vocal presentation.

**Rochester, R News**


# NORTH CAROLINA

Tell a story like you're selling a story. For 1:45, it's your product. You are a tour guide. If you're not interested, the viewer won't be!

**New Bern, WCTI-TV, Doug Spero**


On-air talent should get in touch with their delivery system—from breathing to diction. But don't "put on," be natural and real.

**Raleigh, WLFL-TV, Jonathan Knopf**


Be natural, conversational. Also work on your everyday speaking voice—as it improves your on-air voice improves.

**Winston-Salem, WSJS/WSML, Radio, Bob Costner**

Strive to be natural and conversational in delivery. Be enthusiastic without being sensational—put energy into delivery.

**Charlotte, TV**

When you speak you also have to think.

**Greensboro, TV**

Any regional accent will limit your marketability. Don't sound like a booming announcer—the #1 reason to hit the eject button.

**Raleigh, TV**

Tape a newscast and let a news director comment on your delivery. This should be no later than the beginning of the junior year!

**Raleigh, Radio**

I believe one of the most important points students aspiring to become broadcasters fail to realize is that they must become excellent readers. If you do that well, in most cases, voice training is possible. It's not always important to have what we in the profession call "deep pipes." If you can read well and express yourself to the viewer or listener, a deep voice is not the key to getting that elusive radio or TV job.

**Raleigh, Radio**

# NORTH DAKOTA

Conversational is in. We can no longer announce the news to the people. They want to hear the news from our announcers the same way they would hear it from a relative across the dinner table.

This is all complicated, of course, by the fact that while they want us to be conversational, they also want us to come across as authoritative and professional. Talent today must be a jack-of-many-styles.

**Bismark, TV**

If you read your story like you think it's interesting and important, the listeners are more likely to think so, too.

**Fargo, TV**

1) Speak with a natural voice, unaffected delivery.
2) Breathe from the diaphragm.
3) Strengthen your voice by singing.
4) Don't fool around and misuse your voice in trying to be comical. It can be permanently damaged.

**Fargo, TV**

There is a very special balance that needs to be struck in your delivery between being conversational, credible, authoritative, friendly and natural.

**Fargo, TV**

# OHIO

Relax—deliver news as if you are talking to a friend.

**Cincinnati, Channel 6-TV, Kathy Lehr**

Do not force your delivery. Analyze what kind of voice and delivery is comfortable to you personally and try to improve based on those parameters.

**Twinsburg, TV, Classic Teleproductions, Virgil Dominic**

Be yourself and don't try to imitate!

**Ada, WONG, Radio/Cable, Richard Gainey**

If you understand what you're reading, you'll convey it better. Pay attention to *what* you're saying rather than *how* you're saying it.

**Canton, WHBC, Radio, Amanda Wilson**


Be yourself. Don't try to perform.

**Dayton, WKEF/WRGT-TV, Allen Beckner**


Speak like you are talking to a friend: comfortable, energetic.

**Toledo, WNWO-TV, Michelle Sloan**


It's difficult for some people to understand what is meant by the term "conversational." Some think that it means raising and lowering voice pitch frequently. That produces an unwanted singsong quality, however. Others think it means sounding breathy and warm—qualities that are OK for 900-number commercials, but not that great for newscasts. A common problem for many people who don't have a conversational delivery is producing the word "the" as "thee" (e.g., Thee mayor is delivering thee report). Or the word "a" as "ay" (e.g., Ay new study says drinking ay glass of beer ay day is healthy).

**Cleveland, TV**


I think a radio background is best for broadcasters. If it comes down to two equal candidates, I always choose the person with radio experience. I think too often young broadcasters try to force their delivery to be like the network. I always preach "conversational." Be yourself!

**Steubenville, TV**


Although times have changed, "voice" is still the main ingredient in my hiring method. What good is twelve years of college if the newsperson sounds like a teenager with influenza? Some years back we radio types listened for deep, super-authoritative voices, but that has changed. Nowadays, a person with a good, solid, interesting voice can make the grade . . . but he or she had best be able to get 100 percent flexibility out of what voice they have.

Additionally, there's an element of "show biz" or "acting" that a person must develop. That can be explained as "style/believability/confidence" rolled into one.

I don't mean to suggest that a person should "fake it." I mean most of us have never met Gorbachev in person. Yet, newspeople must go on the air and sound as if they know all there is to know about Gorbachev, foreign affairs, the KGB, etc. We rarely have personal knowledge of the persons and places involved in some national, and certainly international stories. But for the listener, we must sound convincing. They need to believe we had lunch with Gorby at Burger King last week. That's the kind of credibility and authority to shoot for at least. I am not saying we ever lie to the audience. I only paint this confident style as a goal. I want a news anchor who can say "the sky is green" and be believed. The integrity must also be there to make the journalist well balanced. Great delivery with no morals or integrity makes for an egocentric jerk!

**Cincinnati, Radio**

Probably my best advice is to tape yourself . . . review the tape for yourself . . . and then, ask a qualified broadcast professional for his or her observations.

When someone does give you advice . . . listen closely to what they are saying . . . solicit several opinions and find out if they have a common criticism. If they do, listen to your tapes again . . . if you hear it, act on it.

I like to encourage beginners to find someone whose broadcast style they like listening to . . . and emulate it. Later on, of course, once you get the basics down . . . branch out and develop your own unique way of delivering a story, through excellent writing and creative delivery.

**Cincinnati, Radio**

TV news does not require overly powerful voices. Rather, voices need to be comfortable for the listener. Authority, credibility, and trust, along with good articulation need to be combined with a conversational delivery.

**Cleveland, TV**

I think a good newscaster has the ability to "see" a story as they read it—that is, they are able to add the inflection, emotion, and character to their delivery, just as if they were standing in front of an event doing a play-by-play. This takes a certain degree of experience and imagination. It also requires a person to step out from behind the social barriers we erect around us. You have to let the you come through in your delivery. If all we wanted was the facts, ma'am, and nothing but the facts, we could read a paper or watch a teletype. People listen to the radio not only to be informed, but to be entertained, stimulated, and connected to a larger world. They want to hear people—not automatons conversing with them.

**Columbus, Radio**

Put variation in voice; watch what words are accented; avoid ending each sentence at a lower pitch; act interested in what you are saying!

**Mansfield, TV**

# OKLAHOMA

Voice quality and delivery can often be successfully altered through coaching—we use this for our on-air talent several times a year.

**Oklahoma City, TV**

Good anchors know their copy and relate that knowledge to the listener by using proper inflection. It also is important to realize the job of a good anchor is not to fill every moment with the sound of his or her voice. A well-placed pause can be very effective.

**Tulsa, Radio**

# OREGON

One challenge many on-air people face is caused by the stress involved in the job. For some, it results in poor breath control or an unnatural voice; for others, the stress causes physical tension that interferes with articulation by stiffening the jaw or hampering the flexibility of the tongue. Stress control is a real, ongoing issue in our newsroom and/studios. The suggestions made in earlier edition of the *Broadcast Voice Handbook* are put to use here on a regular basis.

**Portland, John Erickson, KKCW-FM**

- Don't listen to yourself—as you read you'll make mistakes!
- Read for meaning.
- Talk to one person as you're reading, not to "thousands."
- Relax, relax, relax!

**Portland, Radio**

Voice quality is certainly an important part of our business, but, in my opinion, even more important is reading with understanding. Too many people read words with no idea of the overall meaning of what they are reading. Viewers and listeners have only one shot at knowing what we are trying to communicate. It has to be delivered in a pleasant, straightforward manner with a pleasant, well-modulated voice. A nasal, high-pitched, unpleasant voice can be an instant turn-off and we may never get a chance to make our point.

**Eugene, TV**

It is important to realize how your voice and the tone in that voice affect people—not just over the air but in person, around the office, and with sources.

If you sound like you know what you're talking about, people will believe you do!

**Medford, TV**

Don't force the voice. It could be damaging.

**Portland, TV**

As audiences get older, understandable delivery will become more important. We often forget that we are in the communication business and that means effective basic oral communication.

**Portland, TV**

Don't read the copy; say it. Use punctuation as a delivery aid. Quit smoking. Fight allergies. Relax!

**Portland, Radio**

# PENNSYLVANIA

Broadcast journalists need to sound not only believable—but as if *they* believe in what they're saying. If you're not . . .

**Moosic, WNEP-TV, Paul Stueber**

Try to be conversational, like you are relating a story to your mother, not "announcing" the news to the masses.

**Philadelphia, WPHL-TV, Richard Scott**

Training in radio prior to television seems to provide anchors and reporters with the best prep. (Voice training is not a bad idea for off-air people, either. They must communicate effectively with on-air people, peers, public, and management.)

**Harrisburg, TV**

Don't forget about your voice with tracking a package. It's part of the overall presentation that can be as impactive as the pictures.

**Johnstown, TV**

The best advice for young people getting started is to work in radio. Radio has traditionally been the place that separates those with good voices from those with bad voices. Since fewer young people want to consider radio first, they must have a similar experience in their college work. Since job applicants outnumber the available jobs, stations will be selective about the people they hire. Those with poorer voices will be left behind.

For everyone in broadcasting, practice, practice, practice! Read out loud to your kids or to yourself. Then if things still have not greatly improved in your voice, seek professional help.

**Lebanon, TV**

The single recommendation I make to on-air talent is to develop an appropriate range in their voice. Different assignments require different tones of voice.

**Philadelphia, TV**

People should cut their tracks as if they're talking on the phone. Write and speak in more of a conversational tone.

**Philadelphia, TV**

# SOUTH CAROLINA

Work to be conversational. Use your voice and delivery to "talk with" viewers—not "at them."

**Columbia, WLTX-TV, Larry Audas**


Tell me the story, do not shout at me.

**Columbia, WIS-TV, Randy Covington**


Be conversational. Tell me a story as opposed to delivering a report.

**Florence, WBTW-TV, John Wessling**


I would recommend radio as a means of developing one's voice. Whether it's through a campus radio station or internship, training through radio gives people better opportunities to develop their voice and more practical experience than they can have when they're limited to cutting audio only for television packages.

**Columbia, TV**


Lack of formal voice training and the assumption that their voices are good are the two biggest problems with news people on our staff. Not one has had a course in broadcast announcing. During the day-to-day rush, only a simple correction now and again is possible. In addition, the news people do not understand the psychology of the broadcast microphone, how to speak to one person at a time who is listening and tell him/her the story. A course in broadcast announcing is one of three during college I believe I use each week during my work.

**Columbia, TV**


Do some radio—learn to think and talk at the same time—breathe—leave your "broadcast voice" at home and be natural.

**Florence, TV**

One doesn't have to be blessed with a perfect voice to do well in broadcasting anymore. Reporters and anchors should simply be able to do a little "storytelling" . . . to be comfortable for viewers to watch and hear. Network anchors Brokaw and Jennings do a terrific job of "storytelling."

**Charleston, TV**

Few young interns are prepared to read well. Even those who had courses in this do not do well as a whole. We have had theater majors, or some with a drama background, do better than journalism grads. These drama folks, though, can't write. I consider voice preparation as essential as typing and basic newswriting. It should be learned already when someone comes into a newsroom.

**Columbia, TV**

I hire entry-level or second-job reporters. I've noted a tremendous weakness with delivery. Recently, I had a reporter-candidate with a Master's Degree from a major journalism school. She was willing to come to work for entry-level money and certainly had the credentials, but her delivery just wasn't good enough for me. I suggested she get a job as a radio reporter or anchor and work on her delivery every day. I gave her specific pointers, the most important of which was to listen to her tapes at home at night. Four months later, she had improved to the point that I hired her, and I'm very satisfied with her. I have another similar candidate to whom I made the same suggestion. She called recently to tell me she's accepted a radio job and is working hard on her voice and delivery. This is an important and very overlooked topic!

**Florence, TV**

Stop sounding like a news authority and talk normal with a full range of highs, lows, dramatic pauses, even sighs when appropriate. Inflect your personality.

**Columbia, Radio**

# SOUTH DAKOTA

Be calm, comfortable, and credible; watch phrasing.

**Yankton, WNAX, Radio, Jerry Oster**

When evaluating on-air talent I think voice is important only because it must convey a conversational style, be credible, precise and authoritative. The need for deep, resonant baritone sounds is long since past. Most broadcasters want people who sound real.

**Sioux Falls, TV**

# SOUTH KOREA

- Keep it conversational
- Talk to your "best friend"
- Good energy level

**APO, AP, AFKN-TV, Christine McGuire**

# TENNESSEE

Speak to the viewer as you like to be spoken to; be clear, conversational, and say it "like you mean it."

**Knoxville, WVLT-TV, Desirée Landers**

Practice; record your voice and listen to it. Many people don't like sound of his or her own voice.

**Kingsport, WKPT-TV, Betty Payne**

Listen to as many established broadcasters as you can and choose a style that fits you. If your delivery is "natural" it will be believable.

**Knoxville, WNOX, Radio, Channing Smith**


No matter how poor the quality of a voice it can be improved with hard work to an acceptable quality.

**Johnson City, TV**


Too many television reporters are more concerned about their appearances than their voices. Certainly, appearance is important—but so is delivery.

So much can be accomplished in terms of effective communication through the use of good vocal technique. Authority, credibility and emotion are just some of the images that are conveyed through voice.

It isn't necessary to have a "big" voice . . . but it is necessary to learn how to best use the voice you have.

**Nashville, TV**


Relax. . . talk to the camera like you're talking to your best friend.

**Chattanooga, TV**


Authoritative delivery with easy to follow verbal interpretation of the copy. (In other words, be *both* a news person and an actor.)

**Murfreesboro, Radio**


# TEXAS


Stop talking to microphones, start talking to people. Imagine telling your story to a friend.

**Austin, News 8, Cable, Kevin Benz**

Talent can overcome a less than perfect on-air voice with good inflection and conversational yet authoritative delivery.

**Austin, KLBJ-AM, Radio, Dave Isaacs**

Be natural. Viewers are sophisticated enough to know when you're not being yourself.

**Austin, KXAN-TV, Bruce Whiteaker**

The first thing I do when I play an audition tape is I close my eyes. I "listen" first. If the candidate passes that test, then I'll go back and watch the tape.

**El Paso, KFOX-TV, David Bennallack**

Be conversational.

**Temple, KCEN-TV, Gary Darnell**

Voice and delivery can be "refined" after you get that first job, but to get that first job, you have to show you have something to develop. Vocal delivery always has and always will play a major part in broadcast news, obviously. And while content is how a good piece should be judged, the audience has to hear the story first. And if they don't like how you sound, they'll miss the news.

**Abilene, TV**

Do radio in college. Read aloud. Listen to Dr. Ann!

**Beaumont, TV**

The advice I give most often is: "understand and convey." Understand the emotions inherent in the copy, and convey those emotions to the listener through your interpretation of the copy with your delivery. I also encourage reporters and anchors to sustain their energy level through the story or newscast and fight the urge to let their deliveries drop off toward the end of the copy. Since I have a background in music, I also draw a musical analogy concerning performance and execution reminding my staff that they are, above all else, performers and that their interpretation/delivery directly affects the listeners' level of interest. And remember, we aren't "delivering the news" to the masses. We're "telling a story" to one person at a time.

**Ft. Worth, Radio**

Reading a news story so the viewer/listener will understand it, is not as easy as it sounds. Being conversational does not mean being sloppy or regionalistic. It takes constant work and study to make the audience listen to what is said, not who is saying it. The job of a communicator is to make it sound easy to do, even though it isn't.

**Abilene, TV**

When they are voicing something, they should really think about what they're saying. Put themselves in the place where the story occurred. That way, they'll sound as if they really know what they're talking about, as if they're really telling someone about the story.

**Austin, TV**

At the very least, get yourself a job at the campus radio station and read news on the air as much as they'll let you. Listen to the network anchors and top reporters. Don't try to copy them, but listen for what they share in common.

**Corpus Christi, TV**

Some surveys show that voice may be the single most important aspect of viewer preference when it comes to anchor preference.

**Dallas, TV**

Slow down—take your time to pause after each "thought group" of words in a sentence, so the listener can absorb and "feel" what you are saying.

**Houston, Radio**

Some of the best advice I've ever received in this business came from long-time KPRC News Director Ray Miller: "Write like people talk. Talk like you talk." I like to hear genuine enthusiasm and energy in a broadcaster's voice. Every word should convey "This is interesting!" to the listener. Too many people try to lower their voice pitch and end up with a loud monotone. One of the more difficult tasks I've encountered in this profession is that of instilling confidence in basic voice quality so that people can then learn to use what they have to best effect.

**Houston, Radio**

A voice is the most visible tool of our trade. If you do not develop the best voice possible you are trying to do the job without the proper tools. It's like trying to do surgery with a penknife.

**Odessa, TV**

We put anchors in a formal setting and ask them to be "natural" . . . this also means their voice and this is tough to do. What I look for and encourage is the anchor and/or reporter to be themselves. The more natural and conversational they sound, the better. So many reporters have a lot of spark, then when the lights and camera go on, they become monotone, almost flat. Strive to have them put that spark in their delivery when the lights go on . . . strive for a "talking" tone.

**Wichita Falls, TV**

People need to take speech and voice classes or training along with journalism and Radio-TV. They need to listen to themselves.

**Houston, TV**

# UTAH

When delivering a story, *don't* think about the number of people you're talking to. Deliver the story to *one* person.

**Salt Lake City, KNRS, Radio, Phil Riesen**

# VIRGINIA

Be authoritative, yet communicate with your audience.

**Alexandria, SRTV, TV/Radio, Terry Anderson**

Get coaching. Too few broadcast journalists have had any, so even a little will make you more competitive in the race for jobs.

**Charlottesville, WVIR-TV, David Cupp**

The same as Edward R. Murrow—it's much more important—what you say than *how* you say it. I'd take a good writer/reporter over a good voice any day.

**Orange, WJMA, Radio, Phil Goodwin**

Don't listen to yourself while you are on air or taping. Concentrate on the meaning of what you are trying to get across.

**Roanoke, WVTF, Radio, Rick Mattioni**

Often preach emphasis/inflection as a way to improve speed and articulation and urgency in delivery.

**Springfield, Newschannel 8TV/Cable, Wayne Lynch**

Find a "happy medium" that's comfortable for you. Don't overdo it (like a bad 1960s DJ) or underdo it by assuming voice work isn't important.

**Springfield, Newschannel 8, TV/Cable, Kim Wright**

Vocal problems on the air are like a dripping faucet. Initially you hardly notice them; but over time they can drive you (and your viewers) nuts. They can also be very difficult to fix. I consider vocal problems so important that when I'm screening tapes from applicants, I pop the tape into the machine, hit the play button, and then turn my back. I do not even check what an applicant looks like until I have listened to him or her for a while without being distracted. If I hear a voice that will evolve into Chinese water torture for our viewers, I will reject the applicant before I even look. I'd rather do that than respond to the letters of complaint that will surely come streaming in as time passes.

**Charlottesville, TV**

Voice is probably the #1 criterion used in hiring. When news directors punch the eject button fifteen seconds into an applicant's tape, they do it because that applicant sounds like an amateur, not a professional. Yet, sadly, far too many broadcast journalism programs ignore vocal training and few other resources are available. Probably ninety percent of our daily communications are verbal throughout our lives, yet no one really teaches us the correct way to speak. We breathe the wrong way, we develop bad habits, and many of us never shake them or learn better. It's simple. If you're going to make your living with your voice, you should learn to use your voice effectively. It is as basic as learning how to type, and for a broadcaster it is just as important.

**Charlottesville, TV**

Radio newscasters will, in their careers, be asked to deliver news in a variety of different styles. Anchors must be flexible.

I always like to work with people who have had musical training. Then, you can coach using terms like "accent," "staccato," "legato"—and be talking in terms you both understand.

In broadcast, either in news or in commercial production work, your voice is your instrument and your delivery must be "musical" to be both credible and understood.

**Norfolk, Radio**


While newspapers and television can use pictures to supplement their news coverage, in radio, voices are all we have. That's why it's particularly important for job applicants to have at least practiced their delivery on a tape recorder and listened to network newscasters for an idea of how news is presented. Newscasters should retain their individual style of delivery, while understanding communication is the main goal. Anything that interferes with effective communication on the radio will stand in the way of a successful career.

**Richmond, Radio**


Relax and talk to viewers, not at them.

**Roanoke, TV**

# WASHINGTON

Be natural and conversational. Don't read copy cold. "Tell," don't "read" to your audience.

**Tacoma, KPLU, Radio, Erin Hennessey**


Make sure you understand the meaning, importance and impact of your material and then make your total focus be "making sure the viewer gets exactly what the story is." Make *them* the focus, not you!

**Yakima, KNDO-TV, Dave Ettl**

Be natural! News readers must understand the *distinction* between reading and telling a story. Many broadcasters I have worked with want to overarticulate because they think it "sounds right." Fact is it sounds unnatural and uncomfortable.

**Seattle, Radio**

Some on-air talent fail to grasp the meaning of the story they are reading and without that understanding they are unable to convey the meaning to their viewers. To be a good reader, the talent must first understand, and be knowledgeable of his copy. Knowing when to inflect your voice is also vital.

**Yakima, TV**

The voice isn't likely to make a reporter's career, but it could break it—or keep it from starting.

The proper use of voice is more important than any other element of a person's delivery.

**Yakima, TV**

# WEST VIRGINIA

Develop your own best broadcast voice—be the best you. Don't try to imitate someone else's voice. Seek feedback and help from others in the business.

**Clarksburg, WBOY-TV, Bob Walters**

Develop your own natural vocal quality into a delivery that is easy to listen to. Do not force another vocal quality that's unnatural.

**Bluefield, TV**

The days of the stiff, robot-like delivery seem to have left us and now the reporter who can communicate in an authoritative yet conversational manner will be the most effective. It is accepted by the viewer as if it is coming from a person rather than just a reporter.

**Huntington, TV**

In most cases, good voice broadcast quality can be obtained with practice. Early and constant work will help anyone willing to practice, even after a few years in broadcasting.

**Oak Hill, TV**

# WISCONSIN

Listen to your TV stories without looking at the video to "hear" how it comes across. "Overdo" your delivery to make it sound more energetic. Gesture while delivering scripts. It may feel funny but helps with emphasis. Mark words you want to emphasize. Think of the "mood" of the script—upbeat, sad, neutral. Push your breath through your voice box, not your nose. Listen to others who are especially good narrators and emulate what they do well—but don't try to copy their style.

**Eau Claire, WQOW-TV, Mike Rindo**

Using your voice well is a learned skill. It requires practice.

**Las Crosse, WKBT-TV, Anne Pappe**

Regular coaching—practice in studio. Sounding natural seems to be the biggest challenge.

**Madison, Wisconsin Public Radio, Connie Walker**

Don't *read* the copy, *tell* me the story.

**Eau Claire, WAYY, Radio, Chris Ouellette**

RELAX! Have TOTAL familiarity with copy—know what you're talking about—this leads to quality vocal delivery.

**Eau Claire, TV**

People need to practice reading more. Voice quality is important.

**Green Bay, TV**

Study grammar. So much of what we do is *live*. A journalist's credibility is destroyed by usage errors. In live reporting, no editor can save you. Newsrooms should develop a culture in which appropriate English usage is paramount and immediate feedback is given.

**Milwaukee, TV**

Seek to find training in breathing and presentation. Get a double major in speech or drama. Learn your craft in radio or live public speaking. Continue to practice, practice, practice. Don't just read when it's time to read, record and read aloud everything. Be open to critique.

**Green Bay, TV**

Gone are the days of the stereotypical radio voice: the booming voice which caused us radio-types to proclaim "what pipes!" I look for an unusual voice quality, one which contributes to style!

**Madison, Radio**

Practice makes perfect! And breaking old habits may be made easier through exercises!

**Milwaukee, TV**

Be natural—don't force it.

**Madison, TV**

# WYOMING

Keeping people within their range, proper pacing and breathing. Pacing is the biggest problem new hires have. Many try to go too fast! They also don't breathe correctly, which leads to poor sound.

**Laramie, Wyoming Public Radio, Bob Beck**

# Pronunciation Tests and Word Lists

The broadcast copy that follows may not be the most interesting material you have read or the best broadcast writing. What is significant about these stories, however, is that each one includes all 40 of the phonemes of our language.

Tape-record these stories and listen to them critically. Ask others, such as your teacher, voice coach, or news director, to listen to them. You may find that you are mispronouncing certain phonemes or dropping sounds. These stories will help you analyze your pronunciations and isolate particular phonemes that cause you difficulty. Once you have found your problem phonemes, consult the practice word lists that follow.

## News Copy—Phoneme Test #1

```
If you are not planning to travel
this weekend, you might want to plan
a trip to the county fair. It begins
tomorrow and continues until the
```

twentieth. They put up the tents
last night and will pull them down
when it ends. You can try your hand
at knocking over bottles, running
races, popping balloons, and testing
your strength in the lifting
contest. Real animals will provide
action as usual on Friday night as
well as Sunday in the large arena.
Officials thought boys and girls
ought to be able to attend for under
a dollar. Now that is the case.
Admission is twenty-five cents for
children and one dollar for adults.
Lunch is available at the
fairgrounds.

## News Copy—Phoneme Test #2

Returns are trickling in from
yesterday's primary election. The
results were delayed due to a
faulty computer in the Richmond
Center. Democrat Hinton Royal is
ranked first to overcome union
official, Jim Sheffield, for
council president. Controversial
candidate, lawyer Roy Pool, put
his position in jeopardy with
awful standings in his own county.
He was chosen by three delegates
to start ahead, but he has yet to
win. Pool needs just nine counties
to get a victory.

# A Comparison of
## AP, IPA, and Dictionary Symbols

# Vowels

| AP | IPA | DICTIONARY SYMBOLS | KEY WORDS |
|---|---|---|---|
| (ee) | /i/ | ē | b<u>ee</u> |
| (i) | /ɪ/ | i | b<u>i</u>t |
| (ay) | /e/ | ā | s<u>ay</u> |
| (e) | /ɛ/ | e | b<u>e</u>t |
| (a) | /æ/ | a or ă | <u>a</u>t |
| (ah) | /ɑ/ | ä | sp<u>a</u> |
| (aw) | /ɔ/ | ô or ȯ | c<u>aw</u> |
| (oh) | /o/ | ō | <u>oa</u>k |
| (u) | /ʊ/ | oo or u̇ | p<u>u</u>t |
| (oo) | /u/ | o͞o or ü | tw<u>o</u> |
| (ur) | /ɝ/ | ûr or ər | fath<u>er</u> |
| (uh) | /ə/ | ə | <u>a</u>bove |
| (y, eye) | /aɪ/ | ī | <u>eye</u> |
| (ow) | /aʊ/ | ou or au̇ | c<u>ow</u> |
| (oy) | /ɔɪ/ | ȯi | t<u>oy</u> |

## Practice Word Lists

If you found that certain phonemes are difficult for you to pronounce correctly, the following word lists will help you practice the phonemes in words until you hear an improvement. The lists are arranged by vowel and consonant phonemes.

# Consonants

| AP | IPA | DICTIONARY SYMBOLS | KEY WORDS |
|---|---|---|---|
| (p) | /p/ | p | pop |
| (b) | /b/ | b | boy |
| (t) | /t/ | t | to |
| (d) | /d/ | d | do |
| (k) | /k/ | k | key |
| (g) | /g/ | g | got |
| (f) | /f/ | f | fit |
| (v) | /v/ | v | van |
| (s) | /s/ | s | say |
| (z) | /z/ | z | zip |
| (h) | /h/ | h | hit |
| (l) | /l/ | l | love |
| (r) | /r/ | r | run |
| (w) | /w/ | w | was |
| (m) | /m/ | m | miss |
| (n) | /n/ | n | now |
| (θ) | /θ/ | th | thin |
| (ð) | /ð/ | th or th | them |
| (sh) | /ʃ/ | sh | she |
| (zh) | /ʒ/ | zh | casual |
| (ch) | /tʃ/ | ch | chip |
| (j) | /dʒ/ | j | Jim |
| (w) | /w/ | hw | while |
| (j) | /j/ | y | yet |
| (ŋ) | /ŋ/ | ŋ or ng | sing |

Reprinted courtesy of The Defense Information School.
Key words from Chapter 4 have been added.

# Vowels

### /i/ bee

| | | |
|---|---|---|
| plea | seen | relief |
| eager | creep | achieve |
| beet | free | week |
| feel | key | illegal |
| easel | tease | intrigue |
| keep | sneeze | conceive |

### /I/ bit

| | | |
|---|---|---|
| trip | hit | city |
| pit | fit | pity |
| wit | mitt | pretty |
| lick | drip | his |
| grin | thin | rib |
| skin | wrist | visit |

### /e/ say

| | | |
|---|---|---|
| race | lame | tame |
| case | way | waste |
| ace | rage | awake |
| pay | state | trait |
| lace | date | dismay |
| fray | make | neigh |

### /ɛ/ bet

| | | |
|---|---|---|
| head | check | pest |
| debt | step | red |
| left | edit | exit |

| | | |
|---|---|---|
| kept | men | theft |
| get | thread | deaf |
| wreck | guess | ten |

## /æ/ at

| | | |
|---|---|---|
| sat | pat | lamb |
| cap | sand | plan |
| gap | hack | trap |
| match | laugh | plant |
| jam | than | answer |
| last | mad | parrot |

## /ɑ/ spa

| | | |
|---|---|---|
| calm | odd | argue |
| car | harsh | bark |
| smart | shark | father |
| palm | cargo | heart |
| arbor | armor | Hawaii |
| parked | dark | charm |

## /ɔ/ caw

| | | |
|---|---|---|
| awful | lost | gnaw |
| clause | coffin | hall |
| fought | dog | sought |
| law | wall | auto |
| mall | August | thought |
| yawn | pawn | straw |

## /o/ oak

| | | |
|---|---|---|
| own | soak | pillow |
| cone | tore | explore |
| bone | omit | both |
| zone | dough | willow |
| clove | toe | oration |
| beau | hotel | cooperate |

## /u/ two

| you | who | school |
| food | crude | tattoo |
| June | gloom | spoon |
| two | grew | moon |
| shoot | ooze | rule |
| blue | screw | drool |

## /ʊ/ put

| wool | poor | roof |
| full | look | nook |
| should | shook | wood |
| bush | bull | crook |
| book | stood | brook |
| tour | cook | push |

## /ə/ above

| alone | cut | money |
| summer | brother | jump |
| rug | love | circus |
| truck | luck | lion |
| run | hut | spud |
| done | plum | sofa |

## /ɚ/ father

| amber | alter | dirt |
| deserve | otter | squirm |
| return | ponder | rehearse |
| worth | favor | jerk |
| verb | mirror | disturb |
| skirt | birth | confirm |

# Diphthongs

### /ju/ use

| | | |
|---|---|---|
| union | funeral | humiliate |
| mute | uniform | music |
| pupil | puberty | numerous |
| view | bugle | fabulous |
| human | amuse | tabulate |
| eulogy | refusal | unify |

### /aɪ/ eye

| | | |
|---|---|---|
| sky | alive | strike |
| fire | iodine | light |
| time | nice | pantomime |
| reply | fight | China |
| deny | whine | biceps |
| bias | rhyme | bright |

### /aʊ/ cow

| | | |
|---|---|---|
| mouse | cloud | how |
| powder | ouch | devour |
| allowance | loud | blouse |
| couch | scowl | South |
| foul | sour | impound |
| anyhow | found | endow |

### /ɔɪ/ toy

| | | |
|---|---|---|
| hoist | doily | oily |
| annoy | avoid | exploit |
| loiter | Joyce | loyal |
| boy | voice | toil |
| joy | tabloid | spoil |
| coil | coy | choice |

# Consonants

## /t/ to (Voiceless)

| Initial | Medial | Final |
|---------|--------|-------|
| tea | attend | light |
| tool | Utah | suit |
| talk | rotate | elite |
| tube | intend | sweet |
| turn | utensil | missed |
| town | entire | laughed |

## /d/ do (Voiced)

| Initial | Medial | Final |
|---------|--------|-------|
| den | ladder | dad |
| dime | handle | told |
| dole | underneath | yield |
| dollar | ending | ride |
| dame | condition | bird |
| dip | idea | gold |

## /p/ pop (Voiceless)

| Initial | Medial | Final |
|---------|--------|-------|
| pay | reaper | keep |
| peg | clapped | mope |
| poem | carpet | hoop |
| poke | wrapper | weep |
| powder | sweeping | asleep |
| position | typify | pipe |

## /b/ boy (Voiced)

| Initial | Medial | Final |
|---------|--------|-------|
| bay | saber | lab |
| bait | flabby | web |
| bottom | baby | probe |

| | | |
|---|---|---|
| bike | ebony | lobe |
| base | habit | curb |
| band | obey | bib |

## /k/ key (Voiceless)

| **Initial** | **Medial** | **Final** |
|---|---|---|
| curl | packing | risk |
| kitten | echo | ask |
| cash | kicked | caulk |
| keep | chicken | fork |
| come | wicked | slick |
| quit | rocky | dike |

## /g/ got (Voiced)

| **Initial** | **Medial** | **Final** |
|---|---|---|
| gear | haggle | bug |
| guest | toggle | vogue |
| gossip | figure | plug |
| gift | disguise | league |
| gallon | tiger | drug |
| ghost | embargo | jog |

## /f/ fit (Voiceless)

| **Initial** | **Medial** | **Final** |
|---|---|---|
| face | raffle | calf |
| fail | define | life |
| flour | reference | half |
| fun | infest | enough |
| fence | safer | golf |
| physics | coffee | chef |

## /v/ van (Voiced)

| **Initial** | **Medial** | **Final** |
|---|---|---|
| veal | paved | love |
| vein | ravel | prove |
| vapor | avid | forgive |

| victory | driver | revolve |
| vowel | seven | dove |
| vice | heaven | have |

## /θ/ thin (Voiceless)

| Initial | Medial | Final |
| --- | --- | --- |
| thank | method | myth |
| thrill | Catholic | wrath |
| thick | birthday | cloth |
| thigh | pathos | mouth |
| theme | esthetic | path |
| thaw | nothing | faith |

## /ð/ them (Voiced)

| Initial | Medial | Final |
| --- | --- | --- |
| this | mother | teethe |
| though | breathing | smooth |
| that | feather | soothe |
| then | clothing | blithe |
| there | northern | clothe |
| the | heathen | bathe |

## /s/ say (Voiceless)

| Initial | Medial | Final |
| --- | --- | --- |
| such | asset | bless |
| steak | insert | peace |
| stay | essay | mouse |
| spill | tracing | kiss |
| skid | bossy | nervous |
| space | history | purpose |

## /z/ zip (Voiced)

| Initial | Medial | Final |
| --- | --- | --- |
| zebra | spasm | ease |
| zenith | music | lads |
| Xerox | desire | wise |

| | | |
|---|---|---|
| zephyr | reason | rhymes |
| zoom | resign | symbols |
| zircon | used | browse |

## /ʃ/ she (Voiceless)

| Initial | Medial | Final |
|---|---|---|
| shall | anxious | fresh |
| ship | direction | mustache |
| shy | fashion | wish |
| sugar | special | cash |
| chic | tissue | leash |
| shoe | washer | fresh |

## /ʒ/ casual (Voiced)

| Initial | Medial | Final |
|---|---|---|
| /ʒ/ does | vision | beige |
| not occur as | pleasure | camouflage |
| an initial | occasion | garage |
| sound in | usual | rouge |
| English except | persuasion | mirage |
| in a few words | Asia | corsage |
| borrowed from | | |
| French | | |
| (e.g., genre). | | |

## /h/ hit (Voiceless)

| Initial | Medial | Final |
|---|---|---|
| hand | behave | /h/ does not |
| human | perhaps | occur in the |
| hotel | somehow | final position. |
| humid | inherit | |
| whose | overhaul | |
| heart | apprehend | |

## /tʃ/ chip (Voiceless)

| Initial | Medial | Final |
|---------|--------|-------|
| chafe | teacher | much |
| charge | lecture | catch |
| chastise | bachelor | reach |
| chicken | question | lunch |
| challenge | picture | search |
| chalk | fracture | coach |

## /dʒ/ Jim (Voiced)

| Initial | Medial | Final |
|---------|--------|-------|
| jaw | adjacent | age |
| joke | education | badge |
| just | collegiate | rage |
| genius | courageous | cage |
| judge | danger | college |
| jar | soldier | edge |

## /w/ was (Voiced or Voiceless)

| Initial | Medial | Final |
|---------|--------|-------|
| wear | question | /w/ occurs |
| wet | forward | only preceding |
| witch | quarter | a vowel sound. |
| witness | somewhere | |
| water | quack | |
| word | quit | |

## /j/ yet (Voiced)

| Initial | Medial | Final |
|---------|--------|-------|
| yes | lawyer | /j/ occurs |
| yellow | champion | only preceding |
| youth | pavilion | a vowel sound. |
| yearling | genius | |
| yeast | million | |
| year | civilian | |

## /r/ run (Voiced)

| Initial | Medial | Final |
|---------|--------|-------|
| read | error | bar |
| wreck | erode | ignore |
| wrap | moron | mare |
| roof | bury | tour |
| wrote | tarot | chair |
| realize | purely | appear |

## /l/ love (Voiced)

| Initial | Medial | Final |
|---------|--------|-------|
| lip | follow | zeal |
| letter | elope | apple |
| lawn | believe | pearl |
| late | palace | kale |
| lake | blind | style |
| lean | tilt | foil |

## /m/ miss (Voiced)

| Initial | Medial | Final |
|---------|--------|-------|
| may | remove | beam |
| murder | hammer | dime |
| mail | emblem | autumn |
| mock | emanate | bomb |
| middle | remind | custom |
| murky | climbing | theme |

## /n/ now (Voiced)

| Initial | Medial | Final |
|---------|--------|-------|
| not | plaintive | bean |
| gnaw | dawning | spoon |
| pneumatic | sentence | done |
| know | pants | brown |
| nation | respond | began |
| knife | telephoned | loosen |

## /ŋ/ sing (Voiced)

| Initial | Medial | Final |
|---|---|---|
| /ŋ/ does | length | throng |
| not occur | kingly | belong |
| in the | wrongly | among |
| initial | gangster | thing |
| position. | ink | sprang |
|  | youngster | stung |

# Stumbling Blocks— Commonly Mispronounced Words

Correct pronunciation of words is a constant challenge for broadcasters. In addition to the problems of omissions, substitutions, additions, and faulty articulation discussed in Chapter 4, there are other problems that arise.

We have all enjoyed watching bloopers by newscasters. *Spoonerisms*, or reversals of sounds in two words, are often the most humorous. "Show you to your seat," becomes "Sew you to your sheet," as a spoonerism. Another problem called *metathesis* involves the reversal of sounds in a word. Metathesis would change "nuclear" to "nucular" and "ask" to "aks." *Haplology* is the omission of a repeated sound or syllable. If this is a problem for a speaker, you might hear "govner" instead of "governor" or "tweny" instead of "twenty."

The pronunciation list that follows is meant to be a beginning for what should be your personalized list of commonly mispronounced words. You might want to photocopy this list and begin a personal file of your own problem pronunciations. You should customize the list by adding words that are particularly troubling for you. These might include local names and pronunciations, as well as general words. For local pronunciations, check with your news director. Your station should have a policy for regionalisms, such as the Kansas use of a /θ/ ("th") ending in the word "drought," instead of /t/.

As you see, in the list that follows, the correct pronunciations are not given. Just like your spelling teacher in grade school may have told you, the only way to learn a word is to look it up yourself. It is a good idea to check pronunciations in two dictionaries. This is time-consuming, but once you have looked up all the words, you have a list to practice throughout your career. If you look through the list and feel you pronounce most words correctly, be wary. Most speakers think they are saying these words correctly, but they are all commonly mispronounced. You may be omitting sounds such as the plosives in numbers like "eighty" and "ninety." Additions may sneak into words like "athlete" resulting in "athelete." Or you may be reversing sounds or mispronouncing phonemes.

Developing the practice of looking words up in a dictionary is important. Here is a list of recommended dictionaries:

*The American Heritage Dictionary.* 3rd College ed. Boston: Houghton Mifflin Company, 1993.

Ehrlich, Eugene, and Raymond Hand, Jr. *The NBC Handbook of Pronunciation.* 4th ed. New York: HarperCollins, 1991.

Kenyon, John Samuel, and Thomas Albert Knott. *A Pronouncing Dictionary of American English.* Springfield: Merriam-Webster Inc., 1953.

*Webster's Collegiate Dictionary. 10th Ed.* Springfield: Merriam-Webster Inc. 1998.

# 100 Commonly Mispronounced Words

Correct Pronunciation

ABERRANT _____

ACADEMIA _____

ACCESSORY _____

ACCLIMATE _____

ACCOMPANIST _____

ADMIRABLE _____

AFFLUENCE _____

ALLEGED _____

APARTHEID _____

APPLICABLE _____

ARCHETYPE _____

ASBESTOS _____

ASSEMBLY _____

ASSUAGE _____

ATHLETE _____

ATMOSPHERIC _____

AUXILIARY _____

BARBITURATE _____

BEQUEATH _____

BULIMIA _____

BYZANTINE _____

CALM _____

CAPRICIOUS _____

CARIBBEAN _____

CAVEAT _____

CLIQUE _____

COMPARABLE _____

CONSORTIUM _____

CONTEMPLATIVE _____

CONTROVERSIAL _____

DAIS _____

DATA _____

DECIBEL _____

DELUGE _____

DISPARATE _____

DUTY _____

ELECTORAL _____

ENVELOPE _____

ENVOY _____

ERR _____

FACADE _____

FORMIDABLE _____

FORTE        _____

FOYER        _____

FUNGI        _____

GALA        _____

GENUINE        _____

GOVERNMENT        _____

GRIEVOUS        _____

HARASS        _____

HEINOUS        _____

HERB        _____

HOMICIDE        _____

HOSPITABLE        _____

IDEA        _____

ILLUSTRATIVE        _____

IRREPARABLE        _____

IRREVOCABLE        _____

JEWELRY        _____

JUROR        _____

LAMBASTE        _____

LENGTH (STRENGTH)        _____

LIAISON        _____

LIBRARY        _____

LONG-LIVED (SHORT-LIVED)        _____

MEASURE _____

MEMORABILIA _____

MISCHIEVOUS _____

MORES _____

NAIVETE _____

NEGOTIATE _____

NUCLEAR _____

OFFICIAL _____

OFTEN _____

OPHTHALMOLOGIST _____

PALM _____

PENALIZE _____

PIANIST _____

POINSETTIA _____

PREFERABLE _____

PRESTIGIOUS _____

PRIVILEGE _____

PROGRAM _____

REALTOR _____

REPARTEE _____

SANDWICH _____

SCHIZOPHRENIA _____

SIMILAR _____

SPECIES _____

SPONTANEITY _____

STATUS _____

SUCCINCT _____

SUPPOSED _____

THEATER _____

TOWARD _____

TRANSIENT _____

VASE _____

VEGETABLE _____

VENEREAL _____

ZOOLOGY _____

## Personal Pronunciation List

Difficult Word                    Correct Pronunciation

_____      _____

_____      _____

_____      _____

_____      _____

_____      _____

_____      _____

_____      _____

_____      _____

_____      _____

_____      _____

_____      _____

_____      _____

_____      _____

_____      _____

_____      _____

_____      _____

_____      _____

_____      _____

| Difficult Word | Correct Pronunciation |
| --- | --- |
| | |
| | |
| | |
| | |
| | |
| | |
| | |
| | |
| | |
| | |
| | |
| | |
| | |
| | |
| | |
| | |
| | |
| | |
| | |
| | |
| | |

# Suggested Readings

Anderson, Bob. *Stretching at your Computer or Desk.* Bolinas, CA: Shelter Publications, 2000.

Benson, Herbert. *The Relaxation Response.* New York: Avon, 1975. (Reissue ed. 1990.)

Crannell, Kenneth C. *Voice and Articulation.* 2nd Ed. Belmont, California: Wadsworth Publishing Company, 1990.

Ehrlich, Eugene and Raymond Hand, Jr. *The NBC Handbook of Pronunciation.* New York: HarperCollins, 1991.

Fisher, Hilda B. *Improving Voice and Articulation.* Boston: Houghton Mifflin Company, 1966.

Kenyon, John Samuel, and Thomas Albert Knott. *A Pronouncing Dictionary of American English.* Merriam-Webster Inc., 1953.

Kirsta, Alix. *The Book of Stress Survival*. New York: Simon and Schuster, 1986.

Lessac, Arthur. *The Use and Training of the Human Voice*. New York: Mayfield Publishing Co., 1996.

Linklater, Kristin. *Freeing the Natural Voice*. New York: Drama Book Publishers, 1995.

Mason, John L., Ph.D. *Guide to Stress Reduction*. Berkeley: Celestial Arts, 1985.

McCoy, Michelle, and Ann S. Utterback. *Sound and Look Professional on Television and the Internet: A Guide for Broadcasters and Executives*. Chicago: Bonus Books, Inc., 2000.

Rodenburg, Patsy. *The Right to Speak*. London: Methuen Drama, 1992.

*The Sivananda Companion to Yoga*. New York: Simon and Shuster, 1983.

Utterback, Ann S. *Broadcaster's Survival Guide: Staying Alive in the Business*. Chicago: Bonus Books, Inc., 1997.

Utterback, Ann S. Audio Tape Series: *Vocal Exercises, Vocal Expressiveness, Coping With Stress, Relaxation Practice*. Chicago: Bonus Books, Inc. 1991-1997.

# Index

# Remember to
# *Breathe!*

*"Ann Utterback is so much more than a voice coach. Working with her has not only made me  better  at my job, but she's helped me balance my career and my life outside of the newsroom."*

Lauren Ashburn, reporter/anchor
WJLA-TV, Washington, D.C.

---

**Would you like to work with Dr. Utterback to improve your voice and/or reduce your stress? Professional services include:**

- Voice and Performance Telephone Tape Evaluations
- Telephone Stress Reduction Counseling
- Personal appointments in the Washington, D.C., Area
- On-Site Appointments, Workshops, and Lectures

For more information, contact Dr. Utterback
at her website: www.AVoiceDoc.com
or call 301-963-8463

---

*"As a fledgling reporter, I thought I'd never sit behind an anchor desk because of my voice. Dr. Utterback showed me how to make the most of what I have through simple, reporter-friendly techniques."*

Donya Archer, Co-anchor, WTXF-TV
Philadelphia, Pennsylvania

# Also Available

## *Improve Your Delivery*

**BROADCASTER'S SURVIVAL GUIDE: STAYING
ALIVE IN THE BUSINESS, first edition**        **$24.95**
There is no profession more stressful than broadcasting. This book describes survival techniques to help everyone in broadcasting recognize stresses and deal with them in healthy ways. This is a self-help manual to use whenever stress is a problem for on-air staff, producers, writers, news directors, and anyone in the business. It's sure to be a guide that is referred to over and over.

**SOUND AND LOOK PROFESSIONAL ON
TELEVISION AND THE INTERNET, first edition**        **$18.95**
Many people are uncomfortable with how they may look on camera or with their voices. One reason is because there are so few resources to aid in educating people about broadcast performing expectations. Co-authors, Dr. Utterback and Michelle McCoy offer executives representing their companies and students aspiring to work in the broadcast field guidelines to improve their performances.

### THE UTTERBACK AUDIO TAPE SERIES

**VOCAL EXERCISES**        **$19.95**
Dr. Utterback leads you step-by-step through exercises and drills to improve breathing, increase resonance, and polish articulation.

**VOCAL EXPRESSIVENESS**        **$19.95**
Dr Utterback explains two methods to use to bring news stories to life: script marking and an interpersonal communication approach.

**COPING WITH STRESS**        **$19.95**
Dr. Utterback talks about stress—what it is, how it affects the body and the voice, and ways to begin to stress-proof your life.

**RELAXATION PRACTICE**        **$19.95**
This tape offers four different ten-minute relaxation periods that can be done in the office or at home.

---

Books and tapes are available from: **Bonus Books, Inc.**
*phone:* (312) 467-0580 *or call toll-free:* (800) 225-3775
*fax:* (312) 467-9271
www.bonus-books.com

**Dr. Utterback** is available for consultations by telephone or in her office. You will find more information at www.AVoiceDoc.com